Get Linux
Certified
and Get Ahead

Get Linux Certified and Get Ahead

Anne Martinez

McGraw-Hill

New York   San Francisco   Washington, D.C.
Auckland   Bogotá   Caracas   Lisbon   London
Madrid   Mexico City   Milan   Montreal   New Delhi
San Juan   Singapore   Sydney   Tokyo   Toronto

McGraw-Hill

A Division of The McGraw·Hill Companies

1 2 3 4 5 6 7 8 9 0   AGM/AGM   9 0 4 3 2 1 0 9

ISBN 0-07-212333-8

The sponsoring editor for this book was Steven Elliot and the production supervisor
was Clare Stanley. It was set in New Century Schoolbook by Patricia Wallenburg.

Printed and bound by Quebecor Martinsburg.

Contents

2 Opportunities and Benefits   23

3 Inside Perspectives   37

Contents

4 The Certifications 49

Part 2 How to Get (Happily) Certified 63

5 Dollars and Sense: Financial Answers Before You Begin 65

10   All About Linux Tests   183

Part 3   Utilize Your Certification to the Max   201

11   Advertising Your New Status   203

Preface

Ten million users have already latched on to Linux as the next big thing in operating systems. An International Data Corporation (IDC) study reports that Linux was the fastest-growing server operating environment in 1998, accounting for more than 17% of all server operating system shipments in 1998. The same study predicts that the number of Linux shipments is expected to grow 25% per year between now and 2003.

The popularity of Linux is tied to its open source roots. The operating system is free, the source code is available to anyone who cares to tinker with it. This gives users control over their own environment that proprietary operating systems just don't offer. Although Linux's success so far has been largely as a server operating system, it's beginning to make inroads on the desktop as well. IDC predicts that by 2003 it will be the fourth most popular desktop operating system—following behind Windows 98, Windows 2000, and Mac OS.

Even the biggest IT companies have recognized Linux as a force that can't be ignored. Compaq, IBM, Intel, SGI, Oracle, Informix, Netscape, and many other IT heavy hitters are investing in Linux companies, porting to Linux, developing for Linux, or otherwise supporting its growth.

All this interest in Linux translates directly into opportunities for individuals who understand and can work with this new operating system. People are needed to install and maintain the operating system, administer all of those Linux servers that are shipping, port applications, develop new applications, and to inform others on the ins and outs of how to benefit the most from Linux. Take a tour of any good sized IT job board (such as www.dice.com) and you'll find several thousand job openings seeking individuals with Linux skills.

Earning a Linux certification will make you a prime candidate for many of these positions. If you're already a Linux guru, your newly added credential(s) will make that more clear than ever. If you're not quite up to speed on the intricacies of Linux yet, a well-chosen certification program can serve as your learning blueprint, defining what you need to know and even directing you to the resources that will help you gain that knowledge. If you don't know the field, how are you supposed to know what to need to know? A Linux certification can answer the question: what do I need to know to be competent Linux Administrator? Or to step up to the true expert level?

If you're an expert in another operating system, adding a Linux credential will broaden your marketability and further increase your value to potential employers.

In addition to giving employers an additional way to assess your expertise, certification gives you a way to test yourself against pre-defined standards to see if you measure up. It's an opportunity to challenge yourself to become more knowledgeable and increasingly skilled. And, it can provide a stepping stone into fresh, interesting, and even cutting edge work opportunities.

Get Linux Certified and Get Ahead is designed to help both experienced and novice computer professionals harness the power of Linux certification. It is the only book that provides a complete picture of Linux certification options as well as specific guidance on how to choose the right certification, earn it in an efficient and cost-effective way, and really put it to work as a career advancement tool.

In Part 1, "Why Certify?," you'll find the answers to 24 of the most commonly asked questions about Linux certifications, learn how certification has become such an important force in the IT industry, and find out in detail the opportunities and benefits that certification can bring to you. You'll also hear from four individuals who have already earned Linux certifications as they describe what the process was like for them, how well it has lived up to their expectations, and what advice they have to offer those who will follow on their footsteps. And, of course, you will learn about each Linux certification: who will benefit, material covered, what it takes to get it, and the suggested curriculum the certification sponsor has defined to accompany it.

Part 2, "How to Get (Happily) Certified," opens with a chapter covering the financial ins and outs of getting Linux certified. You'll learn how to estimate what you're total expenditure will be and how to apply the tricks and techniques that can substantially lower your out-of-pocket costs. Next you'll find out the most common certification mistakes and how you can avoid them. You will also explore the wealth of training alternatives available to you, along with the strengths and weaknesses of each, develop your personal training and certification roadmap, find out what's needed to get Linux running on your home computer, and learn the study secrets that will make your journey to certification quicker and easier. The final chapter in this section lays out the specifics of Linux certification exams. You'll find out how many questions you can expect to encounter on each exam, what form those questions will take, how long you'll have to answer them, and how and where to register when you're ready for your first exam.

Part 3, "Utilize Your Certification to the Max," focuses on the often overlooked topic of how to get the most benefit from your certification after you've earned it. This begins with specific advice on promoting your new, certified status. You'll also find step-by-step advice on how to utilize your certification as a key to a new job, including where and how to find that job, or, if you are happy with your current employer, how to parlay your new credentials into a raise or promotion. Part 3 also describes how to take full advantage of the perks and privileges that accompany various Linux certifications, shows you how and why to keep your certification and your skills current, and looks at the pros and cons of adding additional certifications in the future.

The resource section of *Get Linux Certified and Get Ahead* puts an extensive collection of publications, Web sites, training vendors, free online documentation, and other useful Linux certification resources at your fingertips.

This is an exciting time in the world of certification for computer professionals: a time when the demand for people with IT skills is expected to continue to outstrip the supply, a time when companies large and small have come to rely on the expertise that computer professionals bring, a time when more and more companies are using certification has a way to identify that expertise. If you've been thinking about getting certified, now is the time.

Acknowledgments

Many individuals contributed in large and small ways to the creation of this book, and because of them it's a more valuable resource than any single individual could possibly provide. The computer professionals who were kind enough to share in extensive detail their experiences with Linux certification include: Jeff Miller, Dee-Ann Le-Blanc, Robin Smidsrød, and Richard Dicaire.

My appreciation also goes out to Dan York of Linuxcare, Kevin Seddon and Tobin Maginnis of Sair, Russell Consentino and Bill Lake of Tek Metrics, and Brian Horkah of Digital Metrics, all of whom graciously fielded my questions about the Linux certifications.

Others who were instrumental to the creation of *Get Linux Certified and Get Ahead* include Steve Elliot of McGraw-Hill, who identified the need for this book and encouraged me to write it; Patty Wallenburg, who consistently does an excellent job of producing well-laid out books; Helen Wallenburg, for conducting some initial research for me; and Martha Kaufman-Amitay, my agent for this and other books.

Get Linux
Certified
and Get Ahead

Part I
Why Certify?

Chapter 1

Linux Certification
Quick FAQs

1. What Is Linux?

Linux is a computer operating system, similar to UNIX. It was created by Linus (pronounced *lee-nus*) Torvalds in Helsinki, Finland, in 1991. Since then, many developers around the world have contributed enhancements and bug fixes. The operating system software is free, as are many development tools for it and lots of applications that have been written for it. Not only is the software free, so is the source code behind it. Although its creator pronounces the name as *leen-uks*, many IT professionals pronounce it as *linn-uks*.

In addition to providing a free operating system, applications, and source code, Linux is very stable and portable. It will run on IBM, Hewlett-Packard, PC, PowerPC, Macintosh, Sun SPARC, DEC Alpha, PalmPilot, Amiga, and other hardware platforms. Because the software and source code is open and freely available, rather than controlled by a single vendor, as is Windows NT, applications and enhancements can be created by anyone who has the inclination to do so. This has resulted in rapid proliferation of available Linux applications.

Linux comes in packages called distributions. A distribution is a collection of software including the Linux kernel (the core of the operating system itself), and utilities and applications configured to work with it. The applications typically include one or more windowing systems that can be used as a graphical alternative to the program's command line interface. There are many distributions available, including those from Debian, Slackware, SuSE, Red Hat, and Caldera.

Linux is becoming hugely popular. In its Best Products of 1999 issue (July 1999), *PC World* dubbed Linux "most promising software newcomer." Oracle, Informix, and Netscape are among the industry giants who have added products and support related to Linux. According to a June 1999 article in the *Linux Journal*, there are currently more than 10 million Linux users and that number is growing "exponentially." Practically every industry publication carries stories about Linux and its advance into the marketplace.

2. What Does Having a Linux Certification Mean?

Being certified on Linux means that you have met the requirements that a certification sponsor has created to identify specific levels of competence in working with the Linux operating system in one or more capacities. This includes demonstrating your knowledge by passing one or more exams and meeting other requirements.

Although that's the technical definition, the practical application is perhaps more pertinent to individuals considering earning such a certification. With Linux capturing a growing share of the operating system market, becoming certified in Linux can add a valuable credential to your resumé. Linux is in the early stages of what is potentially a huge penetration into corporate, governmental, and educational computing environments. Already a recent search of the popular computer job board DICE (**www.dice.com**) turned up over 1,000 job openings seeking people with Linux know-how.

Being certified on Linux means that you are identified by a party other than yourself as an accomplished, skilled administrator of the Linux operating system. It means you have a significant career leg up on individuals who do not hold such a credential. It means that you will be a top candidate to fill one of the many interesting and challenging Linux job opportunities available.

3. Who Benefits from Linux Certification?

Certification programs can benefit people and organizations in the computer field, selling to the computer market, or employing technical people to perform computer-related tasks. Those with the most to gain are:

* Computer professionals
* Certification sponsors
* Employers
* Clients and customers

Virtually any IS professional can get *something* (in addition to the official piece of paper) by pursuing a well-chosen certification. Most will reap many benefits. The payoffs may come in the form of a salary increase, a better job, added confidence, or additional skills that allow you to move into a new area or perform your current functions more effectively. Course work often includes hands-on exercises with up-to-the-minute software and/or equipment, exposure you might not otherwise have.

This is not to claim that every certification program is equally valuable. There are many solid certifications available that can have a positive impact on your earning and advancement potential. Compared to some of the more complex and expansive certifications, Linux certifications come with a bargain-sized investment of time and money.

Certification sponsors benefit from these programs too. In addition to revenue from training courses and materials, certification programs generate product and company recognition. For example, every Red Hat Certified Engineer (RHCE) is a confirmation of the power and importance of Red Hat Inc. The more people Red Hat teaches to master its Linux distribution, the more likely it is that those products will be successfully utilized to their fullest extent, an added plus for both. Each Brainbench Certified Linux Administrator adds to the market penetration of Brainbench certification skill assessment products and every Prosoft Certified Linux Adminstrator serves as a demonstration of ProsoftTraining.Com's training prowess.

To employers, certification serves as independent evidence that you have demonstrated the skills and abilities required to complete the program. It also offers a method for bringing employees up to speed on the latest technologies, as well as a way to provide for the continuing education computer people often crave. Certification training can reasonably be billed as an employee benefit. Research has also shown that certified employees are more satisfied and more productive than their non-certified counterparts. Customers benefit, too, because a certification gives them additional evidence of your qualifications and suitability for the task at hand.

Linux certification also addresses a major stumbling block impeding the widespread adoption of Linux—lack of technical know-how. Companies who run a particular application or operating system need to feel confident that the expertise they need for successful operations will be available. Currently, the ranks of Linux skilled professionals are thin. The advent of Linux certifications will go a long way toward solving this problem, through creating a skills bank of Linux expertise. That will benefit the companies that use Linux, the vendors who port applications to it, and not least, the Linux experts themselves.

4. What Linux Certifications Are There?

The potential for Linux certification has quickly caught the attention of certification vendors, and there are already quite a few certification options open to you. Programs currently underway or in development include:

CyberTech Institute

* Cybertech Linux Certification

Linux Professional Institute

* Linux Professional Institute Certified Level 1 (LPIC Level 1)
* Linux Professional Institute Certified Level 2 (LPIC Level 2)
* Linux Professional Institute Certified Level 3 (LPIC Level 3)

ProsoftTraining.Com

* Prosoft Linux Certified Administrator

Red Hat Inc.

* Red Hat Certified Engineer (RHCE)
* Red Hat Certified Engineer II (RHCE II)
* Red Hat Certified Examiner (RHCX)

Sair

* Linux/GNU certified administrator (LCA)
* Linux/GNU certified trainer

Brainbench

* Certified Linux Administrator

There is quite a large variation in requirements among these certifications. Some, such as Brainbench Certified Linux Administrator, require passing a single exam. Others require passing multiple exams for each level—Sair certifications each include four exams. A few, such as the Red Hat Certified Engineer, incorporate a lab exam. A lab exam is a timed, hands-on test where you perform required tasks using the Linux operating system in a realistic computer environment. The tasks typically include installation, troubleshooting, and maintenance items. Your performance is judged and graded by a proctor.

Although a particular certification may include a recommended selection of courses for you to attend, usually these will be suggested rather than mandatory. The complete requirement details for each of these certifications are spelled out in Chapter 4.

5. What Is GNU and What Does It Have to Do with Linux Certification?

Although not synonymous, GNU and Linux are so often found together that people sometimes forget they are separate entities. GNU stands for "GNU is Not UNIX." Like Linux, it's a free, UNIX-like operating system. Development on GNU started in 1984, but until 1996, GNU did not have its own kernel. So it came to be frequently packaged with the Linux kernel. Thus there are many GNU/Linux installations—i.e. installations that incorporate the Linux kernel and the GNU operating system utilities, tools, and compilers. Thus, many of the distributions mentioned earlier are sometimes called Linux-based GNU distributions.

Because Linux and GNU are such frequent companions, GNU is incorporated into some Linux certification objectives. The Sair certifications further recognize the connection between the two by including both in their certification program names.

6. If Linux Is so Similar to UNIX, Why Shouldn't I Just Get a UNIX Certification?

Linux is based on UNIX, and Linux shares many characteristics of UNIX, but Linux is *not* UNIX. UNIX is a widely used operating system—more widely used than Linux. But Linux is newer, and is the one claiming the headlines in today's IT news. That newness and visibility set up Linux certification to be a big resumé and career booster. There are lots of people who have been working with UNIX for many years; Linux pros, on the other hand, are much harder to come by.

7. How Do Linux Certifications Compare to Other Certifications Such as Microsoft's MCSE?

Linux certifications are obviously not the only career-boosting credentials available. There are currently over 200 computer professional certifications to choose from. Vendor certifications such as the Microsoft Certified Systems Engineer (MCSE) are also valuable routes toward professional advancement. Vendor-independent certifications can prove worthwhile, too. Because context is crucial to defining the value of any credential, it's impossible to definitively place one certification above another. The key to success with certification is to match a credential with your goals. A person who administers a standalone Novell network would find little relevance in a Linux certification or an MCSE.

Due to the new nature of Linux certifications, individuals who hold them are in short supply. This means that, with a Linux certification, your resumé will be one that stands out among others put in for a Linux-related position.

Because they pertain to an operating system, Linux certifications also pair nicely with many other skills—for example a growing number of Web servers run on Linux. And because the certification is narrowly focused, your investment of time and money will be less than it would be for a more complex certification.

8. Will Linux Certification Help Me Earn More?

If you're already a Cisco Certified Internetwork Expert (CCIE) pulling down $100,000 a year, then a Linux certification won't increase your billing rate. Otherwise, it has the potential to do good things for your bank account.

Research into Linux job openings as this book went to press found that most positions offered annual salaries ranging from $45,000–$65,000. The more senior positions promised $80,000–$100,000 per year. The high-end positions typically cited programming and development expertise as well as Linux administration skills. So depending on your current skill levels and area of expertise, Linux certification may well earn you access to a higher-paying position.

But even if you don't manage to parlay your Linux certification into an immediate pay increase, it will, nonetheless, add to your base of knowledge and qualifications, which should pay off in the long term.

9. How Will Linux Certification Affect My Marketability?

There's only one thing that getting a Linux certification is likely to do for your marketability—enhance it. People with any sort of professional certification are enjoying increased visibility in the computer job market, and since Linux is a hot technology topic, Linux certification is poised to be especially valuable. By pursuing Linux certification now, you'll gain the opportunity to work with an operating system that's rapidly gaining market share and shows many signs of becoming an operating system of choice in the future.

The need for Linux-skilled pros is summed up well by writer Greg Shipley in his May 31, 1999 *Network Computing* article titled "Is it time for Linux?" Shipley says: "In the same way that the mass exodus from NetWare to NT screamed for fleets of

MCSEs, any large Linux deployments will need to be fueled by people who know Linux well. These days, such people are few and far between."

In addition to positioning you to benefit from this demand for Linux pros, certification training listed on your resumé demonstrates your ability and your desire to stay current; this is no small task in an industry where skills can become obsolete as quickly as they became cutting edge. It also shows that you take initiative and care about your career, traits many employers find attractive. Yes, there are many ways a Linux certification can have a significant positive impact on your marketability.

10. Can Certification Compensate for Inexperience?

Certification cannot replace experience; however, it can to some degree compensate for lack of it. Certification is certainly far preferable than offering neither experience nor credentials. The ideal combination is to have both certification and extensive work experience. When first starting out, nobody has experience. Think about the new college graduate with a bachelor's in computer science but no on-the-job experience. When it comes to landing a job, or even an interview, in the information technology department of a good-sized company, she's light years ahead of an equally inexperienced non-college grad counterpart because she has a credential. Professional certifications are credentials that operate in the same way that a college degree does—to open doors.

Hands-on experience is still a key criterion in determining your qualifications for a particular position. The importance of it depends upon the level of the job you're after. For the lower-level positions, it's acceptable to have less experience.

The thing about experience is that it takes time, often a lot of it. And there isn't much you can do to accelerate the process. Certification, on the other hand, is something you can add to your resumé in the more immediate future. Even for newcomers to the Linux operating system, the process of obtaining a Linux certification helps you gain experience. Certifications provide a path for learning, and as you work through that path you will gain some of that oh-so-valuable experience. When pursued with the proper spirit, the knowledge you gain while earning a Linux certification will help you do your job better.

The bottom line is that although Linux certification cannot completely substitute for hands-on experience, it will still increase your expertise, marketability, and most likely, your salary too.

11. Which Linux Certification Is Best for Me?

It may seem obvious, but many people underestimate the importance of matching choice of professional credentials with career goals. Part of the problem arises because career plans are sometimes vague and ill-defined, such as "to earn more money." Other times confusion occurs because there are multiple routes to achieving a particular goal, and there isn't enough information available to help you choose. This book will help you past both of those potential road blocks.

Because Linux isn't owned by a single vendor, there are more certifications to choose from, and the programs are more diverse than they would otherwise be. The good news is that this means there's probably more than one Linux certification that will serve as a useful career tool for you. The bad news is that you'll have to sort through a larger number of possibilities to uncover the certification that best fits your time, experience, goals, and budget. Chapter 4 provides the details on all the Linux certifications currently available and Chapter 8 will walk you through the process of selecting the specific Linux certification that will work best for you.

12. How Much Will Getting Certified Cost?

The total cost of certification can be tricky to calculate beforehand, yet that's exactly what you should do. It's important to develop a reasonable estimate so that you know exactly what you're getting into financially. Your estimate will also help you budget accordingly, so that your plans won't get put on hold due to unexpected certification-related expenses.

During the course of obtaining certification, there are several kinds of expenses you're likely to incur: exam fees, training materials (sometimes including software), training instruction, and travel to training and testing sites. Linux certification exams vary in price. The Sair Linux and GNU Certified Administrator (LCA) exam costs $99, the Prosoft Certified Linux Adminstrator exam costs $100. As this book is being written, Brainbench e-certification exams were offered at no charge, and the LPIC exams didn't have a set fee yet. The hands-on lab exam required to earn the Red Hat Certified Engineer comes with a $749 fee. Exam price is obviously not the only consideration for choosing a certification, and these prices are listed just to give you an idea of the costs.

Additionally, for some certifications, you will need access to a copy of the Linux operating system on which you can practice. Although the software is free, you may choose to have it sent to you on CD or elect a distribution with "value added" features. Even if you choose either of these, this particular expense will be very small.

In reality, it's nearly impossible (maybe someone, somewhere has done it) to pass these exams without putting in the requisite study time first, and purchasing some kind of class or material to help you prepare. How much your training expenses will total depends upon which preparation methods you choose and how much you need to learn. For instructor-led courses the price of training materials varies widely. To give you an idea of the costs, during the writing of this book:

* Red Hat's 5 day RHCE course costs $2,498 (including exam).
* Taking Magellan University's 8-week, online, instructor-led *Introduction to Linux 6.0* course costs $1,195, and the self-paced version $895.
* Ziff-Davis University (ZDU) offers an instructor-led online "Intro to the Linux version of UNIX" class. ZDU subscriptions costs $7.95/month.
* The book *Linux Unleashed* by Tim Parker (Sams Publishing, 1998) costs $27.95 through fatbrain (**www.fatbrain.com**).

Monetary expenses aren't the only costs of earning certification. You'll also have to devote time and effort, often a substantial amount.

Although this has given you a general idea of the kinds of expenses you will incur, you'll still want to develop an actual estimate. Chapter 5 will walk you through doing that. It includes a simple worksheet to help you total the various types of expenses. Chapter 5 will also reveal a number of ways to reduce your total outlay and still achieve your goal.

The costs of obtaining certification can obviously become quite substantial. It's important to put them in perspective by considering how quickly you will recoup your investment once you take your new certification to the job market.

13. Is Financial Assistance Available for Certification Training?

As professional certification has become an increasingly popular career choice, the number of ways to obtain funding to pay for it have multiplied. Employers and even recruiting firms are beginning to recognize that certification is important to their employees/clients and is good for their own bottom line. For that reason, it's often possible to obtain direct reimbursements for certification training and/or testing costs. The money may come from the training budget or from the tuition reimbursement program.

If you're an American, the U.S. Government is also interested in seeing you advance your career. Although training expenses have been to some extent deductible for many years, the tax act of 1997 makes it even easier to recoup some of your training costs through your federal income tax return. If you're using the training to advance in your current profession (rather than to change professions) you'll want to explore Form 2106, Employee Business Expenses, or, if you're self-employed, Schedule C, Profit or Loss from Business.

The 1997 tax act created two credits you may be able to take advantage of as well: the Lifetime Learning Credit and the Hope Scholarship Credit. Credits are dollar-for-dollar reductions of your tax bill. Chapter 5 includes specific advice explaining how to take advantage of education-related tax breaks like these.

If you don't have the cash on hand to fund your certification efforts, and you don't have an employer willing to foot the bill, there are several loan programs specifically designed for computer professional certification candidates. You'll find out all about those later in this book too.

Besides using financing, tax breaks, and third-party funding, there are many ways you can cut your certification bill to make the total more manageable. Judicious selection of training and preparation materials is the first place to trim expenses. You can also save money by doing little things such as careful selection of exam options. You'll learn all these tricks later in this book.

14. How Long Does Earning Certification Take?

The time span varies considerably depending on your choice of certification, current experience level, and the learning methods you employ. The biggest portion of your time will go to preparing for exams. For some of the certifications it's possible to compress preparation time into a few weeks—if you're willing and able to put just about everything else aside. It's more common, and more practical for professionals who are earning certification on their own time to start with one exam, determine the requirements, self-study, and then take the exam. The process is repeated for the next exam for that certification.

Although many of the Linux certifications require just one exam, you may decide that one of the more complex certifications will provide more value to you in the long run. In this case, you can expect a longer study period and multiple exams. Whichever route you choose, you should be able to earn certification in less than a year.

15. Where Will I Have to Go for Certification Training and Testing?

For some tests you will be able to study largely from books and/or software preparation materials—which means you can study from home or at work. These materials are available through bookstores that carry technical books. Fatbrain.com (**www.fatbrain.com**) is a good place to find such books, but you can also find them in traditional bookstores as well.

If you choose to take instructor-led training, which may be just what you need to best meet a particular requirement, you'll have to travel to the class site. If you're lucky, that will be nearby, perhaps even through a local college, but you may have to travel to find the class you want, when you want it. You do not necessarily have to get your training from the certification sponsor. Keep in mind that "unofficial" training is often as good as or better than its "authorized" counterpart, and can cost substantially less.

There is another great alternative for individuals who find self-study inadequate and travel to instructor-led courses too expensive and/or time consuming: online learning. It's possible to study for Linux certifications using courseware over the Internet. These online classes can take a variety of forms, and you'll learn all about them in the training alternatives chapter of this book.

To a somewhat lesser extent than many other certifications, some Linux certification testing is administered through Sylvan Prometric testing centers. There are over 1,200 of these testing centers serving 80 countries, so there's probably one not too far away from you. You can find the closest one using the online test center locator available through **www.2test.com**.

A few Linux certification vendors actually make exams available online, via the Internet. These include Brainbench and CyberTech Institute. You can take Web-based tests from your home computer. Some allow you to use reference materials, while others do not.

If your chosen certification includes a hands-on lab requirement, you'll have to travel to the sponsor's site to take the exam. Some sponsors may have multiple testing sites; for others there will be only one.

16. What Will I Receive from My Sponsor When I Get Certified?

When you have completed the requirements for a particular certification, including signing the certification agreement, you will be sent a "graduation kit." These kits vary by certification sponsor, but typically include a certificate and information on taking advantage of additional perks that come with the certification. Such perks often include free or reduced training opportunities, use of a certification logo, access to restricted discussion forums, inclusion in a professional directory, and/or similar benefits.

17. Is Passing Exams the Only Thing I Have to Do to Become Certified?

Passing the tests will not usually qualify you for a Linux certification. You'll also have to sign and submit a document called a certification agreement. Certification agreements are another item that varies among certification programs. Typically they contain terms and restrictions spelling out:

* Allowed usage of logos and marks
* Conditions under which your certification could be revoked
* Recertification requirements
* Notice the certification sponsor has the right to alter the program at discretion
* Your promise not to reveal confidential information—i.e. exam questions
* Clarification that certification does not convey software licensing rights to you

18. Do I Need a College Degree to Get Linux Certified?

You don't even need a high school diploma. What you do need is an urge to excel, along with large amounts of self-motivation, determination, and persistence. If you can learn the material, you can pass the exams and become certified.

That's not to claim that a college degree wouldn't do good things for your career. Adding Linux certification on top of a college degree will open more doors for you than a Linux certification alone, but you don't have to have the degree—the certifications are valuable career boosters in and of themselves.

19. What if I Don't Remember How to Study?

The prospect of going back to studying after a long hiatus can be intimidating, but if it is, that's probably because you didn't develop efficient and effective study skills the first time around. If so, you are not alone. It's amazing how many people manage to make it through formal schooling without learning the techniques that make studying easy. But don't worry, it's never too late to learn how to learn. In fact, you may be among the many people who find studying much easier this time around simply because there are specific reasons and personal goals driving your effort.

But whether your study brain cells never developed much muscle, or if they're simply a little dusty, the tips and techniques in this book will help you brush up on efficient and effective study habits. In the Study Secrets chapter, you'll get a refresher on effective reading, and note-taking skills, as well as help figuring out just how you're going to find study time into your busy schedule. You'll also learn test-taking techniques that will help you achieve the best score you're capable of on certification exams.

20. What Resources Are Available to Help Me Achieve Certification?

You'll find information to help you pass Linux certification exams all over the Internet and on the shelves of your nearest megabookstore. Available resources include:

* Internet forums and discussion groups
* Study guides and text books
* Self-assessment tests and computer programs
* Expert instructors
* Documentation and preparation materials available through your certification vendor
* World Wide Web sites
* And, of course, this book

Thanks largely to the Internet, you'll be able to access many powerful and useful learning aides right from your computer. If you're not already set up with an Internet connection, this is a good reason to get yourself a modem and sign up for service. You'll be giving yourself virtually 24-hour access to others who've obtained your certification already, are in the process of doing so, or who write or teach about it or about related technologies.

There are plenty of offline resources, too. Because the Linux operating system is experiencing such growth and stimulating wide interest among IT professionals, you can expect continued growth in the variety and depth of preparation assistance available.

21. Do I Need Access to the Linux Operating System to Get Certified?

Although it may be possible to earn the lower-level certifications through studying without actually practicing on the Linux operating system, it's not a good idea to do so. For the more complex and difficult certifications, it would be impossible; but why would you even want to?

There's no reason for you to even try to avoid getting hands-on experience because Linux is priced at a level anyone can afford— it's free. You can download Linux from one of the many sites on the Web (see resource section for specific suggestions) or order a distribution sent to you on CD. Follow the installation instructions judiciously, and bingo, you've got a Linux computer at your fingertips.

And no, you don't have to convert your entire system over to Linux. It's possible to install Linux on a computer in such a way that the computer becomes what's called a *dual-boot system*. Such systems give you the option at start-up of choosing which operating system to load up. This way, you can keep your existing operating system and get your hands-on Linux practice too!

22. What are the Certification Tests Like?

Four Linux certification exams are administered through Sylvan Prometric testing centers. Candidates can register by phone. Each certification vendor using Sylvan has a special toll-free number for exam registration. You can find the registration number for your certification vendor in the reference section of this book or by visiting Sylvan Prometric's Web site (**www.2test.com**).

For all tests administered by Sylvan you must register in advance. On the day of the test you go to the center, present two forms of identification, and sign in. You will be escorted to a quiet room with one or more testing stations. You won't be allowed to bring anything into the room with you but your wits and a wipe-off note board. You'll sign onto the computer using your social security number and the test will begin. You may be required to complete an agreement promising not to reveal the contents of the test before you receive any actual questions. The questions themselves are mostly variations of multiple choice formats. Most certification exams last one to two hours. Passing scores vary depending on the exam but generally hover around 65–70%.

VUE (Virtual University Enterprises) is another test administration vendor you may encounter. Although less widely used than Sylvan Prometric, it functions basically in the same way—through a network of testing centers worldwide.

Lab exams typically last at least a several hours and often a full day. The Red Hat lab exam, for example, includes a one- to-two-hour written exam, a two-hour network services configuration lab, and a three-hour troubleshooting lab.

For certification exams administered via the Web, you can expect to be required to agree to non-disclosure rules up front. You'll also have to read and confirm the testing rules, which will specify whether you can use reference materials. The actual format of the exams will vary by vendor, but you can expect primarily multiple choice type questions. Brainbench certification exams limits the amount of time you have to answer a particular question to 1 minute. You'll find more details about individual certification exams in Chapter 10, "All About Linux Tests."

23. How Can I (or Anyone Else) Verify that Someone Really Holds a Linux Certification?

The process for verifying certification is another one of those things that varies between vendors. A few vendors offer no method at all, but many have a procedure in place.

* Brainbench issues a transcript ID to each individual it certifies. The certified individual gives out this ID to anyone who wants to verify the certification. The ID can be used to verify certified status via the Brainbench Web site. Brainbench will also mail your transcript to the employer at your request.
* For certification programs without a specific policy in place, it may be possible to request verification via e-mail from the certification program manager.

24. How Can I Promote Myself and My Certification?

Professional certification has the power to boost your career and increase your job opportunities, but only if you use it! To make the most of your certification, you'll want to learn how to maximize its value as a career tool. Filing it away in a cabinet won't do that. The most obvious thing to do is advertise your new status by adding it to your resumé, business cards, and e-mail signature, but don't stop there. You can also learn to be your own PR person. With a little effort you can get your name out into the world as an expert in your field. The Internet is an excellent tool for this purpose. Through well-planned use of Web pages, forums, and other Internet resources, you can get your name to pop up in association with Linux skill areas. Be careful to abide by Internet etiquette (often called netiquette); indiscriminate self-promotion will annoy other Internet users and ultimately work against you. You can also establish expert status by providing useful information to media outlets such as newspapers and television.

There are also techniques you can use to move up in the ranks at your current company or in billing rates if you're an independent contractor. These include finding ways to demonstrate your enhanced value, and making an airtight case for a raise or promotion. After you obtain a certification, you might also decide that it's time to move on to a new company or perhaps become an independent contractor or consultant. Because this topic is important, you'll find specific advice on how to get the most *oomph* from your new credential in several chapters of this book.

25. What's the Future of Linux Certification?

The computer certification marketplace is in the midst of explosive growth. Consider that there are currently over 200 professional certifications available and that number continues to expand rapidly. Linux itself has been responsible for a half-dozen new certifications and certifications-in-progress in the last two years.

Linux certification is really a multi-vendor marketplace, with different sponsors competing to develop the most valuable, most meaningful, and most widely respected Linux certification. For the IT professional this competition is likely to result in a higher overall quality of certification programs, as well as several clearly defined levels of Linux certification from which to choose. In the future, expect Linux certifications to continue gain recognition and acceptance among computer professionals and employers. Don't be surprised if they make the move from desirable to required.

Chapter 2

Opportunities and Benefits

A major attraction of certification is its flexibility of purpose and application. If you want to move on to a new and better job, certification can help you. If it's a new specialty that's caught your eye, certification can simplify the transition. If you want to become more of an expert at what you already do, certification can serve that purpose as well. When chosen with care and earned in the proper spirit, Linux certifications can be used to accomplish any of these tasks. That's not to say that professional certification is a career cure-all; it isn't. What it does do is offer a powerful set of tools that you can use to make significant, positive changes in your work life.

More Options, Better Pay

When you become Linux certified, you open doors to new and different career options, increase your professional credibility, learn where your knowledge gaps are and how to plug them, and receive an objective measure of your technical accomplishments. Whether you stay where you are or move on to another employer, these benefits will give you a leg up the career ladder.

Jobs, Jobs, Jobs

A recent search of a Web site that caters to job-hunting computer professionals turned up over 1,400 positions that either require or desire applicants with Linux expertise (one of the results pages is shown in Figure 2.1). The site is an electronic repository of open positions posted by technical recruiters and is only one site among many that include job opportunities for certified professionals. The openings were quite diverse and included:

* Linux Developer
* Technical Writer
* Linux/UNIX Systems Engineer
* Kernel Hacker
* Linux Specialist
* Software Engineer
* Sr. R & D Engineer

* Linux Driver Engineer
* Programmer/Analyst
* Component Testing and Porting Consultant
* Linux Technical Trainer
* Linux Technician
* And others

Hiring the wrong person is an expensive mistake that employers strive to avoid. When you present yourself with a Linux certification, you're making it easier (and less risky) for the hiring manager to assess your technical qualifications.

FIGURE 2.1
Internet job postings seeking Linux skilled applicants

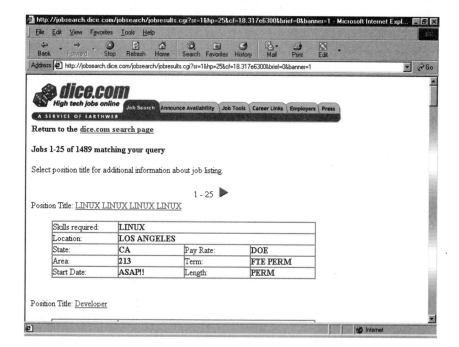

Training to Train

Besides improving your chances for the "standard" mix of technical jobs, you can take advantage of an interesting and potentially lucrative outgrowth of the certification explosion. People are needed to teach the necessary classes, write exam questions, and develop certificate curriculums.

Firms hiring technical trainers like to see people with related certifications and experience. Because training requires a high level of expertise in both the technology at hand *and* the ability to teach and communicate well, salaries can be impressive.

You really have to know what you're doing to be able to handle the questions and problems that arise during a training session, but it's often possible to land such a position without a trainer certification. Based on a review of advertised openings for trainers, it appears possible to break into this field based on nontraining-related technical certifications coupled with other technical skills you hold. Once you're hired, you'll be put through trainer certification, *at the employer's expense*. Employers who hire trainers this way pay less than those who want a certified trainer from the beginning, but the salary is still likely to be quite reasonable.

As this book was going to press, Sair was the only Linux certification vendor offering an instructor certification, but others may well appear soon.

Adding to Your Bottom Line

If you are like many people and one of the main reasons you're considering earning a Linux certification is because you want to increase your earnings, you'll be encouraged to hear what International Data Corporation (IDC) found when it investigated that question. A 1996 study (conducted before certification's current boom) revealed that, on average, certified employees earn 12 percent higher salaries than noncertified employees. That's probably directly related to another statistic from the same study. Seventy-eight percent of IS managers believe that certified employees are more productive.

Honing in on the value of Linux expertise, I conducted a survey of current IT job openings with following results:

✳ There are both contract and permanent openings for Linux pros.

✳ The majority of Linux jobs are systems administrator positions. The compensation for these positions varies widely, ranging from $35,000 to $90,000 in salary, with many in the

$60,000–$80,000 range. Junior positions run $35,000 to $45,000 per year. Hourly rates range from $35/hr to $75/hr.

* The next most frequently occurring openings are for Linux programmers and software engineers. These openings promise from $50,000 to $90,000 per year, with many in the $70,000 range and a few promising "up to" $100,000.

* There are also a fair number of QA/Testing positions. These are often related to porting applications and hardware drivers to Linux from another environment. Most positions fall in the $30,000 to $60,000/year range with senior positions paying $70,000 and even higher. These openings seem to provide more contract opportunities than administrator or developer openings.

* At the lowest compensation level are Linux technician jobs. These are typically involve installing and configuring Linux on new systems. They pay between $20 and $35/hour.

Large Demand Plus a Short Supply
Equals a Higher Market Price

According to the Information Technology Association of America (ITAA), 190,000 information technology jobs are *currently open* in mid- to large-sized companies in the United States. Employers need skilled workers, and, for many, certification rates a premium.

Articles in trade publications confirm the power of certification to boost income. An August 1999 *PC Week* article titled "IT Training, Certification Go Online" said "Ask any IT career counselor for one surefire way to punch up your resumé, and you're likely to hear this answer: Get certified." The article goes on to discuss that although certification is not a career panacea, it is proving to be a valuable yardstick used by computer professionals and their employers.

An April 1999 article in the *Linux Journal* titled "Linux Certification for the Software Professional" analyzed the driving force behind the development of Linux certification and concluded: "We believe certification has significant mutual benefits for employers and employees and it will become a key tool for managers as Linux software is brought into corporate and government environments."

In its February 1998 issue, *Inside Technology Training* revealed that "another name for 'certified employees' may be 'former employees.'" Newly certified workers have been known to bolt from their employers to take advantage of their dramatically increased marketability (to get paid more). From the employer's viewpoint, that's a problem; from yours, it's evidence of the value of certification. The same article suggests that "a manager budgeting for certification should include the cost of the raises certified employees have come to demand—to keep them from leaving." It's fundamental economics in action.

Leading the Crowd

Although it hasn't reached that point yet, it's reasonable to predict that increasing popularity will make this type of credentialling more universal. When and if that eventually happens, people who have ignored the trend will have to play catch-up. Certifying now or in the near future will place you near the leading edge of the trade, at least in the perception of potential employers. Wait too long and certification may become a requirement for basic success rather than a springboard for career advancement. It's well on its way there already.

QUOTE

One Recruiter's Perspective

Since this technology has only recently become common in corporate settings, it will be hard for most [administrators, programmers, whatever] to trace a long history of successful projects. Certification should help reassure hiring managers that a candidate knows their stuff.

—Audrey Chapel, Sr. Recruiter, Entex

Career Shifting

Are you feeling a bit bored and restless within your current computer specialty? Perhaps it's not as hot as it once was, and you like to work with technology that's more cutting edge? Maybe you've simply topped out where you are and would like to move on to something new—like administering Linux-based Web servers. A Linux certification (or two) may be just what the career counselor ordered.

If you want to switch your career focus, then, by definition, you already have one big thing going for you: experience. It probably isn't in Linux, but at least it's there, and that's very valuable. Nevertheless, you still face a resumé and training gap that stretches between where you are and where you want to be.

Although some Linux certifications simply consist of exams, others include a suggested training path that can be used as a blueprint to learn what you need to know about Linux. Especially if there are associated courses you can take online or in person, this can be used to help you move into a new area of expertise. In fact, one of the more prevalent uses of certification is as a springboard to a new job. That makes employers anxious about the subject. They like to hire certified people, but when their current workers get on a certification track, managers may lose a little sleep. They probably wonder if those workers are planning to leave for greener pastures or if another company will attempt to lure them away.

Although some people (but surely not you) might find the idea of stressing out their bosses appealing, the point is that managers recognize the meaning and value of certification. People who get certified are pursuing something more than they already have—something better, something different. They are demonstrating in a public way their commitment to continued professional advancement.

The person who gives you your first job in your new, post-certification area of specialty is likely to be a manager. Remember, managers like to hire people who are already certified, as you'll be. And by getting this training, you have demonstrated that you take initiative and are serious about this career move; it's not just a passing fancy. Perhaps, more important, you'll have gained knowledge and skills relevant to your new domain. *And* you've added a credential directly related to the position you are seeking. If you get asked technical questions during interviews, you'll be able to field them fairly competently.

This is not to say that obtaining a Linux certification will automatically enable you to jump from one computer field to another at the same or higher level of pay and responsibility. But it's likely to ease that leap significantly, and enable you to start in your new field at a higher level than you might otherwise have attained. Who wants to go back to square one?

Power Perks

As an added incentive to professionals and employers contemplating certification, certification vendors often bestow a range of perks on those who complete their programs (Sair's perks list is shown in Figure 2.2). The best perks incorporate elements that help you to perform your job at a higher level. They address your reasons for pursuing the certification and add value to the program for you and for your clients/employer.

FIGURE 2.2
Certification perks from Sair

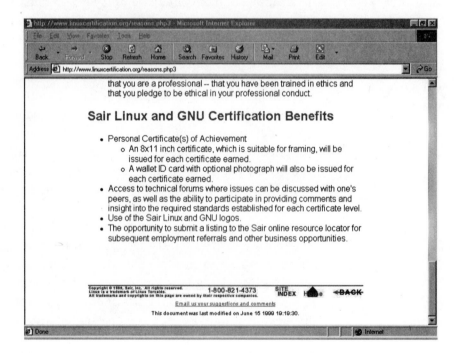

Exclusive Forums

Often certification vendors create forums for the exclusive use of their certified professionals. Digital Metrics, before merging with the Linux Professional Institute, had such a forum. Because these have proven fairly popular among professionals with other, non-Linux certifications, you can expect them to appear more widely as a benefit tied to Linux certifications.

These forums can prove very useful. When you want to hash over an idea, glean some arcane advice, or discuss the pros and cons of a new release, these forums can serve as a valuable resource. Because only individuals with the same certification as yourself can post and respond to questions, there is a much higher signal-to-noise ratio than in unrestricted discussion forums. That means you won't have to wade through dozens of off-topic postings, as you would in a typical Usenet newsgroup. In addition, the employees of various Linux distribution vendors may frequent the forum, so you may even get your feedback straight from the horse's mouth.

Training and Conference Admission

Once you're certified, you can't (and probably won't want to) rest on your laurels. Because of the same rapid pace of change that makes your certification valuable, you'll need to keep updating your skills. Many sponsors recognize this, and require that you complete continuing education each year to retain your designation. Linux certifications are so new that the recertification requirements have yet to be specified for many of them. A few, however, are already in place. Brainbench, for example, requires annual renewal.

Even when retaining your certification isn't the issue, you may want to take advantage of free and reduced-cost training sometimes offered by certification vendors. This typically comes in the form of discounts on new courses or reduced admission to industry events. In some cases the training will be for certified individuals only. This perk can provide reduced-cost opportunities to expand your technical skills and network with others in the computer industry.

Use of Logos and Marketing Materials

Linux certification vendors are interested in helping you promote
your new status (and, along with it, their program). To that end,
they take advantage of a useful product recognition tool—the
logo. A Web page featuring the Brainbench Linux certification
logo is shown Figure 2.3. When you obtain certification, you'll be
granted permission, and even be encouraged, to use the logo to
advertise your status. You'll be able to place it on your business
cards, stationery, Web site, and in other places. The sponsor's
advertising experts expend time and money promoting logo recognition and you reap the benefits.

FIGURE 2.3
A certification logo
on the Brainbench
(formerly
Tekmetrics)
Web site

Independents, especially, may appreciate the ability to include
the logos on marketing materials. The sight of a professional logo
increases customer confidence in your abilities. Suddenly you're
not an unknown or a risky proposition anymore. You're Linux certified after all.

If you work for an employer, you may have less use for these
logos. On the other hand, your employer may wish to place the

logos on company materials in association with your name, which can work out well for both of you. This is especially true for resellers.

You can expect to receive specific instructions on the proper use of the logos. Although this might seem a bit controlling at first, it's actually in your best interest. If the logos are misused, their value may be diminished.

Other Payoffs

The benefits and opportunities mentioned so far are largely concrete and directly related to income or career advancement. But as we all know by now, there are other, less tangible, aspects of career satisfaction that are equally important.

Study Dividends

If you get certified simply by taking a test, you won't expand your knowledge of the subject area. But in most cases, you'll attend one or more classes, participate in a hands-on lab session, or at the minimum, work through a self-study guide. In doing so, you are virtually assured of gaining exposure to new areas in your field and to different ways of doing things.

You already know how to perform the duties required by your current position, but do you know the most efficient ways to do them? And how do you learn about what could be or should be done in the near future? Through the certification process you'll achieve added exposure to the issues related to your area of expertise and answers to these questions. This has the potential to make your work life easier by:

* Augmenting your level of proficiency
* Increasing your personal productivity
* Decreasing downtime
* Familiarizing you with product and technology advances

Peace of Mind

Serenity is probably beyond what any of us can hope to achieve in the workplace and may not even be desirable. Freedom from various job-related fears and anxieties is another story. How can certification bring you increased peace of mind? As you probably have already guessed, it does this in several ways.

Let's start with that most basic of workplace concerns: the possibility of getting downsized, rightsized, released, phased out, riffed (subjected to a reduction in force), or just plain laid off. Whatever your company calls it, it comes down to two little words: job security.

Linux certifications have the potential to address job security in two key ways:

1. By increasing your value to the company
2. By increasing your value to *other* companies

Let's take number one first. By keeping in tip-top technical shape through certification, you multiply your value to your employer, enabling you to keep your employer's customers satisfied. In fact, the more integral you are to smooth daily operations, the more painful it would be for your employer to let you go. In addition, if an employer who helped finance your certification has invested in you and has an added incentive to keep you on board.

By demonstrating your desire to excel at your current duties (through earning certification) you simultaneously communicate your ability to take on new or different tasks (for increased compensation, you hope), should the need arise. Transfer within the company then becomes a distinct possibility when layoffs threaten.

In reality, you only have control over your own actions, not those of "the boss." That's what makes job security key number two so critical. Suppose that one day the dreaded pink slip does land in your mail slot. If you've chosen your certification wisely, it won't be as big a deal as it might otherwise have been. Yes, losing your job would still be stressful (unless you're lucky enough to receive a generous severance package). But by adding to your technical credentials, you'll have secured a competitive advantage over many other job seekers; you'll have greater marketability.

During a time in which companies are hungry for the latest technical expertise, recent training and certification is likely to translate into quicker and more lucrative job offers. If you're any good at all, you're not likely to be idle for long. And because changing jobs is one of the most effective ways to obtain a significant salary boost, you may actually find yourself thanking your employer for pushing you out the door.

Food for Your Ego

Last but not least, is an extremely personal benefit of professional certification: self-satisfaction. Individuals often report a feeling of pleasure and accomplishment after achieving certification. It arises from the professional recognition conferred by your peers within the industry, from the knowledge that your skills and expertise have been assessed by someone other than yourself, and from the fact that you've successfully measured up to professional standards.

Chapter 3

Inside Perspectives

Four professionals who have earned Linux certifications report on what the process was like and what certification has and hasn't done for them.

The Way In

No matter which Linux certification you choose to pursue, the process of achieving certification is straightforward. The basic steps are:

1. Choose a certification.
2. Identify gaps between what you know and what you need to know.
3. Determine what you will do to fill those gaps.
4. Choose an exam and prepare for it.
5. Take the exam.
6. Repeat steps 4 and 5 until all requirements are met.
7. Put your certification to work for you.

Each of these seven steps can be further broken down and will be later. But this is the basic process for obtaining a certification. Depending on your choice of certification and your current level of experience and skills, the commitment needed to go through this process will vary considerably. Significant time and expense may be involved, and self-motivation is an absolute must. The bottom line is that you should know what you're getting into.

Reports from the Field

If you wanted to find out what skydiving is like, you might begin by asking someone you know who's seen parachutists in action. But that would only give you a partial picture—the pieces that a spectator can observe and convey. To fill in the details, you'd also want to ask a participant, perhaps a parachutist or the pilot of a jump plane. Better yet, ask more than one.

In the same way, when it comes to getting a good sense of the roles certification can play in the careers of computer professionals, statistics, study, and trend observations can provide only part of the story. The most meaningful insights come from people who've been through the certification process and/or encounter it on a daily basis.

The interviews that follow offer the inside scoop on Linux certification. Four computer professionals who've taken the plunge share their personal perspectives on these certifications and the process of obtaining them. Because these certifications are relatively new in the marketplace, these professionals haven't had much time to utilize them to their fullest potential. Nonetheless, the experiences they've already encountered may prove useful you.

Jeff Miller, RHCE, dmCLA

Job title: Corporate Communications Manager, Old National Service Corp.
Certifications held: RHCE, dmCLA, MCNE, CCNA, and others
Years of experience in computer field: 5

When did you obtain your Linux certifications?
DmCLA 3/8/99; RHCE 4/23/99, Currently working toward Sair Linux/GNU certification

In August 1999, the Digital Metrics program, which launched the dmCLA designation, merged with the Linux Professional Institute's Linux certification program. The dmCLA is no longer available as a separate designation.

What made you decide to pursue Linux certifications?
To me, it is a validation of the many sleepless nights I've spent learning Linux at home. Now that I work in a Linux/UNIX environment, these skills have proven necessary. Certification is just a way to reflect the work it took to gain the skills.

How did you prepare?
Self-study. There are few Linux certification books. The ones I've seen aren't released yet. I spent considerable time reading FAQs and HOWTO files and experimenting with services I've had little experience with, such as INN and NIS.

Who paid for your training and testing?
My employer paid for the training and testing. The dmCLA cost
$15, the RHCE $2,495.

How has being Linux certified affected your career?
It really hasn't had any effect yet. I believe that it will affect my
opportunities should I decide to leave my current employer.

*What do you think of the need for and value of Linux certifica-
tions?*
There is a definite need. With the explosive growth of Linux in
the Enterprise, it's a must for employers to have measurements to
judge an applicant's skills. Certification is one way of doing that,
as long as Linux certification doesn't become corrupted by people
simply reading books and taking tests instead of learning through
experience and study.

I realize that this *will* happen but for now, the possession of a
certification such as the dmCLA, Sair or RHCE actually does
reflect skills possessed by the candidate simply due to the lack of
published study materials.

What do you feel is the best way to prepare for certification exams?
Self-study and experience.

*What do you think is the biggest misconception about Linux certi-
fications?*
I know many system administrators that could easily study and
pass several certifications but won't take the time. I think the
biggest misconception is people thinking that certification "doesn't
matter." In the IT industry, like it or not, certification is the foot
that gets you in the door. Once you're in, you still have to prove
your skills.

*What do you think is the most common mistake people make when
pursuing a Linux certification?*
Lack of study. (I know—I've done it).

*What advice do you have for anyone who is considering earning a
Linux certification?*
Be over-prepared (if that is possible). Prepare much more than
you think you should.

Dee-Ann LeBlanc, dmCLA, RHCE

Job title: Technical writer, author of *The Linux Install and Configuration Little Black Book* (Coriolis) and *Linux Exam Prep* (Coriolis).
Certifications held: dmCLA, RHCE
Years of experience in computer field: 9

When did you obtain your Linux certifications?
DmCLA March 1999; RHCE May 1999.

What made you decide to pursue Linux certification?
I needed the certifications to work on Linux exam preparation book projects.

What did you do to prepare and what was the process like?
The Digital Metrics Web site listed a number of books which they felt were useful for those trying to prepare for the exam. I went to a bookstore known for its well-stocked computer section and bought several books to round out my Linux book collection since I had never gotten around to going out and buying any Linux-specific books before. One of the smartest ones I picked up was *Linux in a Nutshell* from O'Reilly. I also teach introduction to UNIX courses so I studied partially by very carefully researching all of my students' questions.

Who paid for your training?
LANWrights paid for it so I could work on some Linux writing projects for them, $15 for the Digital Metrics exam, $2,500 plus airfare plus hotel plus food plus time for RHCE.

How has being Linux certified affected your career?
Tremendously. There are a number of writing projects I could not work on without it, and seeing that I'm certified via my Web page has gotten me a few interesting phone calls regarding work on site.

What do you think of the need for and value of Linux certifications?
I can understand the need for businesses and others to have some sort of gauge to help them decide who knows what they are doing, and who is not quite ready to be responsible for their production-level systems and sensitive data. The difficulty is, as always,

designing an exam that assesses not just how quickly people can look things up in a book, or how good they are at memorizing, but how well they actually function doing the tasks covered by the exam. Certification exams that cover this last point, in my opinion, that will be of value to the consumer looking for Linux consultants.

What do you feel is the best way to prepare for certification exams?
A combination of things. One of the foremost seems simply to play around with items on the exam topic list you are unfamiliar with. Even better for people like me who learn better by doing than just from reading a book is to answer people's questions, perhaps on a newsgroup or mailing list. As more study guides become available these will be a great boon to those who are preparing for the exams, because they will be specifically aimed at what needs to be learned. The course I took at Red Hat before the exam also helped quite a bit, filling some gaps in my knowledge base.

What is the biggest misconception about Linux certifications?
That you can cram and learn enough quickly to pass them without a prior thorough grounding in Linux.

What do you think is the most common mistake people make when pursuing a Linux certification?
Taking the exam before they're ready. Even the exams which have courses leading up to them assume a certain knowledge base going into the course. If you don't have that background and understanding already, you may not be able to keep up.

What advice do you have for anyone who is considering earning a Linux certification?
Do some research on the Linux certification options and choose one or two that you feel have a good future. The others can be good practice for taking the weightier exams, especially those which are inexpensive. Also, watch Linux discussion forums, especially those regarding certifications to see what people are saying about the exams. When exam-specific books are available to study with, use them. I took them without such a luxury.

Robin Smidsrød, dmCLA

Job title: System Administrator / IT Consultant
Certifications held: Digital Metrics Certified Linux Administrator (dmCLA)
Years of experience in computer field: 11

When did you obtain your Linux certification?
March 1993.

What made you decide to obtain it?
The certification exam was easy to access, and I felt that it was time I proved to myself what I was good for. An added bonus was that it didn't cost a lot of money.

How did you prepare?
I checked out the prerequisites list and checked up on the subjects I was uncertain about. I really didn't prepare much, I just made sure I was on a network with low latency, and was sure not to be interrupted while I was taking the test.

Who paid for your training and testing?
Myself. The whole registration process and the exam cost me no more than $20.

How has being Linux certified affected your career?
It hasn't really boosted my career in any way, but it makes me a lot surer that I know what I'm talking about. A colleague of mine (who I consider much smarter in the field of network security) actually failed the test, something I didn't quite understand, because I've always considered him smarter than me. This probably means that I know more about the overall system, something which is essential if you're going to be a good system administrator.

What do you think of the need for and value of Linux certifications?
Linux is an Open Source OS, this way it's easy for everybody to think that they know a great deal about it. But in this area, experience is everything. If you are an employer and plan to employ somebody, it's more probable that you'll employ the person with the certification, if their experience/education is almost identical [to that of a candidate without a certification].

Linux is definitely a product if the Internet age. If you plan to keep up with this OS you need to be online with the Internet and know how to extract important information from this medium. If you've got a Linux certification you're certain that you know what people expect you to know. That's the value of a certification.

What do you think is the best way to prepare for certification exams?
Read documentation and use the system in ways you haven't tried before. Try to understand and set up things you haven't touched (either because they haven't interested you, or you feel they're to hard to understand).

What is the biggest misconception about Linux certifications?
As with any other certification: Employers think a cert means you know everything about a product/idea. This isn't necessarily the truth. People without certifications often know the products just as well, but they may haven't had the time or opportunity to show it.

What advice do you have for anyone who is considering earning a Linux certification?
Learn Linux. Use it every day. Do things you haven't tried before. Install it at home. Explore the options and possibilities, don't be satisfied with the way things are. Always try to improve either the stability or the usability of your system. If you do this regularly, you'll probably get into all the important areas a system administrator (or programmer) needs to know about the system. Versatility is your best tool.

Richard Dicaire

Job title: System Administrator/IT Consultant
Certifications held: Brainbench Certified Professional Master Linux Administrator
Years of experience in computer field: 6

When did you obtain your Linux certification?
August 15, 1999.

What made you decide to obtain it?
My love for the Linux operating system, the need for credible acceptance for my knowledge of Linux, and the desire to have proof of that knowledge.

Our business (K&R Information Technologies, owned by my wife and me) pushes Linux and having credible certification separates us from the "Tom, Dick, and Harry" Linux users that make claims to be able to offer services etc., and have no formal degree/certification for same. From a client's point of view, I feel they'd be more comfortable going with a company that's certified in what it does—not unlike the function any Microsoft certification performs.

How did you prepare for and earn it?
I undertook no preparation. I just took the test straight. This, in my opinion, gave me the best gauge for my knowledge.

Who paid for your training and testing?
The only costs incurred were for PCs, mail-order Linux CDs, and a number of books purchased on specific subjects like DNS, Apache (Web server), Perl, HTML, and the C programming language. I've undergone no formal training whatsoever in computers: I'm self taught, and I read a lot.

How has being Linux certified affected your career?
It's too early to tell, at this point I've only been certified for less than a month.

What do you think of the need for and value of Linux certifications?
Without going into the hype and hyberbole surrounding Linux right now, the need for certification and value of same isn't very high, *yet*. As Linux gains more headway into the corporate world, the demand for certification, and the value of it, will increase; based on the growth of Linux over the last two years—exponentially.

What do you think is the best way to prepare for certification exams?
I've never been one to believe in "cramming" for an exam. The best teacher is experience, the best lessons learned are the ones taught by experience. It's one thing to just read documentation,

quite another to use the knowledge gained by reading. Linux, and all other UNIX-like operating systems, are best learned by trial and error. This is the reason I took the Linux certification test without "studying" first.

What do you think is the most common mistake people make when pursuing a Linux certification?
I think the most common mistake is the thought that the certification test itself will be Linux distribution specific: Red Hat specifically, seeing as how Red Hat Linux is the most used of all the various distributions available.

When I started the test, I was under the misconception it *would* be distribution specific, it wasn't. I understand that Brainbench will be offering distribution-specific certifications in the future.

I think another mistake is those people who get the certification for no other reason than to stroke their own egos. They may not take the certification seriously enough and use it to their advantage.

What advice do you have for anyone who is considering earning a Linux certification?
Know your stuff! And don't be afraid to make mistakes; you can't learn if you don't make mistakes to learn from.

Personally, I plan to make the most of my Linux certification, for both my career, and my business. Linux IS an alternative to the cost-driven operating systems currently available. It's stable, runs better on older hardware than other commercially available operating systems, and is for the most part free. From a small-business owner's point of view, I can't go wrong offering reduced costs to my clients, and excellent performance for both my own business, and my clients.

Putting the Pieces Together

As you can see, these professionals agree that certification is a useful career tool. It can add valuable credentials to your resumé and provide a learning path to help you achieve Linux expertise.

It's important to note that these certification will open doors for you, but it's up to you to keep them open, which is a good sign of effective and reasonable use of credentialing in any industry. Those extra letters on your business card or resumé signify that you have (or once had) particular expertise. Although that will get you a quicker and closer look, you'll still be required to provide evidence of your accomplishments in additional ways. That's as it should be, and if you've pursued certification in the proper spirit, backing up your credentials should be no problem. Strive to learn the material as thoroughly as possible instead of attempting to cram in just enough knowledge to pass the next exam.

Certification processes provide a method and motivation for keeping up on the latest products and technologies, a key to career success in the computer field. Although a few computer professionals have been disappointed by their efforts in the certification marketplace, by and large, individuals who have obtained one or more certifications report that the experience has been both personally and professionally satisfying. So much so that they rarely stop at one.

Chapter **4**

The Certifications

The newness of Linux as a significant force in the operating system marketplace, combined with the open-source nature of the software, creates a unique certification situation: multiple vendors offer Linux certifications, and many of these are very new or even still under development. Additionally, there is as yet little stratification of the marketplace. No single Linux certification or vendor has risen above the rest, in the eyes of either IT professionals or their potential employers. With no clear top, middle, and bottom, it becomes a bit more challenging to choose which certification to pursue. However, this slightly chaotic situation also means that by earning a Linux certification now, you can become one of the first, rather than the 30,000th, to offer this credential to potential clients and employers.

To get the most benefit from professional certification, it's important to take the time to choose the certification that best matches your goals, current skill level, and the amount of time and effort you're willing to invest. Choosing a certification because it's the one everyone is currently talking about won't serve you as well as making your selection based on your background and future goals. It's also important to balance the cost, time, and effort required to earn a particular certification with the benefits you hope to obtain and the time span that you find acceptable.

To help you make these decisions, this chapter discusses each Linux certification in detail and includes tables to help you compare various paths. Chapter 10 presents detailed information about the individual tests. The certifications are presented in alphabetical order to help you quickly locate those that you're most interested in.

CyberTech Institute

This company's sole business is creating and administering certification programs that cover a large array of technical and nontechnical topics. Rather than using one of the existing exam delivery companies, they have created their own network of test centers. The number of testing centers is rather limited, and they are only available in the United States. More recently CyberTech has begun introducing some online testing, which would help alleviate the test center location problem. Unlike other certification programs, they package preparation materials and the exam at a single price ($95).

CyberTech Linux Certification

This is a one-exam certification for Linux administration at a proficiency or master level. Coverage encompasses multiple distributions of Linux. For example, you'll be expected to know how to install Red Hat Linux and Caldera Open Linux Lite. You'll also encounter questions on:

* RPM and vi
* Managing file and directory systems
* Using Samba
* Linux shells
* Multiple processes
* X-Windows
* Managing a Web server
* And more

Linux Professional Institute

The Linux Professional Institute (LPI) began as a collaboration of members of the Linux community who were interested in developing standards for professional certification. In January 1999, after certification discussions had been going on for several months via Internet mailing lists, these individuals formed themselves into an entity called The Linux Institute. For legal reasons the name was changed to The Linux Professional Institute shortly thereafter.

Since then, LPI has been working through the process of creating a tiered set of vendor-independent Linux certifications. Along the way they have garnered the support of such industry participants Caldera Systems, Red Hat Inc., and SuSE. Their advisory board also boasts representatives from IBM, Lotus, CompUSA, and ExecuTrain Corp.

As this book went to press, the overall structure of the program had been defined, and the objectives for the level-one certification had been released, with exam objectives for levels 2 and 3 to follow. Exams will probably last 1-to 2 hours. Although no suggested training curriculum has been defined at this time, LPI is seriously considering developing courseware to help candidates prepare.

As with many other Linux certifications, the implementation is still in progress. You'll want to check the LPI Web site (**www.lpi.org**) for the current status of this program. Meanwhile, the initial LPI certifications are as follows:

Linux Professional Institute Certified Level 1 (LPIC Level 1)

LPIC Level 1 certification is geared toward the serious power-user/help desk individual. Candidates are expected to be able to install and configure workstations and perform basic maintenance tasks such as backup and restore functions.

To earn this certification you must pass three exams. The first two test general Linux, nondistribution-specific skills. They cover GNU, X, TCP/IP networking, and PC Linux specifics such as understanding hardware, boot process, kernel, and file system subtypes. The third exam tests distribution-specific knowledge and skills. The Linux Professional Institute plans to have one of these exams for every major Linux distribution. The exams will cover distribution-specific installation, administrative tools, file locations, and package and software management. Currently the list includes Caldera, Red Hat, SuSE, Slackware, and TurboLinux. Candidates may choose to take more than one of these exams. Figure 4.1 illustrates this certification path.

Linux Professional Institute Certified Level 2 (LPIC Level 2)

Predictably, LPIC Level 2 certification requires substantially higher skills than LPIC Level 1. Candidates must already hold LPIC Level 1, and pass two additional exams: an advanced administration exam and a Linux internals exam. The advanced administration exam covers administration tasks like problem tracking and resolution, script writing using sed and sh, and general internetworking knowledge. The internals exam encompasses configuration and compiling the Linux kernel and modules, applying patches, managing libraries, monitoring processes, and similar tasks. Figure 4.2 shows this certification.

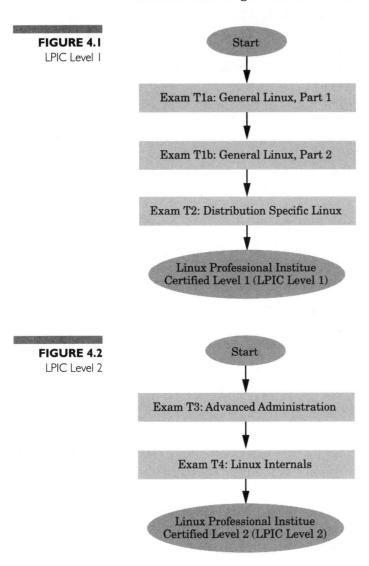

FIGURE 4.1
LPIC Level 1

FIGURE 4.2
LPIC Level 2

Linux Professional Institute Certified Level 3 (LPIC Level 3)

Earning the top-level LIPC designation requires holding Level 2 certification and passing at least two specialization exams. Currently planned specializations include:

* Windows integration (working together with NT-server, many Win/9x clients)
* Internet server (listservs, newsserver, FTP, HTTP, DNS, ISP, NFS, maybe Perl scripting)
* Database server
* Security, firewalls, encryption
* Kernel internals and device drivers; creating distribution packages

Figure 4.3 shows this certification.

FIGURE 4.3
LPIC Level 3
certification path

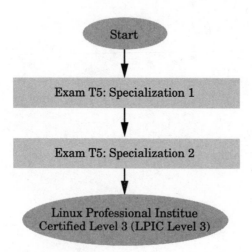

ProsoftTraining.Com

Originally named Tel-Fed in 1985, this company has gone through a series of name changes—first to Prosoft Development, then to Prosoft I-Net Solutions, and most recently this company officially changed its name to ProsoftTraining.com. It got into the certification business in 1998 when it acquired Net Guru Technologies, founders of the Certified Internet Webmaster credentials. Their primary products are instructor-led training and courseware, and they design a complete curriculum to accompany each certification they offer, as well as provide training for other certification programs.

Prosoft Linux Certified Administrator

The Prosoft Linux Certified Administrator, initiated in 1999, is a straightforward, single-exam certification. It's intended for individuals who use Linux in a production environment. A corresponding curriculum is available, for individuals who already have UNIX experience. The five-day curriculum includes a two-day Linux Fundamentals course followed by a three-day Linux System and Network Administration course. Exams are administered through Sylvan Prometric and cost $100.

Red Hat Inc.

Red Hat Inc., formerly Red Hat Software, is, not coincidentally, the vendor of a popular Linux distribution called Red Hat Linux. Although you can download the Red Hat distribution for free from the **redhat.com** Web site, obviously this is not how the company produces profits. Red Hat's business is creating and selling boxed sets of its distribution, along with support for the operating system. These sets come with manuals, installation technical support, and many extra applications. Some of those applications are open-source software, others are not.

Red Hat is one of the leading players in the Linux marketplace. The name is well recognized and their certification program is one of the better known for Linux. Red Hat Linux is a three-time winner of *InfoWorld*'s Product of the Year award. Quite a few high-tech firms have taken an equity stake in Red Hat, including Compaq Computer Corp., IBM Corp., Intel Corp., Netscape, and Oracle Corp. Because of the company's visibility and its early entrance into Linux certification, Red Hat certifications are off to a stronger start than many of the other Linux certifications.

Red Hat Certified Engineer (RHCE)

The Red Hat Certified Engineer designation was launched in 1998. It is designed for individuals who have significant experience with Linux and UNIX, and is specific to the Red Hat distribu-

tion. The RHCE is also version specific: you'll have to recertify as
new versions are released. Red Hat says certifications are valid for
a least a year, and will not immediately expire upon the release of
a new version.

To earn the RHCE certification you must pass a hands-on lab
exam ($749). The lab exam is intended to verify that you can install
and configure Red Hat Linux, understand limitations of hardware,
configure basic networking and file systems, configure the X Windowing System, configure basic security, set up common network
(IP) services, carry out basic diagnostics and troubleshooting, and
perform essential Red Hat Linux system administration.

The closed-book exam consists of three elements: a written test
(1–2 hours); a server installation and network services configuration
lab (2 hours); and a diagnostics and troubleshooting lab (3 hours).

Although it's not required, Red Hat does strongly suggest that
you take its preparation course unless you have a great deal of
experience with UNIX and Red Hat Linux. The RHCE preparation course runs 5 days and costs $2,498 including the lab exam
on the final day. This course is not for complete novices, but
assumes significant UNIX and Linux knowledge. Additional,
lower-level Linux courses are also available.

Red Hat Certified Engineer II (RHCE II)

The RHCE II certification was still under development as this
book was going to press and was expected to appear late in 1999.
Basically, it will cover more advanced system administration,
server administration, and networking, security skills than the
RHCE does.

Red Hat Certified Examiner (RHCX)

The Red Hat Certified Examiner (RHCX) designation is for individuals who want to proctor RHCE exams—these individuals
would be working for an authorized training partner. The certification is very specific to downloading and administering the
RHCE exam and setting up the RHCE lab environment. The
examiner certification test is administered at Red Hat's Durham,

North Carolina location and in Stockely Park, Uxbridge, England. This certification is only offered in conjunction with Red Hat's Train The Trainer class and cannot be taken separately. To become an RHCX you must be an RHCE as well.

Red Hat Developer

Red Hat recently introduced a Red Hat Developer training program. As this book was going to press, this was *not* a certification—there was no exam, just a curriculum. However, there's a good chance this could become a certification, so if it interests you, check out Red Hat's training and certification site at **www.redhat.com/products/training.html** for the latest status. So far there's a foundation course and then tracks for kernel and device driver development or application and GUI development.

Sair

Sair (pronounced *zair*) is an acronym for "Software Architecture Implementation and Realization." Sair Inc. is a software development company that's been in business since 1992. In 1999 it made a major investment of time and effort toward developing a Linux certification program. The program was developed with the participation of numerous Linux industry insiders as well as representatives from various Linux distribution vendors.

Much like the offerings of the Linux Professional Institute, Sair's program has three certification levels. It's organized around what Sair calls a "knowledge matrix." This means that each certification is based on a level of proficiency in four system usage areas:

* Linux installation
* Network connectivity
* System administration
* Security, ethics, and privacy

Each of these areas has six areas of competency:

* Theory of operation
* System base

* Shells and commands
* Utilities
* Applications
* Troubleshooting

Figure 4.4 illustrates this matrix. Each Sair certification follows this matrix format, but with different expectations depending on the level of the certification. Each level requires passing four exams, corresponding to the four system usage areas.

FIGURE 4.4
Sair's knowledge
matrix

Linux installation	network connectivity	system administration	security, ethics, & privacy
theory of operation	theory of operation	theory of operation	theory of operation
system base	system base	system base	system base
shells and commands	shells and commands	shells and commands	shells and commands
utilities	utilities	utilities	utilities
applications	applications	applications	applications
troubleshooting	troubleshooting	troubleshooting	troubleshooting

Individuals who obtain Sair certification will receive a certificate, wallet ID card, and permission to use the Sair Linux/GNU certification logo. Successful candidates also receive a listing in a directory of Linux-certified professionals and access to restricted Linux forums.

Linux/GNU Certified Administrator (LCA)

The Sair Linux/GNU Certified Administrator designation follows Sair's knowledge matrix from the perspective of Linux knowledge that a power user or system administrator should have. For example, under the installation: shells and command, you'll be expected to "Compare and contrast environmental versus shell variables." Figure 4.5 shows the exam path for this certification.

As this book was going to press, the first two LCA exams were available through Sylvan Prometric, at a cost of $90 each. The additional LCA exams are likely to be available as you read this.

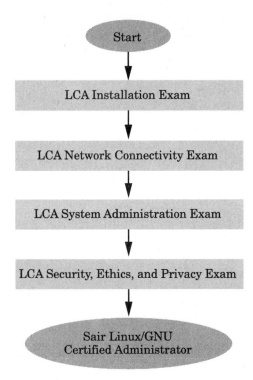

Linux/GNU Certified Engineer (LCE)

The Sair Linux/GNU Certified Engineer is Sair's advanced Linux certification. This certification revisits the knowledge matrix from the perspective of the expertise characteristic of a full time system manager. Although exams for this certification weren't available as this book was going to press, they were expected to appear in the near future. Figure 4.6 shows the exam path for this certification.

Master Linux/GNU Certified Engineer (MLCE)

The top Sair certification is the Master Sair/Linux GNU Certified Engineer designation. Once again following the knowledge matrix structure, according to Sair, this certification "represents the kind of detailed understanding and mastery of Linux knowledge that the senior system administrator and manager should have."

FIGURE 4.6

Sair's Linux/GNU
LCE certification
path

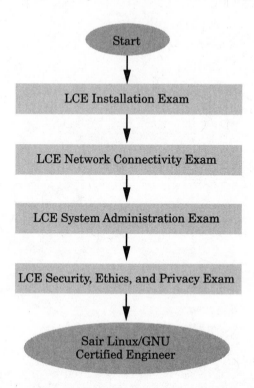

Linux/GNU Certified Trainer

Sair Linux/GNU Certified Trainers are authorized to teach Sair Linux/GNU certification preparation classes at Accredited Center for Education (ACE) sites. To become a Certified Trainer, you must already be a professional trainer, and attend a five-day train-the-trainer session. The session covers installation and setup of five Linux distributions, basic features, and important commands. At the close of the session candidates will be required to demonstrate mastery of the material.

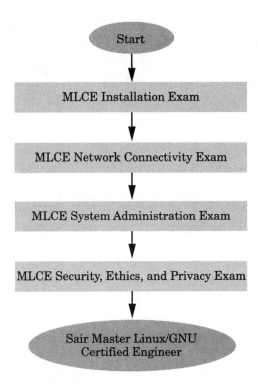

FIGURE 4.7
Sair's Linux/GNU
MLCE certification
path

Brainbench

Brainbench is neither a Linux-related organization nor an Linux vendor; rather, this company specializes in creating and administering online certification tests covering a variety of technologies. The Linux Administrator exam was added on June 5, 1999. Within two months, over 1,000 individuals had obtained the certification.

Certified Linux Administrator

To become a Brainbench Certified Linux Administrator, individuals must pass the Web-based Linux administration exam with a score of 2.75 or above out of a possible 5. Individuals who achieve a score of 4.0 or higher are granted a Master Linux Administrator certification.

The exam uses computer adaptive testing (CAT) technology, which means the sequence of questions is determined by the candidate's answer to the previous questions. Each exam is comprised of 40 questions, drawn from a much larger test bank. Brainbench exams cost between $25 and $50.

This certification must be renewed annually. The charge for recertification exams hadn't been officially determined as this book went to press, but was expected to be between $15 and $20.

Digital Metrics

Digital Metrics is a corporation based in Southern California. It was originally founded as a nonprofit entity called the Linux Foundation, but for various legal reasons, incorporated and changed its name to reflect its new organization. Digital Metrics was one of the first vendors to sponsor a Linux certification, and the first to offer Linux certification exams via the Internet. The company mission is limited specifically to the creation and administration of certifications that measure proficiency with a Linux operating system. In mid-1999, Digital Metrics merged certification efforts with the Linux Professional Institute. If you meet someone with the designation of Digital Metrics Certified Linux Administrator (dmCLA), it came from Digital Metrics before this merger. Digital Metrics no longer operates a Linux certification program.

Still Under Development

As you can see, there are quite a few Linux certifications to choose from. Due to the recent boom in the popularity of Linux, these programs have appeared quickly and are still in the early stages of implementation. Even more may appear in the near future.

Part 2

How to Get (Happily) Certified

Dollars and Sense: Financial Answers Before You Begin

Depending upon the program and training methods you choose, obtaining a Linux certification can entail a substantial investment. Because there are numerous possible routes to a single certification, it can be difficult to make an accurate assessment of what your actual cost will be. However, it's worthwhile to work up an estimate in advance so you won't be blindsided by unexpected expenses.

A detailed expense estimate can also help convince your employer to pay for part or all of your certification costs. When you itemize the figures on paper, you demonstrate that this is not just a whim; you have carefully considered the path to your goal, its costs, and its consequences. You'll also be better able to compare certification to other career-boosting alternatives, such as earning a traditional degree.

As certification continues to gain popularity, the number of ways to pay for it are increasing. Don't assume your own bank account is the only source of certification funding.

Once you've developed your initial estimate, you'll also be able to create alternate scenarios. This will enable you to compare the costs of various approaches. With that information, you'll be able to decide, for example, whether the classroom training courses are worth X dollars more to you than the self-guided CBT course covering the same material. You'll also be able to identify potential savings points, which can prove very useful if your funds are in short supply.

Throughout the process of estimating your expenditure, it's important to remember that while you may be laying out a substantial chunk of change today, you're doing so in expectation of an even larger payback in the future. That payback comes in the form of increased income, a better job, and increased personal and professional satisfaction.

Total Expenditure

Standard certification expenses include study materials, training costs, testing fees, and application fees. Depending upon the certification, you may also find yourself paying for travel to a training site or lab test, purchasing equipment or software, or incurring other charges.

Another expense you'll encounter is opportunity cost. Opportunity cost addresses the value of what, besides money, you'll be giving up in order to pursue certification. If you'll be studying during your usual work hours, then you won't be producing the income you otherwise would. If that will be the case, then your opportunity cost is measurable in dollars.

Some might argue that another opportunity cost is time out from other career advancement or networking activities. But focusing on certification is really a shift in method rather than a replacement for such activities; the time is still being dedicated to the same purpose but in a different way. In fact, you'll most likely be spending more time (or at least more effective time) on career-enhancement activities than you would otherwise.

If you plan to do the majority of your studying outside your usual business hours, then you won't be trading income for study time, but you'll still be taking time from somewhere else, such as family time or other areas of personal life, and dedicating it to your professional goals. That's an opportunity cost that's more difficult to quantify but still important to keep in mind.

Table 5.1 lists both the monetary and opportunity costs of certification.

TABLE 5.1
Certification costs

Out-of-Pocket Expenses	Opportunity Costs
Training tuition	Forgone earnings
Study materials	Reduced personal/family time
Test/lab fees	
Practice equipment	
Application fee	
Travel to testing/training facilities	

Creating a Worksheet

In estimating your total expenditure, it's helpful to use a spreadsheet like the one in Figure 5.1, or you can develop your own. You can make it the old-fashioned way—with paper and pencil—but a spreadsheet generated using Excel, Quattro Pro, or other program will be quicker and more versatile. An electronic version of the spreadsheet in Figure 5.1 can be found on **www.gocertify.com**.

FIGURE 5.1
Expenditure
worksheet

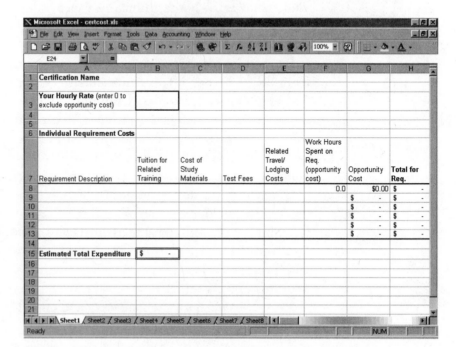

To calculate your total expenditure using the worksheet in Figure 5.1, first enter the certification name at the top of the sheet. If you prepare multiple worksheets (to compare various certifications), the name will make it easy to identify which worksheet goes with which certification program.

Next, enter your hourly pay rate. Your hourly rate is needed to calculate your opportunity cost. If you don't wish to include opportunity cost in your estimate, simply enter 0 (zero) for hourly rate.

The next section contains the meat of the worksheet. Beginning with the first requirement needed to obtain the certification, enter a brief description of the requirement. Then go across the row, filling in estimated tuition, cost of study materials you'll need to meet the requirement, any test fee related to the requirement, associated travel costs if you'll need to attend training elsewhere, and, last, the number of hours you'll take from work and apply to meeting this requirement. If you're using the electronic spreadsheet from the **gocertify.com** Web site, the opportunity cost and total cost for meeting the requirement will calculate and fill in automatically. If not, you'll need to perform the calculations and fill in the blanks by hand.

To determine the opportunity cost manually, multiply your hourly rate by the number in the "Work Hours Spent On Req." column. The total cost of the requirement is calculated by summing all numbers in the requirement row *except* the entry in the "Work Hours Spent On Req." column.

For each requirement you need to meet, fill in another row. Don't be afraid to make an educated guess at figures you don't know. You can dig up the actual numbers by calling vendors, surfing the Internet for course listings, or asking friends.

The estimate of your total certification expenditure will appear at the bottom of the spreadsheet. If you're completing the worksheet manually, add up the requirement expenses to obtain the same number. Figure 5.2 shows a worksheet completed by an RHCE candidate.

FIGURE 5.2
Completed worksheet

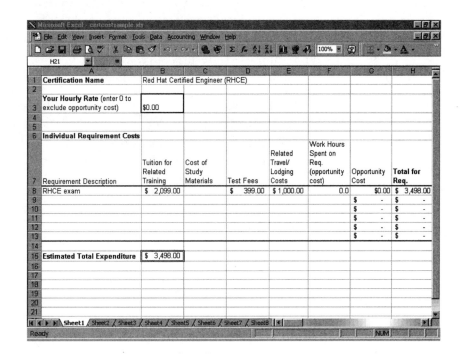

Save the completed worksheet, or print it out. Then you can go back and play with the numbers to create "what if" scenarios. If you complete the necessary training through CBT self study instead of instructor-led training, how will the total expenditure be affected? If you work on certification strictly outside your regular business hours, how much will you save in opportunity cost? To go back to your beginning worksheet, you can simply reload the version you originally saved. Additional scenarios you want to keep should be stored under other file names or printed out.

How to Cut Your Costs

You can significantly cut your certification expenditures in a number of ways. Some of them will come with one or more trade-offs that you'll have to measure against your savings. As we all know, cheaper isn't always better and sometimes may not even be adequate. Deciding which cuts make sense in a particular situation is a highly personal decision that involves factors such as your available free time, your individual learning strengths and weaknesses, your financial situation, the extent of your employer's support, time pressures, and so on. With that in mind, the basic ways you can make certification more affordable are:

* Convince an employer to shoulder part or all of the cost.
* Cut your training costs.
* Spread out your expenses over time.
* Take any related tax deductions for which you qualify.
* Consider taking out an education loan.

Getting Subsidized

As part of its fourth annual salary survey of professionals who have obtained or are in the process of obtaining one of the Microsoft Certified Professional (MCP) designations, *MCP Magazine* asked respondents who paid for the last certification/training program they attended. Well over half (62%) of respondents reported receiving financial support for their training from their employer. Half (50%) of respondents said that their employers footed the entire bill, while 12% shared the expense with an employer. Thirty-eight percent of respondents paid for their own training. Although there's no comparable study available about Linux certification, it's likely the numbers are somewhat similar. Clearly, the odds are good that you'll be able to convince an employer to subsidize your training, at least to some extent. But, first, you have to know where the available money is.

Tapping the Company Budget

At least two areas of the company budget are potential contributors of certification funding, especially at larger organizations: the departmental training budget and the company-wide tuition reimbursement program. Your employer's department training budget is likely to cover a broader variety of training options than the tuition reimbursement plan. Still, it may have been created largely with manager-selected and in-house training in mind, so you'll have to approach your manager (or the appropriate human resources person) and convince him or her that certification training and/or testing is an appropriate use of the funds. Be prepared to explain how your certification training would provide value to the company and why the company should fund it. Think of this as a business presentation, and prepare for it by collecting the necessary facts and practicing beforehand in private.

When taking your case for certification to your boss, it often helps to present independent verification of the value of certification. Even though only one of these is Linux specific, the following sources can be used to argue the benefits of certification:

* *Linux Certification for the Software Professional* by P. Tobin Maginnis, published in the April 1999 issue of *Linux Journal*, takes an in-depth look at the need for and benefits of Linux certification. You can find it at **www.linuxcertification.org/ art5.html**. Figure 5.3 shows the online version.
* The IDC (International Data Corp.) white paper *Benefits and Productivity Gains Realized Through IT Certification* (**www.ibm.com/Education/certify/news/proidc.phtml**).
* Microsoft Corporation's *Microsoft Certified Professional Program Corporate Backgrounder* and several certification case studies (**www.microsoft.com/mcp/mktg/bus_bene.htm**).

✱ Novell's *Novell Certification: A Strategic Investment; An Executive Brief for Employers* throws some pretty impressive numbers your way too (**education.novell.com/general/stratinv.htm**).

FIGURE 5.3
Benefits of
Certification
white paper

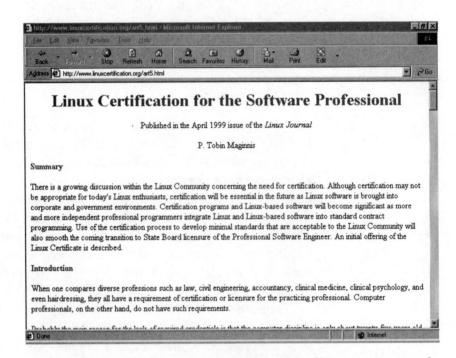

A tuition reimbursement plan is typically more narrowly defined than a training budget; it's often limited to courses that qualify toward a traditional degree. But that doesn't mean it can't fund certification training. If you are working toward a degree of some kind, many certification courses and programs are accepted by colleges as transfer credits and applied toward your degree. If you can demonstrate to your company that the programs will count toward your degree and the company has a tuition reimbursement policy, there's a good chance you'll be able to get certification training coverage.

If you hope to receive funding from your employer, it's important to investigate both the tuition reimbursement and training budget possibilities *before* you begin your program. There may be steps you'll have to take to qualify for the funds, and you'll want to find out just how much of which kinds of training will be covered.

QUICK TIP

Questions to Ask the Budget Minders

At a large corporation, there's usually a human resources department, and within it, an individual who is in charge of employee benefits. That person is the one to bring your questions to. In smaller companies, start with your manager or supervisor. If she can't answer your reimbursement questions, she'll be able to direct you to someone who can. Here are the important questions to ask:

✳ If you take certification courses that are recommended for college credit, will the company cover the tuition?

✳ If the certification and/or training will benefit your job, will the company cover your costs?

✳ Besides tuition itself, will the company reimburse you for related expenses such as books and travel? If so, which expenses are covered?

✳ Do you need to obtain official advance approval in order for your curriculum to qualify? From whom?

✳ What evidence will you need to provide in order to obtain reimbursement?

✳ Are there limits on the total reimbursement you can receive?

In addition to the above questions, take care to clarify any reimbursement-related concerns you have. It's a good idea to present your queries in the form of a memo, and to request the answers in writing, signed by the person who provided them. Then, if a difference of opinion arises later over just what was promised, you'll have indisputable evidence to support your side.

The Payback Plan

When you can't obtain funding as part of an existing budget category, consider working out an arrangement with your employer. One reason that employers may be reluctant to finance certification is the fear that the newly qualified employee will jump ship. You can understand how, from the employer's perspective, spending money on an employee to enable that person to leave (taking their expensive training with them) for another job would be counterproductive. So you may have to offer some reassurance.

One of the more common methods of overcoming this impediment is to form an agreement with your employer that insures the company against your departure. Basically, you agree in writing that if you leave the company within a certain period of time after receiving company-financed certification training, you will reimburse the company for its expense. If you decide to move on after the end of the specified period, you won't owe the company anything.

An arrangement like this often allows for prorating the amount of refund you would owe the company, based on how long you remain with your employer after training. Recruiting companies may also agree to an arrangement like this in return for your promise to continue to use them as your placement agency.

Look ahead. If you're very dissatisfied with your current position (or recruiting company) and expect to leave in the near future, this probably isn't a good way to pay for certification.

Hitting the Road

Your current employer isn't the only potential source of certification funds. Another route used by computer professionals is to begin training on their own and then look for a new position. Some employers consider an individual who has already embarked on the road to certification to be a superior job candidate. As an incentive for you to switch jobs, a new employer may well agree to pay for the rest of your certification program, as part of your new employment contract.

To follow this route, go ahead and complete your first requirement and test. Then begin searching online databases and elsewhere for job opportunities that appeal to you. Your resumé should note that you're in the process of obtaining certification. When you reach the negotiating table, work to include funding for continuing training as part of your employment contract.

Linux distribution vendors typically have Linux certified professionals on staff. This translates into job opportunities that include certification training. Your chances are especially good if you already have one Linux certification under your belt or are well on your way. They will also have access to equipment and software you can practice on. To find opportunities with Linux distribution vendors, visit the vendor's Web site and look for a "careers" or "join the team" link.

Training on the Cheap

One of the most effective ways to cut your certification expenditure is also perhaps one of the simplest: be budget conscious when selecting and purchasing training for your certification. Because of the popularity of certification, there are many vendors and an extensive array of training options to choose from. Linux certification candidates don't have quite as many options as candidates for certifications that have been available for longer periods of time, but preparation materials are appearing quickly. A few rules of thumb to keep in mind are:

* Self-study is less expensive than instructor-led training.
* A training package is often cheaper than purchasing the components separately.
* Special discounts are frequently available, if you ask for them.
* Training time span affects costs.
* Prices vary significantly among training vendors.

Training Methods and Costs

Self-study is radically cheaper than instructor-led training. Although the 5-day Red Hat Certified Engineer (RHCE) course taken through Red Hat runs around $2,099 (not including the exam), you can purchase a self-study book such as the *RHCE Exam Cram* by Kara Pritchard (Coriolis, 1999) for $23.95 through **fatbrain.com**. Depending on your learning style, abilities, existing knowledge, and access to other resources, you may be able to get by with a study guide or even just studying the manuals that accompany Linux distributions and other free papers available through the World Wide Web.

You'll also find "study kits" and CBT software on the market. The kits incorporate several training media, such as videotaped presentations, text material, and self tests, into one package.

The price and quality of training products vary widely, so don't commit to any of them without a solid preview. This book's companion Web site (**gocertify.com**) contains links to CBT programs and training materials, but you'll find even more by searching the Internet and reading trade magazine advertisements.

Professionals who've taken the self-study track often recommend study materials that include practice tests, so that may be an important feature to look for. You'll also find that some companies actually guarantee that if you use their materials (or take their classes) that you will pass the associated test, but don't be misled; the best guarantee in the world isn't as meaningful as your personal determination—you're in this to get certified, not to get your money back.

If you don't feel confident that self-study will work for you, the next level up is facilitated training online. Courses offered via the Internet are cheaper than their classroom cousins and offer some of the same benefits. You'll have access to an instructor and interaction with other students, but you won't have to travel to a training center or follow as rigid a schedule. Magellan University (**www.magellan.edu**) offers several different online Linux training choices.

Step up another price level and you'll encounter another option that may prove just the ticket if time isn't in short supply: college classes. Increasingly, exactly the same certification classes offered by authorized training companies are available as college courses. The major difference is the time span; instead of blasting through requirements with several intense, sequential days of training, you'll complete them at a more leisurely pace. For some people, the pace is a bit too leisurely. But when instructor-led training appears to be what you need, colleges will save you money over commercial training centers. Linux training has begun to appear at an increasing number of community colleges.

The top tier of certification preparation, in cost, is the authorized training center class. For some people and for some requirements, it can be irreplaceable. You'll have the equipment, trained and certified instructors, and other resources at hand. But you will pay for it. This type of class may be the way to go for requirements you find especially daunting, but in other cases, lower cost options will do the job handily. Table 5.2 illustrates the comparative costs of the various options. The table provides a general expense assessment based upon typical market prices, but individual products may sometimes fall outside their category.

Of course, price isn't the only consideration in choosing a training method, or necessarily the most important. Additional pros, cons, and characteristics of available training options, including resources that are free, are discussed in detail in Chapter 8.

Method	Standard Price Level
Self-study book/manual	$
Single CBT program	$$
Online class	$$$
Self-study kit	$$$
College course	$$$$
"Unauthorized" training vendor	$$$$$
Authorized training vendor	$$$$$$

Package Deals

Just as stocking up in a supermarket can pay off, bulk purchasing training can, too. If you're preparing for one of the more complex certifications, there will be multiple requirements and corresponding exams. Training vendors want to keep your business, and one way to do that is to hook you in for an extended period. In exchange for customer loyalty, they offer substantial savings.

Consider Learning Tree International's Alumni Gold Tuition Discount. Everyone who attends a Learning Tree course receives the discount card, which entitles the holder to a significant discount on the tuition for additional courses you take in the following 12 months. Many training providers offer similar bulk purchase discounts.

Make any bulk certification training purchase with extra care. It's a good idea to try a single course first to make sure the training style and materials are a good fit with your needs. Ask for the names of satisfied customers and talk to them about what they liked and didn't like in their dealings with the company. Signing up for a package training deal only to discover afterwards you don't like that certification, training company, or learning method can be a costly error.

You may come across deals, especially with the newer "online universities," where you pay one fee in return for all the classes you can or care to complete within a given period of time. These sound like a great deal, and for some people, they may be. If this is an option you're considering, carefully assess:

* The quality of the classes
* The selection of classes offered
* How many you will realistically complete within the stated time period

You may find a great deal or, instead, discover that although the offer sounds like a bargain, the quality of the courses or your ability to utilize them makes it much less so.

Another type of package deal is one that your employer can enter into, especially if yours is a medium- to large-sized company. Your employer agrees to use the vendor as the company's trainer of choice, and employees receive discounted tuition in return. Ask your employer if there is a similar arrangement with a training organization. If not, suggest implementing one.

Special Discounts

Make sure you ask about any available discounts. You may find that government employees or other specific groups that you may belong to are eligible for reduced rates at a particular vendor.

Shop Around for the Best Deals

In contrast to purchasing the entire shebang from a single vendor, you can also purchase a piece here and a course there. This method requires a greater investment of your time and legwork (or keyboardwork), but will allow you to purchase each training item at the lowest price you can uncover.

To locate training vendors in your area, you can contact the sponsor of the certification you're pursuing. But that's only a starting point because the listing is likely to be limited to authorized trainers. Internet search engines are a powerful tool for uncovering training vendors. A few places to start your search are:

* **www.yahoo.com/Business_and_Economy/Companies/ Computers/Software/Training/**—Yahoo's indexed compilation of software training companies. Yahoo has recently added a certification subcategory on this page (shown in Figure 5.4).
* **www.nerdworld.com/nw190.html**—Nerd World Media's list of computer training companies. Each entry contains a brief summary and link to a related Web page.

Part of effective price shopping is to ask others who've pursued the same credentials where they obtained training and materials, how much they paid, and how they rate the vendor they purchased from. In this way, you can gather tips that will spare you both search time and quality problems.

FIGURE 5.4

Yahoo's certification training companies index

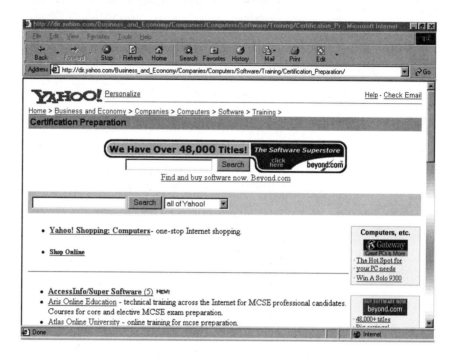

Make Your Funds Do Double Duty

If you can't trim your training costs appreciably, perhaps you may be able to get double mileage for your money. A certification training course may qualify for college credits toward a degree program, so be sure to check with your academic institution beforehand to see if and how you can get your training applied toward your degree.

As valuable as certifications are, don't overlook the importance of college degrees. For better or worse, many employers use a college degree as a break point for getting an interview. You may be able to get around this with a combination of certification and experience, but you will face greater challenges than if you have that college degree. This means it's really worth checking into the possibility of applying certification training toward a traditional four-year diploma.

Condense Training

Getting back to opportunity cost, one of the simplest ways to cut your expenses is to reduce the amount of time you spend earning certification. When work time is being devoted to certification, it isn't being used to generate income. That's the age-old time-equals-money equation.

Correspondingly, less time equals less money. That is, reducing the amount of time away from work can drastically reduce total certification costs. For example, if your income works out to an hourly rate of $35 per hour, and you cut 20 hours off your certifiagtion training time, you've trimmed $700 from your certification bill (or conversely, returned that 20 hours to the income side of your budget, resulting in an additional $700 to your bank account).

Another way to compress certification time is to take intense, condensed courses or sequences of courses which are often called boot camps. Because the vendor doesn't repeatedly have to set up the training environment, coordinate staff and facilities, or lay out other one-time costs, the vendor's cost is lower if the same material were offered over a more extended period of time. The savings are often passed on to the students.

Stretch It Out

If paying for certification will just put too much of a squeeze on your budget, you may be able to manage it more easily by meeting the requirements over time. Your overall cost may well be higher than if you didn't follow this route, but it will be spread out into more manageable outlays. You may even find that once your certification is under way, you'll be able to boost your billing rate, and financing your education will no longer be a problem.

It's important to remember that, other than death and taxes, nothing in life is guaranteed, including an income boost from certification. So if you're considering relying on your credit cards (with their high interest rates) to pay for certification, look for another way or risk carrying the balance and paying the high interest rates longer then you planned on. Perhaps a loan at a more reasonable rate from a bank or family member will tide you over. Otherwise, seriously consider putting off certification until your financial picture improves.

Join the Exchange

Certification training materials (software and printed matter), especially "authorized" materials, don't come cheap. A price tag of $75 to $100 or more isn't unusual. After the exam, they become like last semester's college textbooks; an expensive reminder of courses gone by. College students cope with the issue by selling used textbooks to each other, and, now, certified professionals have begun doing the same thing. In gocertify.com's SwapShop (**www.gocertify.com/swapshop.html**), you can buy, sell, or swap Linux or any other certification preparation course materials. The site does this strictly as a public service, at no charge to participants. The SwapShop is shown in Figure 5.5.

FIGURE 5.5
The gocertify.com certification SwapShop

Taking Advantage of Tax Breaks

Although taxes may be an inevitable price of life in the United States and elsewhere, that doesn't mean you have to pay more than your fair share. Luckily for Americans pursuing professional training, Uncle Sam smiles on citizens who work to improve themselves and their economic position. A strong worker makes for a strong economy, and all that. So employees who pay out of pocket for certain types of education get to deduct their expenses from their federal tax return. The available deductions apply whether you're self-employed or on the payroll of a national conglomerate. If you're not self-employed, you'll need to itemize your deductions in order to claim these, too, and the amount will be subject to the two percent limitation.

This section details federal tax deductions in force at the time this book was written. Tax consequences vary depending on individual situations and circumstances, and although I'm not qualified, nor do I intend to advise you on your personal tax position, this book can provide a good overview of some potential deductions. Because of the ever-shifting nature of the tax landscape, it's a good idea to consult a tax professional or study up, using publications from the IRS for the latest details and tax laws.

Do You Qualify?

To calculate your deduction(s), the first thing you'll have to determine is whether your courses are considered "qualifying education" according to the IRS definition. Specifically, the education must either:

1. Be required by your employer or the law to keep your present salary, status, or job (and serve a business purpose of your employer) or
2. Maintain or improve skills needed in your present work.

That sounds pretty straightforward, and as long as you already work in the computer field, your certification training is likely to fall squarely under number 2, which, according to the IRS, includes refresher courses, courses on current development, and academic or vocational courses.

But, the tax code being what it is, there are complicating exceptions—namely, education is not "qualifying" if it:

1. Is needed to meet the minimum educational requirements of your present trade or business, or
2. Is part of a program of study that can qualify you for a new trade or business, even if you have no plans to enter that trade or business.

Again, assuming that you are already a computer professional, neither of these is likely to invalidate your certification expenses as qualifying education. If this seems confusing, check out Figure 5.6, which contains a reproduction of a handy decision flowchart included in IRS Publication 17 to clarify the definition of qualifying education.

FIGURE 5.6

IRS flowchart: Are your educational expenses deductible?

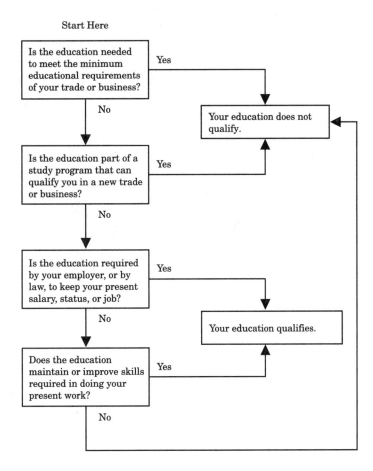

What You Can Deduct

Once you've determined that your training qualifies, you'll need to know which expenses are deductible. They are:

* Tuition, books, supplies, lab fees, and similar items
* Certain transportation and travel costs
* Other educational expenses, such as costs of research and typing when writing a paper as part of an educational program

You can't deduct personal or capital expenses (which include opportunity expense).

The IRS further defines "certain transportation and travel costs." Basically, you can deduct your transportation from work to school and then school to home, as long as you're attending school on a temporary basis (defined as a matter of days or weeks). If you go to school from home, again, on a temporary basis, you can probably deduct your transportation both ways. Longer-term educational engagements may only be eligible for mileage from work to school.

Cab, subway, and bus fares; car expenses; and parking fees and tolls are all transportation costs. Car expenses can be either your actual expenses or at the standard mileage rate.

If your training takes you away from home overnight, then you've moved into the realm of travel expenses. As far as education-related travel expenses, the IRS says that you can deduct expenses for travel, up to 50 percent of the cost of your meals and lodging, if you travel overnight to obtain qualified education and the main purpose of the trip is a work-related course or seminar.

Claiming Your Deductions

If you're self-employed, your qualifying education expenses can be deducted on your Schedule C Profit or Loss from Business or Schedule C-EZ Net Profit from Business. When using Schedule C (see Figure 5.7) your tuition, lab fees, books, and similar items will fall under Part V Other Expenses. Other amounts should go under their matching headings elsewhere on the form.

If you're an employee, the form you're after will be 2106 Unreimbursed Employee Business Expenses (or its shorter cousin

2106-EZ). Form 2106 is shown in Figure 5.8. Note the word unreimbursed in the form title; if an employer already refunded your expenses, you're not allowed to double dip. Especially if you file a Schedule C, you might find it more financially beneficial to utilize these pre-1997 Tax Act methods of claiming education expenses.

FIGURE 5.7
Schedule C
Profit or Loss
From Business

SCHEDULE C (Form 1040) Department of the Treasury Internal Revenue Service (99)	**Profit or Loss From Business** (Sole Proprietorship) Partnerships, joint ventures, etc., must file Form 1065 or Form 1065-B. Attach to Form 1040 or Form 1041. See Instructions for Schedule C (Form 1040).	OMB No. 1545-0074 19**98** Attachment Sequence No. **09**
Name of proprietor		Social security number (SSN)

A	Principal business or profession, including product or service (see page C-1)	**B** Enter NEW code from pages C-8 & 9
C	Business name. If no separate business name, leave blank.	**D** Employer ID number (EIN), if any

E   Business address (including suite or room no.)
    City, town or post office, state, and ZIP code
F   Accounting method: **(1)** ☐ Cash   **(2)** ☐ Accrual   **(3)** ☐ Other (specify)
G   Did you "materially participate" in the operation of this business during 1998? If "No," see page C-2 for limit on losses   ☐ Yes   ☐ No
H   If you started or acquired this business during 1998, check here   .   .   .   .   ☐

Part I   **Income**

1	Gross receipts or sales. **Caution:** If this income was reported to you on Form W-2 and the "Statutory employee" box on that form was checked, see page C-3 and check here . . . . . ☐	1	
2	Returns and allowances	2	
3	Subtract line 2 from line 1	3	
4	Cost of goods sold (from line 42 on page 2)	4	
5	**Gross profit.** Subtract line 4 from line 3	5	
6	Other income, including Federal and state gasoline or fuel tax credit or refund (see page C-3) . . .	6	
7	**Gross income.** Add lines 5 and 6	7	

Part II   **Expenses.** Enter expenses for business use of your home **only** on line 30.

8	Advertising	8		19	Pension and profit-sharing plans	19	
9	Bad debts from sales or services (see page C-3) . .	9		20	Rent or lease (see page C-5):		
				a	Vehicles, machinery, and equipment .	20a	
10	Car and truck expenses (see page C-3)	10		b	Other business property . .	20b	
11	Commissions and fees . .	11		21	Repairs and maintenance . .	21	
12	Depletion	12		22	Supplies (not included in Part III) .	22	
13	Depreciation and section 179 expense deduction (not included in Part III) (see page C-4) . .	13		23	Taxes and licenses . . .	23	
				24	Travel, meals, and entertainment:		
				a	Travel	24a	
14	Employee benefit programs (other than on line 19) . .	14		b	Meals and entertainment .		
15	Insurance (other than health) .	15		c	Enter 50% of line 24b subject to limitations (see page C-6) .		
16	Interest:						
a	Mortgage (paid to banks, etc.) .	16a		d	Subtract line 24c from line 24b	24d	
b	Other.	16b		25	Utilities	25	
17	Legal and professional services	17		26	Wages (less employment credits) .	26	
18	Office expense	18		27	Other expenses (from line 48 on page 2)	27	

28	**Total expenses** before expenses for business use of home. Add lines 8 through 27 in columns .	28	
29	Tentative profit (loss). Subtract line 28 from line 7	29	
30	Expenses for business use of your home. Attach **Form 8829**	30	
31	**Net profit or (loss).** Subtract line 30 from line 29. If a profit, enter on **Form 1040, line 12,** and ALSO on **Schedule SE, line 2** (statutory employees, see page C-6). Estates and trusts, enter on Form 1041, line 3. If a loss, you MUST go on to line 32.	31	
32	If you have a loss, check the box that describes your investment in this activity (see page C-6). If you checked 32a, enter the loss on **Form 1040, line 12,** and ALSO on **Schedule SE, line 2** (statutory employees, see page C-6). Estates and trusts, enter on Form 1041, line 3. If you checked 32b, you MUST attach **Form 6198.**	32a ☐ All investment is at risk. 32b ☐ Some investment is not at risk.	

For Paperwork Reduction Act Notice, see Form 1040 instructions.   Cat. No. 11334P   Schedule C (Form 1040) 1998

FIGURE 5.7

continued

Schedule C (Form 1040) 1998   Page **2**

| **Part III** | **Cost of Goods Sold** (see page C-7) |

33 Method(s) used to value closing inventory: **a** ☐ Cost   **b** ☐ Lower of cost or market   **c** ☐ Other (attach explanation)

34 Was there any change in determining quantities, costs, or valuations between opening and closing inventory? If ™Yes,∫ attach explanation . . . . ☐ **Yes**   ☐ **No**

35	Inventory at beginning of year. If different from last year's closing inventory, attach explanation . .	35	
36	Purchases less cost of items withdrawn for personal use	36	
37	Cost of labor. Do not include any amounts paid to yourself	37	
38	Materials and supplies	38	
39	Other costs	39	
40	Add lines 35 through 39	40	
41	Inventory at end of year	41	
42	**Cost of goods sold.** Subtract line 41 from line 40. Enter the result here and on page 1, line 4 . .	42	

| **Part IV** | **Information on Your Vehicle.** Complete this part **ONLY** if you are claiming car or truck expenses on line 10 and are not required to file Form 4562 for this business. See the instructions for line 13 on page C-4 to find out if you must file. |

43 When did you place your vehicle in service for business purposes? (month, day, year) . . . . . . / . . . . / . . . .

44 Of the total number of miles you drove your vehicle during 1998, enter the number of miles you used your vehicle for:

a Business . . . . **b** Commuting . . . . **c** Other . . . .

45 Do you (or your spouse) have another vehicle available for personal use? . . . . ☐ **Yes**   ☐ **No**

46 Was your vehicle available for use during off-duty hours? . . . . ☐ **Yes**   ☐ **No**

47a Do you have evidence to support your deduction? . . . . ☐ **Yes**   ☐ **No**

  b If ™Yes,∫ is the evidence written?. . . . . ☐ **Yes**   ☐ **No**

| **Part V** | **Other Expenses.** List below business expenses not included on lines 8±26 or line 30. |

. . . .	
. . . .	
. . . .	
. . . .	
. . . .	
. . . .	
. . . .	
. . . .	
48	Total other expenses. Enter here and on page 1, line 27	48	

⊕

FIGURE 5.8

Form 2106
Employee Business
Expenses

Form **2106**	**Employee Business Expenses**	OMB No. 1545-0139
Department of the Treasury Internal Revenue Service (99)	See separate instructions. Attach to Form 1040.	19**98** Attachment Sequence No. **54**

Your name	Social security number	Occupation in which you incurred expenses

Part I   Employee Business Expenses and Reimbursements

STEP 1 Enter Your Expenses		**Column A** Other Than Meals and Entertainment		**Column B** Meals and Entertainment
1	Vehicle expense from line 22 or line 29. (Rural mail carriers: See instructions.) **1**			
2	Parking fees, tolls, and transportation, including train, bus, etc., that **did not** involve overnight travel or commuting to and from work . . **2**			
3	Travel expense while away from home overnight, including lodging, airplane, car rental, etc. **Do not** include meals and entertainment **3**			
4	Business expenses not included on lines 1 through 3. **Do not** include meals and entertainment **4**			
5	Meals and entertainment expenses (see instructions) **5**			
6	**Total expenses.** In Column A, add lines 1 through 4 and enter the result. In Column B, enter the amount from line 5 . . . . . **6**			

Note: *If you were not reimbursed for any expenses in Step 1, skip line 7 and enter the amount from line 6 on line 8.*

STEP 2   **Enter Reimbursements Received From Your Employer for Expenses Listed in STEP 1**

7	Enter reimbursements received from your employer that were **not** reported to you in box 1 of Form W-2. Include any reimbursements reported under code ™L[in box 13 of your Form W-2 (see instructions) **7**			

STEP 3   **Figure Expenses To Deduct on Schedule A (Form 1040)**

8	Subtract line 7 from line 6 . . . . **8**			
	Note: *If both columns of line 8 are zero, stop here. If Column A is less than zero, report the amount as income on Form 1040, line 7.*			
9	In Column A, enter the amount from line 8. In Column B, multiply the amount on line 8 by 50% (.50). If either column is zero or less, enter -0- in that column. (Employees subject to Department of Transportation (DOT) hours of service limits: Multiply meal expenses by 55% (.55) instead of 50%. For more details, see instructions.) **9**			
10	Add the amounts on line 9 of both columns and enter the total here. **Also, enter the total on Schedule A (Form 1040), line 20.** (Fee-basis state or local government officials, qualified performing artists, and individuals with disabilities: See the instructions for special rules on where to enter the total.) **10**			

For Paperwork Reduction Act Notice, see instructions.   Cat. No. 11700N   Form **2106** (1998)

FIGURE 5.8
continued

Form 2106 (1998) Page **2**

Part II Vehicle Expenses (See instructions to find out which sections to complete.)

Section A–General Information

		(a) Vehicle 1	(b) Vehicle 2
11	Enter the date vehicle was placed in service	11 / /	/ /
12	Total miles vehicle was driven during 1998	12 miles	miles
13	Business miles included on line 12	13 miles	miles
14	Percent of business use. Divide line 13 by line 12	14 %	%
15	Average daily round trip commuting distance	15 miles	miles
16	Commuting miles included on line 12	16 miles	miles
17	Other miles. Add lines 13 and 16 and subtract the total from line 12	17 miles	miles
18	Do you (or your spouse) have another vehicle available for personal purposes?	☐ Yes ☐ No	
19	If your employer provided you with a vehicle, is personal use during off-duty hours permitted? ☐ Yes ☐ No	☐ Not applicable	
20	Do you have evidence to support your deduction?	☐ Yes ☐ No	
21	If "Yes," is the evidence written?	☐ Yes ☐ No	

Section B–Standard Mileage Rate

22	Multiply line 13 by 32½¢ (.325). Enter the result here and on line 1	22	

Section C–Actual Expenses

		(a) Vehicle 1	(b) Vehicle 2
23	Gasoline, oil, repairs, vehicle insurance, etc.	23	
24a	Vehicle rentals	24a	
b	Inclusion amount (see instructions)	24b	
c	Subtract line 24b from line 24a	24c	
25	Value of employer-provided vehicle (applies only if 100% of annual lease value was included on Form W-2–see instructions)	25	
26	Add lines 23, 24c, and 25	26	
27	Multiply line 26 by the percentage on line 14	27	
28	Depreciation. Enter amount from line 38 below	28	
29	Add lines 27 and 28. Enter total here and on line 1	29	

Section D–Depreciation of Vehicles (Use this section only if you own the vehicle.)

		(a) Vehicle 1	(b) Vehicle 2
30	Enter cost or other basis (see instructions)	30	
31	Enter amount of section 179 deduction (see instructions)	31	
32	Multiply line 30 by line 14 (see instructions if you elected the section 179 deduction)	32	
33	Enter depreciation method and percentage (see instructions)	33	
34	Multiply line 32 by the percentage on line 33 (see instructions)	34	
35	Add lines 31 and 34	35	
36	Enter the limit from the table in the line 36 instructions	36	
37	Multiply line 36 by the percentage on line 14	37	
38	Enter the **smaller** of line 35 or line 37. Also, enter this amount on line 28 above	38	

The Tax Act of 1997

The Tax Act of 1997 contained several education provisions that change how much and in what ways you can claim tax breaks for education expenses. The provision most relevant to computer professionals obtaining certification is the one called the Lifetime Learning Credit.

Unlike a deduction, which reduces the amount of income you pay taxes on, a credit is a dollar for dollar reduction of your tax bill. The Lifetime Learning Credit equals 20 percent of the first $5,000 of your qualifying education expenses (a $1,000 maximum per family per year). That amount will increase to 20 percent of the first $10,000 in expenses (or a $2,000 maximum), after the year 2002. The amount of the credit is reduced for filers with higher incomes. The actual amount of the credit depends on your family's income, the amount of qualified tuition and fees paid, and the amount of certain scholarships and allowances subtracted from tuition.

The Hope Scholarship credit is an option you'll want to explore if you'll be enrolled at least half time in an eligible program leading to an undergraduate or graduate degree at an eligible school during the calendar year or enrolled at any enrollment level in any course of instruction at an eligible school to acquire/improve the student's job skills during the calendar year. This credit has a maximum limit of $1,500 a year per qualifying student, and begins to phase out at an modified adjusted gross income of $40,000 ($80,000 if married filing jointly). If your modified AGI is over $50,000, ($100,000 if married filing jointly) you won't be eligible for this credit. Current law specifies that schools will supply this information in the form of a "return" to individual taxpayers and to the IRS. More information about the return will be available after the Treasury Department issues regulations to implement this law. The definition of qualifying expenses for the credits is different than for the deductions. Check with the IRS or your tax preparer for the nitty-gritty details.

QUOTE

Qualifying for Credits vs. Deductions

There are entirely different requirements for the education credits than for the deductible education expenses. The deductible education expenses are considered "business expenses," and so don't have to be from a school that meets the IRS's requirements. And a wider range of expenses can be included. The IRS's requirements focus on the *purpose* of the education.

On the other hand, the new credits are designed to encourage education in general. Most accredited public, nonprofit, and proprietary post-secondary institutions are eligible under the education credits. The credits can be taken for education used to meet the minimum requirements of your trade or business, or to qualify you in a new trade or business. And many people either don't itemize their deductions, or they have education expenses totaling less than 2% of their AGI, and as a result are unable to use them at all on the Schedule A.

—*Sally Rothenhaus-Faulkner, Certified Financial Planner*

There may be other additional provisions of the 1997 act for which you qualify, so be sure to check with your tax advisor before filing your return for any year in which you spent money on professional education. It may be your duty as an American citizen to pay taxes, but there's no reason to pay more than you're legally obligated.

As always, when dealing with tax matters, document, document, document. Collect and keep all receipts related to your education expenses, whether they're for $2,000 worth of tuition or a $1.20 highway toll, and keep an expense log that includes mileage records. Store the documents with your personal copy of your return. You'll probably never have to look at them again; but should the need arise, they'll be there.

QUICK TIP

Related IRS Forms/Publications

The following forms and publications pertain to various aspects of deducting education expenses. If you don't care to wade through them all, start with the bible of individual tax returns, Publication 17 (fondly referred to by tax professionals as Pub 17). It may adequately answer your questions.

You can retrieve the most recent versions of any of these items (and a vast quantity more) from the IRS Web site at **www.irs.ustreas.gov/**. Or call **1-800-TAX-FORM** and ask for them to be mailed to you.

Publication 17 Your Federal Income Tax
Publication 334 Tax Guide For Small Business (C or C-EZ filers)
Publication 508 Educational Expenses
Publication 529 Miscellaneous Expenses
Publication 535 Business Expenses
Publication 552 Recordkeeping For Individuals
Publication 553 Highlights of 1997 Tax Act Changes
Publication 970 Tax Benefits for Higher Education
Form 1040 U.S. Individual Income Tax Return

Schedule A Itemized Deductions
Schedule C Profit or Loss from Business
Schedule C-EZ Net Profit from Business
Form 2106 Employee Business Expenses
Form 2106-EZ Unreimbursed Employee Business Expenses

Taking Out a Loan

Although using your credit cards to fund certification is an iffy proposition, there are other options that are more desirable. You may be able to obtain a low-interest loan, grant, or scholarship. If you attend training at a professional school or college, you may qualify for a student loan from the Federal government. To find out more about federal student loans, call 800-557-7395 or visit the Direct Loan Web site at **www.ed.gov/offices/OPE/DirectLoan/index.html**. For information about other federal financial aid programs, call 800-4-FED-AID.

There are a number of loan programs popping up that cater specifically to IT professionals and cover certification training. These include:

* CCLC (**www.techloan.com**) provides loans for all technology training.
* The Key CareerLoan (**www.key.com**).
* National Association of Communication Systems Engineers (NACSE) has a training loan program for its members (**www.nacse.com**).

There are many other educational financial aid options open to you. Visit your local library for help uncovering them. If you have Internet access, you'll find the Financial Aid Information Page at **www.finaid.org** a tremendous resource (see Figure 5.9). Remember, if you do take out a loan for education purposes, the interest may be tax deductible.

FIGURE 5.9
Using the Web to
find financial aid

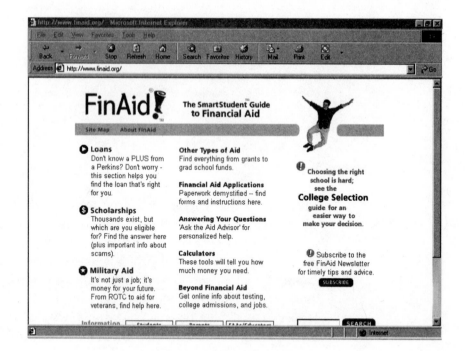

Chapter 6

Certification Mistakes You Don't Have to Make

The amount of time, money, and effort you put into achieving certification in Linux will depend upon the certification you choose and how much it is a natural extension of your current skill set. It will also depend on if and how far you stray from the direct path to your goal: certification. Although few computer professionals think of themselves as one of the herd, this is one time when staying on the beaten path is usually the best choice.

Fortunately, such a path has been blazed for you by computer professionals who have been embracing certification since early on. Even though Linux certifications haven't been around very long, plenty of other certification programs have been. Whether for Microsoft networking, IBM hardware, or the Linux operating system, the process of earning a certification is basically the same, and so are the pitfalls. By understanding where earlier certification candidates have gone astray, you can avoid making the same mistakes. What follows is an exploration of the certification errors most commonly made, and how to steer clear of them.

The errors are grouped into three categories:

* Choosing the wrong certification
* Mistakes made while working toward a chosen certification
* Mistakes made after achieving certification

Each of these areas contributes to your overall success and satisfaction. Although a small misjudgment here or there isn't going to cancel out all of your hard work, you might as well benefit from other people's hindsight. After all, that's one type of vision that's almost always 20/20.

Choosing the Wrong Certification

Choosing the wrong program is one of the more common mistakes people make when pursuing certification. What makes a certification a bad choice? Either it's chosen for wrong reasons, or it's lacking in some way that could easily have been detected with a little research. This type of mistake is easier to make than you might suspect. Here's why it happens.

Error 1: Choosing a Certification Because It's "Hot"

There's no doubt about it, the Linux operating system is enjoying hot status right now. So is certification. The combination of increasing demand and the cachet of working with the latest technology is very attractive. But it's still very possible that these certifications aren't right for you; just because you've heard great things about them doesn't mean they'll do great things for your career.

QUOTE

Quick & Easy May Not Be Best

Right now there are a number of different certifications available. It will take a while for the Linux certification industry to shake itself out as far as who employers and the Linux community decide to favor (and these may very well be different). I think it is a mistake to run out and get the easiest certification you can find and then feel secure in having it.

—*Dee-Ann LeBlanc, dmCLA, RHCE, author of several Linux books*

For a certification to achieve its fullest measure of career-boosting power, it must be chosen with care and closely matched with your existing skills and long-term interests. The certifications discussed in this book deal with the Linux operating system, and in most cases, the associated utilities and applications. If you're a Windows programmer, you're probably better off with a different certification. If you administer a Novell Network, this certification won't do as much for a you as a Novell MCNE. If you're out for top-of-the-heap salary and technical respect, Cisco's extremely challenging CCIE certification may be worth considering. You don't have to make a lifetime commitment to Linux to benefit from a Linux certification, but doing so is making a choice of career direction. Choose it because it's something you enjoy doing and learning about. Take the time to find the certification, Linux or otherwise, that fits your long-term plans and success will follow.

Error 2: Unrealistic Expectations

Do you anticipate a significant career boost will result from gaining the certification of your choice? Are you planning on earning more money? Incrementing your level of expertise? Moving into a new specialty? Switching to a different (and better) job?

All these goals are indeed possible outcomes of certification. However, it's important to remember that certification isn't a guaranteed cure-all for what ails your career. If your boss is a jerk, getting certified won't change him. It may, however, enable you to find employment somewhere with a boss who has more positive attributes. Or it might serve as an impetus to go independent and become your own boss.

Similarly, the skills you add in the course of earning a Red Hat Certified Engineer (RHCE) certification will improve your ability to implement and administer Red Hat Linux, but won't transform it into a stress-free job. Certification can be a powerful career tool, as long as you take care to select the proper tool for the particular career goal.

Error 3: Underestimating Cost

There are so many variables to consider when estimating how much certification will cost that it's not surprising that the calculation is often done wrong. Sometimes, it isn't done at all.

Why is underestimating the cost of certification such a big deal? Consider these potential scenarios:

* You run out of funds before you're done. If you end up taking an extended break from your certification program, some of your qualifications may expire and you'll have to meet them again. At best, you'll have to spend time reviewing to get back up to speed once your budget gets back on track. At worst, you'll never pick it up again and your efforts will have been largely wasted.

* Based on ball-park figures you described, your employer agrees to pay for certification training and testing. Then you submit a bill that's double what you initially suggested. How will that go over?

* You decide that a particular certification will more than pay for itself. But as the bills mount up you realize you've grossly miscalculated the figure in question. What will you do if it

isn't still worth it at the "new" price, yet you've already committed significant time and resources?

As you can see, miscalculating the cost or failing to calculate it at all can be a big mistake. It's a mistake that happens because naming a figure isn't always a simple process. Part of the confusion arises because there are usually several different routes to achieving any particular certification. The largest variance comes under the heading of training expenses. Whether you self-study from manuals or attend instructor-led, sponsor-approved training can make thousands of dollars of difference in your total tab.

Then there's the somewhat nebulous question of opportunity cost. To some people, an estimate that doesn't include it is meaningless. Others consider adding opportunity cost an inaccurate inflation of price. Either way, coming up with a reasonable figure for it requires a little math.

But given the potential consequences of underestimating the price tag of a particular certification path, it's worthwhile to work out a few figures. The worksheet in Chapter 5 will walk you through the steps. When in doubt, guess a little high. Having extra money left over is a problem you can no doubt live with.

Mistakes While Working Toward Certification

When you're undertaking something new and exciting, like professional certification, it can be tempting to rush ahead full speed. After all, you want to see results as soon as possible, don't you? But haste has its costs. People in a hurry tend to make assumptions in order to save time. While these assumptions may seem reasonable at the time, they sometimes turn out to be wrong, and end up disrupting your plans.

The following mistakes often result from eagerness and the desire to get on with it as much as anything else. Although these errors have less dire consequences than choosing the wrong certification, they can still cost you time, money, and frustration. Happily, forewarned is forearmed. Once you read about the snags that other professionals have encountered, you can easily dodge them.

Error 4: Purchasing a Complete Certification
Package Right Away

When you're offered a significant discount to purchase a package deal, it's tempting to leap at it. You'll get all your arrangements taken care of with one vendor and grab a discount besides. But—and this is a big but—it's a good idea to hold off making such a major investment until after you pass your first exam, at the earliest. Only then can you be fairly confident that the certification you've chosen is one you can work with. There's always a chance that you'll discover you've bitten off more than you care to chew or have a sudden change of heart over the direction you want to pursue.

If you buy a package up front, there's another risk: if this is your first foray into certification, how can you know which learning alternatives will become your favorites? What if you invest in a series of computer-based, self-preparation programs only to discover that you can't bear to sit down and face your PC each evening after doing the same all day at work? If it's instructor-led training that you've purchased in bulk and you discover that you don't need such a degree of support and instruction, you'll be faced with thousands of dollars of training you don't need but have already contracted for—a truly costly mistake.

 Don't overlook product documentation and information available on the World Wide Web as study tools. They are free and contain many, if not all, of the intricacies you'll need to master.

It's fairly simple to protect yourself from this particular pitfall. Start with one test and one preparation package. In fact, it's not a bad idea to see how you feel working strictly from free study guides and product manuals. Then if you want to escalate to third-party preparation materials, such as workbooks' computer-based training Web-based instruction or a classroom staffed by a living, breathing technical trainer, you can easily do so. And if you discover that the resources that are free will serve your purposes adequately, you won't have expended a single extra penny.

Error 5: Assuming Your Employer Will Pay for Your Training

This is a big mistake and a totally avoidable one. It happens when people recall that educational incentives were mentioned somewhere in the slew of paperwork they received as part of new employee orientation, but don't spend the time to pin down the details. Perhaps you don't just think so, you *know* that the company pays for continuing education, making it unnecessary to research further.

The problem is, even if your employer does as a rule pay for continuing education, the definition of just what that encompasses may be limited. Some companies only reimburse for courses completed as part of a degree program. Others further require that the degree be related to your job functions.

It also occurs when a coworker mentions in passing that the company paid for his certification training. But perhaps he neglected to mention that it was through a special arrangement, or that a dollar limit was imposed. Or maybe he really meant that the company paid his certification test fees, but you missed that clarification.

The bottom line is that what another employee got isn't necessarily something that you will receive too, and vice versa. It's important to check into employer funding/reimbursement before you begin. If the purse strings do open, which they often will, you'll still need to be aware of which paperwork needs to be submitted when, time limits, restrictions, and so on. Before you can comply with any guidelines, you need to know about them. To know about them, all you need to do is ask.

Error 6: Assuming Your Employer Won't Pay for Your Training

Just because it isn't in the employee handbook doesn't mean your employer can't be persuaded to share the expense of continuing education with you. Chapter 5 offers advice on how to bring this about. Why spend your own money on professional training if someone else is perfectly willing to foot the bill for you? Lately even independent contractors are having success at convincing someone else to finance professional training.

Error 7: Failing to Shop Around

Don't you hate it when you buy something at what you think is a good price only to see it advertised a week later somewhere else for a third less? It happens all the time with consumer purchases and it can happen with training purchases too.

You might not be willing to expend much effort to save three dollars on a pair of shoes, but when it comes to training packages, your potential savings are much higher. For a one-time investment of an hour or less, you may save $50, $100, or even $1,000. In addition to financial dividends, when you give yourself more training options to choose from, it's more likely you'll find one that closely matches your learning preferences and style.

Why then, do so many people neglect to shop certification training? Often because they:

* Aren't aware that drastic price differences exist
* Don't know where to look
* Are unsure of how to compare vendors and products.

Because each of these items is addressed in this book, you can totally avoid this mistake. Chapter 7 explores the wide selection of learning alternatives you can choose from. Chapter 8 explains how to find certification preparation training and tools, such as through the Internet, telephone book, and Linux distribution vendors. It also describes what to look for in a training center, and how to assess the quality of an instructor.

If you were in the market for a new television or lawn mower, you wouldn't purchase the first one you came across. Give your selection of certification training at least as much attention, and preferably more. Pay attention to the features each option has to offer, and weigh benefits against cost. Because prices vary widely between vendors, your dollar savings alone will make it worth your while, unless, of course, money is no object.

Error 8: Ignoring/Missing Time Constraints

When you begin your program, inquire up front if there are any time limits specifying how long you have to complete the entire program or any element of it. As of this writing, several of the

Linux certifications had time limits on recertification, but none had limits on the initial certification process. Recertification may involve passing an update exam, attending specific educational events, or meeting other requirements. The important thing to note is that if you don't complete the specified activities before the recertification deadline, you lose your certification and must start over again from the beginning. Some recertification requirements are annual, more run on a two-year cycle. Distribution-specific certifications often require update exams or complete recertification with new version releases.

Error 9: Failing to Get Certified After Your Employer Agrees to Pay for It

Once you've announced your intentions, failure to deliver isn't going to reflect well on you. This is especially true if you've approached your supervisor or boss and secured a promise of financial reimbursement. Fortunately, changing one's mind after starting a certification program is a rare occurrence.

Your goal in pursuing certification is to use it as a tool to further your career. It would be quite ironic if you end up damaging your image instead. If you find yourself faced with completing a certification that you've changed your mind about, one that your employer already approved, consider completing it anyway to avoid risking a reputation as someone who doesn't follow through.

The best course of action for this potential mistake is prevention. Develop a solid feel for the program before you enter it, including how much time you'll have to put in, and what benefits you hope to achieve. If you've done your homework in advance, it's unlikely that you'll find yourself pursuing a certification that isn't what you'd hoped for, and highly probable you'll obtain a credential that will be worth much more than the time and effort you spent earning it.

Error 10: Neglecting Your Job in Order to Study for Certification

Even if your employer has agreed to let you study during regular working hours, it's important not to allow your normal duties go unattended. This can be a difficult balancing act, especially if you have a demanding schedule, but it can be done.

> Although you probably don't have the facilities to set up a clustering scenario at home, you most likely could install a standalone version of Linux, or even a Linux-based Web server, to practice on outside work time.

Keep in mind that there's nothing like hands-on, on-the-job training for learning how to perform specific tasks. Try to apply the technology you're studying to your duties at work. If you don't have access to the equipment or software in question, but a coworker does, take him to lunch and explain your situation. Ask if you can shadow him during your lunch hour or at other times. Once you've learned how a particular task is done, try to get a chance to do it yourself.

When taking this approach, it's important to recognize that the person you're learning from may feel threatened. If you're after his/her job, then this plan is a bad idea. But most likely you're not, in which case it's a good idea to explain clearly what you are after as reassurance. Try to offer something in return, perhaps sharing skills you have.

But even if you get plenty of hands-on practice, you're going to have to hit the books to pass exams. Even in the busiest schedule, there's room for study time. You just have to find it. The time management guidelines in Chapter 9 can help you with that. Another trick to keep study time from encroaching on work time is to study less. Learning efficient and effective study habits will drastically reduce the quantity of time you'll need to prepare. Chapter 9 can help you on that front, as well.

The key to keeping your certification plans from interfering with your current job duties is to pay attention. In your eagerness to get certified, you may devote more time to preparation than you realize. Setting up a schedule will help you keep study and work hours in the proportion you want them. With the world being the unpredictable place that it is, you can expect to find your schedule disrupted at one time or another. When it is, simply get back on track as soon as you can.

Throughout the process, keep your certification goals in sharp focus. The purpose of certification is to enhance your career. If you irritate your employer in the process, getting ahead is going to be that much harder. But if you manage to juggle work and study effectively, you'll create the impression of a capable professional who takes initiative and follows through.

Error 11: Assuming You Don't Need to Study

Obtaining certification requires two forms of competency: knowing what to do, and being able to prove that you do. These are really two separate skills. The first has to do with the extent of your experience and understanding. The second reflects your ability to perform well on a test. A shortfall in either area will hinder your success.

The person who makes the mistake of assuming there is no need to study is likely be someone who is quite masterful in handling the technology in question, as demonstrated by performance at the current job. Consider a help desk professional or LAN technician pursuing a Linux Professional Institute Certification (LPIC) Level One. As a person who sorts out Linux questions and perhaps installs Linux as needed day in and day out, this person probably has an excellent grasp of what it takes to install and run Linux on the particular type of machines and for the particular applications in use within the organization. But what would happen if this professional arrived at work one day to find a new TCP/IP network in place, additional hardware needing to be configured for every Linux-based computer, and a formerly Windows NT-based Web server utilizing NTFS waiting to be converted to Linux? Probably, that person would feel a lot less expert.

Although this help desk professional/LAN technician's company computing environment would never change so dramatically overnight, such a setup could easily occur in written format, on a certification exam. Don't assume that a certification test you'll be taking will be limited to the environment in which you're an expert. In fact, expect it not to be.

The second component of successful certification is the ability to recall information in a test setting. You'll need to respond in theory instead of in practice. A situation that you may handle easily when you've got your command line utilities at your fingertips can suddenly seem foreign when it's presented as words on an exam. But spend time studying, and the written version will become second nature too.

QUOTE

Installation Is Just the Beginning

One of the biggest mistakes is that people think they know the whole system if they know one or two things well. They know how to install the system, and thereby think they know how to work it. For example: If your average Linux-newbie made an error in the install-procedure (and forgot to include a program), he would install the system again. The experienced user would just add the program afterwards. The average user would reboot when he has changed a configuration option and needs to see if it's working. The expert user would never reboot unless hardware is faulty, or a new kernel image needs to be installed (unless you're on a debugging phase).

—*Robin Smidsrød, dmCLA, Systems Administrator*

Error 12: Assuming You Know the Best Way to Study

Studying doesn't just consist of opening a book or manual and reading it through, perhaps several times. It's a lot more than that, and a lot less. Effective study techniques enable you to learn new information and recall it as needed. Enhancing your study skills can trim the amount of time you'll have to devote to studying and even make it possible for you to accomplish through self-study what perhaps earlier required expensive classroom instruction.

Reading skills are the foundation of much of learning. You already know how to read, but do you know how to read to learn? A skilled learner knows the tricks that make it possible to read faster and remember more. But even something as overtly straight-forward as reading can be done ineffectively and inefficiently for the simple reason that many people have never received specific instruction on reading to learn. The same is true of such basics as note taking and exam preparation.

There are also many techniques you can apply to make test preparation fairly painless. These methods will serve you well for certification tests, as well as for future tasks that involve learning and remembering technical information. Even if you already know how to study effectively, you'd probably benefit from brushing up on your skills. Doing so is as easy as reading Chapter 9.

Error 13: Failure to Set Deadlines for Yourself

You've no doubt heard the saying, "the squeaky wheel gets the grease." If you have multiple priorities competing for your time, you may well find yourself playing the role of grease monkey and running from project to project, applying the lubrication that will keep the critical things from freezing up. Meanwhile, projects that aren't in crisis go untended, until they begin to squeak, too, or are completely forgotten. Certification preparation is rarely one of the squeaky wheels. Because of that, it often falls low on the scale of daily priorities. Unless you take action to keep this from happening, your certification plans will languish and your goals will go unmet.

The best way to avoid the pitfall of inaction is to create deadlines for yourself. This should occur as part of the process of creating your personal certification plan. Each requirement should have a deadline date. If the requirement is that you pass a test, go ahead and schedule the test. As each deadline approaches, the urgency of finding time to train and prepare will grow until, like the proverbial squeaky wheel, it demands your attention. Tending to these artificially induced squeaks will keep your "certification wheel" turning.

A second challenge to your progress is the big P: procrastination. If you're the type of person who doesn't get things done until the last minute, then deadlines will generate time pressure to keep you on track.

Mistakes After Certification is Achieved

Once you've completed all the requirements for a certification, it may be tempting to sit back and enjoy your accomplishment. But if you do that, you won't be taking full advantage of your new status. It would be rather like buying a new sports car and leaving it in the garage most of the time. To get the most benefit from certification, you need to use it at every opportunity, and maintain it in tip-top condition. Correspondingly, the mistakes that occur after certification is achieved are largely due to inaction or inattention. Consider the following.

Error 14: Forgetting About Continuing Requirements

Don't count on your certification's sponsor to remind you when updates to your certification are due. Such a reminder is a bonus, not a given. It's up to you to track how often professional development activities or update exams are required and to fulfill those requirements.

Record professional development deadlines on your calendar, allowing plenty of time to complete them and their accompanying paperwork. Once you've completed a recertification requirement, such as attending a technical seminar, immediately collect and submit the necessary information to your certification vendor and verify that it's been properly recorded.

Error 15: Failing to Take Advantage of Perks and Privileges

Some of the benefits of certification will accrue to you even if you do nothing else once you have your certification in hand. Free subscriptions and early product news, for example, will arrive in your mailbox whether or not you request them. But other perks and privileges are provided to you on an as-needed basis. To benefit from them, you have to access them. What if someone offered you free valuable services such as:

* Priority technical support
* Access to special forums
* Marketing tools and assistance
* Certificate

Wouldn't be an incredible waste to ignore them? But that's exactly the mistake that newly certified people make. Although the specifics vary depending on the certification, perks like these come with most Linux certifications. Figure 6.1 shows Sair's list of certification perks you can expect to receive. These are tools you have earned access to. They are (or should have been) part of the reason you chose the certification in the first place. Use them.

FIGURE 6.1
The perks list

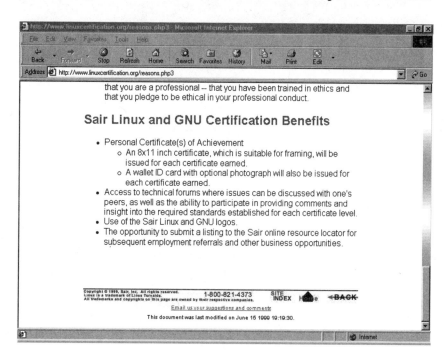

Error 16: Failing to Advertise Your New Status

The first thing to do with your certification is add it to your resume, but that's not the only way you can promote your new status. Certification is a marketing tool that can be applied in a variety of ways. Don't neglect to put it to work for you.

The simplest methods are as basic as redesigning your business cards and stationery to incorporate the certification logo, and adding the designation to your e-mail signature. Include logos on your Web site too. If you don't have one, create one. Basic Web page design tools are available for all levels of site developers, from beginners through experts, and at affordable prices too. Some, such as AOLpress (**www.aolpress.com/press/**) can be downloaded via the Internet free. The AOLpress Web site is shown in Figure 6.2. Advice on these and other methods for marketing yourself as a certified expert is provided in Chapter 11.

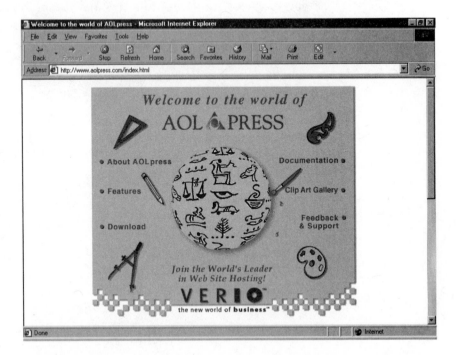

Completing the requirements for certification is 90% of the job, but the remaining 10% is important too. With a little effort, you can use certification as a launching pad to develop a reputation as an expert on the related technology, or simply to add to your credibility. You can bet that your competitors will be doing just that.

Plan, Perform, and Follow Through

If there's one key to successful use of certification as a career booster, it's attention. You control each stage, starting with how carefully you develop your personal certification plan, continuing through how closely you follow it, your application of certification as a marketing tool, and whether or not you devote attention and effort to stay current over time.

A mistake here and there won't keep you from reaching your certification goal. Individuals who are eager to earn their certification may make some of these errors through haste. The most constructive step you can take to avoid wasting time and money is to plan ahead. Each time you move on to a new step in the certification process remember the mistakes you read about here, and make sure you don't repeat them. If you find yourself making one of these mistakes, correct your error, and get back on track as quickly as possible. Above all, keep moving forward toward your goal of certification.

Chapter 7

Understanding
Training Alternatives

Although it's possible to obtain Linux certifications solely on the basis of exam scores and signing the certification agreement, few people can walk in, take the tests cold, and walk out certified. This is especially true of the Linux certifications that require a lab exam in addition to the written exam. If you feel confident about your skills after reviewing the objectives for a particular exam, you can consider taking the exam with only your existing experience to draw upon, but it's unlikely that you'll be successful. If you approach testing this way, it's likely to cost you extra time and money; you won't get your money back if you fail and you may have to wait before you can get rescheduled to try again.

It's difficult to pass a certification exam without studying because an individual's knowledge is usually limited by job function. Imagine for a moment that your current job is to install and maintain your company's sole Linux-based development machine. You may be quite the wizard when it comes to managing that machine and its current configuration, but if you were suddenly placed in charge of implementing a Linux-based Web server or clustering multiple Linux machines for greater processing power at Company B instead, you'd likely find yourself stumbling around a bit, at least at first. That's because every organization's computing environment is unique. Hardware and software are combined in different ways and configured to serve specific purposes. Company B's usage of Linux may be completely different from the setup you're used to working with.

In the above scenario, you'd probably pick up what you needed to know by turning to documentation and technical coworkers, but certification tests don't offer the same opportunities. They aren't open book and you can't bounce ideas off of the person at the next desk. Questions won't be limited to one company's computing environment, either.

This doesn't automatically mean that you need to sign up for thousands of dollars worth of intensive training before you can pass certification exams, but you do need to prepare in one way or another. Fortunately, you have many options to choose from.

Thanks in large part to the computer industry, the classroom and textbook are no longer the only, or even the primary, education venues. Current alternatives include:

* Computer Based Training (CBT) prepared by the certification sponsor
* CBT and training programs offered by independent vendors
* Online classes and training communities
* Courses at authorized training centers
* Self-paced workbooks and study guides
* Product documentation
* College courses
* Video tapes

Each has attributes that may make it attractive to you, and each has drawbacks. To select training that will serve your purposes, it helps to distinguish between two types of learning you'll need to undertake: adding to your body of knowledge and learning new practical skills.

Think of the first item as the what and why of your subject area. Extending your knowledge of Linux would include things like understanding the various distributions available and the differences between them, learning the different types of things you can do with Linux—such as networking, multi-processing, hardware requirements for installation, types of file systems available, and so on. This kind of learning revolves around concepts, theory, and case studies. You can reasonably expect to master the material through absorption methods: reading, listening, and watching presentations of the material. And yes, repetition and regurgitation of what you've just learned to help lock it into your memory.

Learning new practical skills is equivalent to the how of your subject area. It involves applying the knowledge you've gained; you perform instead of observe. You'll install and configure Linux, you'll deploy a Linux-based Web server, you'll become a master of X-Motif (a graphical user interface). The ideal way to accomplish this is to have the applicable hardware and software at hand, along with someone who can answer any questions and help if you get stuck. But that's not the only way. You may be astonished by what can be accomplished via simulation these days.

Both types of learning are valuable and important. How much you need of each kind will depend on the gap between your current knowledge and experience, and what you'll require for the certification you've decided to pursue. Self-study will carry you a long way. For some people and for some certifications, it's all that's needed. Other certified professionals swear that formal training classes are the way to go. A combination of the two may best meet your personal training needs. Let's explore the education options that you're likely to encounter.

Workbooks and Study Guides

Text materials, including study guides, workbooks, instructional texts, and product manuals, are very attractive to certification candidates (Figure 7.1 shows a page from **fatbrain.com**'s collection of Linux study guides). A big factor working in their favor is cost. You can frequently obtain workable study guides and exam preparation outlines directly from the certification sponsor via mail, or as downloads from the certification Web site. Texts that must be purchased are relatively inexpensive when compared to other routes for learning similar material. They are available through major bookstores and computer-specialty book outlets.

Because Linux is part of the open source movement, you'll find an exceptionally generous amount of free documentation on the Internet. This includes how-to manuals, technical explanations, step-by-step instructions for particular tasks, and of course lots of source code.

If you aren't strongly motivated, learning by reading about a topic may not be the best alternative for you. But then, if motivation is really a problem, perhaps you should rethink your career goals with that in mind.

People may also bypass basic reading as a route to learning because they find it a slow and tedious way to learn. Whipping through the latest best-selling novel may be pure pleasure, but page after page of dry technical exposition can seem like torture in comparison. Fortunately, you can drastically increase your reading speed and comprehension level by investing $6 and a bit of effort (see Speed Learning sidebar).

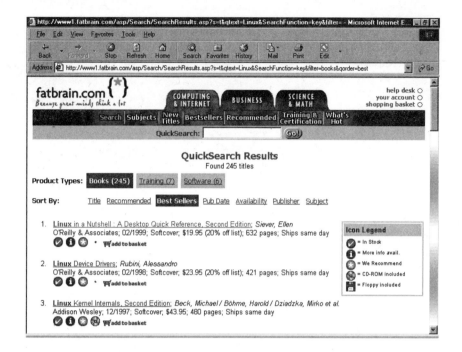

FIGURE 7.1

fatbrain.com offers a large selection of books packed with Linux expertise

Speed Learning

If you've made it this far in this book, you can obviously read at a decent level. But what exactly does that mean? The average reader proceeds at a rate of about 250 words per minute. Especially "fast" readers race along at 400–600 words per minute. But the limits of human reading speed are vastly higher: 1,200–3,000 words per minute can be achieved through training. And that same training will improve your comprehension and recall. You'll not only read faster, you'll understand and be able to recall more of what you read.

What kind of practical difference would this make in your certification training? If you have a 200 page manual to plow through (about 100,000 words), and your reading speed is above average at 300 words a minute, you'll need nearly six hours of reading to get through the manual. Up your speed to 900 words a minute, and you'll be able to read that same manual in under two hours.

But how can you accomplish such a vast increase in your learning rate? By purchasing and following the advice contained within of the more than 70 books written to help you learn to do so.

The book *The Evelyn Wood 7-Day Speed Reading & Learning Program*, by Stanley D. Frank, Ed.D. (Avon Books, 1992) for example, costs just $5.99. Even if you just read and follow the steps in the first two chapters (about 40 pages), you'll dramatically increase your reading speed. The later chapters in this book are less useful, but still may prove helpful to you. You can even get an abridged version of this book on tape and listen to it during your drive time.

But going through a lot of pages in a little time is only one aspect of leveraging your reading abilities. Along with step-by-step instruction on how to accelerate your reading, you'll find study tips and advice on how to increase your comprehension and recall and on how to prepare for exams.

When it comes to squeezing learning into a crowded schedule, this is one method that can really pay off. You can pick up one of these books at most major book stores. You can also order them online from Amazon Books (**www.amazon.com**) or any major online bookseller.

For some purposes, reading is no substitute for doing, but it's been a solid way to gain new knowledge or to expand upon what you already know. Table 7.1 lists learning characteristics of books. A book is the ultimate portable classroom. You can use it beneath the fluorescent lights of the company cafeteria, inside a clattering subway car, or deep in the shade of an ancient oak in your favorite park. And the battery never runs out.

TABLE 7.1
Learning characteristics of workbooks and study guides

Advantages	Disadvantages
Very portable	Not interactive, therefore less engaging
Can serve as a reference	May not be completely current
Relatively low cost, some free	No external motivation, easy to get off track
Proceed at your own pace	Predetermined linear format

Product Documentation

One of the most overlooked preparation materials is product documentation. It's free, widely available, and goes into technical detail. Distribution-specific Linux documentation is available from each distribution's vendor, often via the Web site. But there's another documentation source you should become familiar with: The Linux Documentation Project.

The Linux Documentation Project (**metalab.unc.edu/LDP/**), shown in Figure 7.2, is a collaboration of volunteers working to create "good, reliable docs for the Linux operating system" that are freely available. They've already compiled an impressive collection of documents, including texts on installation, the ins and outs of the Linux kernel, a Linux programmers' guide, a Linux system administration guide, and a user's guide. All of this is available to you, absolutely free of charge, on the LDP Web site.

FIGURE 7.2
Free and plentiful Linux documentation from the LDP

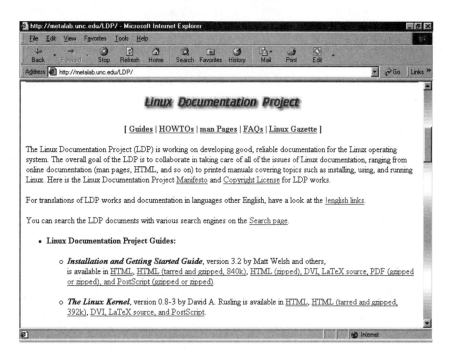

Computer-Based Training (CBT)

The term computer-based training refers to educational software developed and delivered via computer technology. It's also referred to by many other names, including computer-aided instruction (CAI), computer-based instruction (CBI), and courseware.

Good CBT programs are interactive. By requiring you to answer questions, step through tasks, and perform other actions, CBT *involves* you. By responding to the program, you become an active learner. Most people find that participation in this way increases their enjoyment of the process.

Another way CBT eases learning is by adding a "wow" factor. CBT software increasingly is a blend of multimedia wizardry, with voice tracks, video clips, animation sequences, and a big bag of tricks for transforming mundane information into, well, fun.

CBT software also provides freedom from the predefined, linear format, of many other educational formats. You can largely elect to work with the topics in the order you prefer, and at the pace you choose. If you already have a particular area down cold, you can skip right over it. If a lesson misses the mark, you can return to it as many times as you like.

On the down side, the software is limited in what its instructions include. There's no trainer to answer free-form questions or to urge you onward, and you have to be sitting at a computer (usually equipped with a CD-ROM and loads of memory) to use it.

Current CBT software seems to be developed in one of two styles: task oriented or knowledge focused. Task-oriented programs lead you step-by-step through the procedures native to the software, hardware, or environment you're studying. If the topic of the CBT is administering Linux, a single lesson might cover how to create a group ID for a new user. In a textbook you would read about it. In a traditional classroom, you would hear about it and possibly observe a demonstration by the instructor. With CBT, the operation is simulated on your computer screen. You'll be instructed, often by text, but sometimes via voice clips, on the proper sequence of steps to perform. You'll follow the instructions as if you were actually adding a new user, clicking on the appropriate menu items, filling in variables, and coding switches. You can concentrate fully on what you're doing with no worry that you'll inadvertently bring the system crashing down.

But don't get too used to all that hand-holding because it will diminish as you advance through the course. Procedures that were spelled out in detail the first time won't be later on. You'll have to "create a user and initial environment for him." Step four might be to specify a group ID for the user. Because you already learned that procedure, you won't be walked through it this time around. This building block, hands-on, simulation-type of learning can prove very successful when your goal is to acquire a specific, concrete set of skills.

Knowledge-focused CBT takes a completely different approach. Instead of facing the simulation of a particular program's GUI and being given the goal of completing a specific task, you'll find yourself in more of an open-ended, exploratory environment.

Learning Tree International (**www.learningtree.com**) is one company that makes impressive use of this style for some of its CBT courses. When you fire up the "Client/Server Computing" course, you are greeted by Ken, leader of the AcmeTech development team you've just joined. You're introduced to other team members, each with a particular perspective and area of expertise. You'll probably call on them later. Or they may have questions for you. Your job? To help develop and implement a client/server environment at a prestigious university. Get to work. Although Learning Tree didn't have any Linux-related CBTs as this book was going to press, hopefully some will appear soon. Table 7.2 pinpoints learning characteristics of CBT.

TABLE 7.2

Learning characteristics of computer-based training

Advantages	Disadvantages
Somewhat portable	Less practical as a reference
Interactive	Requires fairly powerful personal computer to use
Moderate cost	No external motivation, easy to get off track
Proceed at your own pace	Often available in PC-compatible only, not Macintosh
Multimedia format is engaging	
Can review as desired	

Not all CBT software is created equal. Some programs place block after block of text on the screen, which will quickly fatigue your eyes. Others fail to utilize multimedia capabilities in an interesting and beneficial way. These and other shortcomings can limit the value of CBT software. Investigate your CBT options, preferably by test-driving a demo, before purchasing a CBT program. Most CBT vendors have demo versions available to download from their Web sites and/or available via mail. New programs are constantly appearing, so don't rely only on what other certification candidates report they have used. Don't limit yourself to software that includes the word "certification" in the title. There are plenty of concepts that are not certification specific that you will need to learn.

Online Classes

One of the more recent developments in technical training is the use of the Internet as a delivery medium. Although online classes might appear to fall under the umbrella of CBT, they're distinct enough to deserve a category of their own.

Because online courses typically cost substantially less than their traditional classroom counterparts, training online is a cost effective option. But perhaps more important are the savings in time and aggravation. Distance learning makes it possible and practical to study at your own pace, on your own schedule, from anywhere you can link to the net. Courses often come with 24-hour access to subject experts, and if you want to, you can even earn continuing education units (CEUs) while you explore the intricacies of the Linux kernel or catch up on the features of the GNU C++ compiler. Learning doesn't get much more convenient than this.

Distance education, while not an utter newcomer to the Web, is still a young industry. Technology barriers, such as the ever-present bandwidth bottleneck, place significant constraints of the format and delivery of course material. At the same time, distance learning offers an opportunity to develop entirely new learning models that take advantage of the delivery medium. The result is a menu of three flavors of course delivery from which to choose: online multimedia courseware, the virtual classroom, and hybrids that combine features of each.

Courses that are delivered using online multimedia software are much like those that come on CD-ROM: they may incorporate snippets of video, audio clips, text-based instruction, software simulations, and self-tests to measure your progress. Typically, a student signs onto the service, connects to the next module in the series she's currently following, and either works through the module online or downloads the module and completes it offline. Once a lesson is completed, the student takes an electronic self-test and then move on to the next lesson in the series. The self-tests usually consist of multiple choice questions, with a score calculated and provided immediately on completion of the quiz. The test program reports on missed questions, identifying the correct answer and/or identifying areas for additional student review.

Virtual classrooms, on the other hand, attempt to create an electronic parallel to a school setting. They do so by adding interaction with human instructors and other students as well as academic record-keeping and access to additional resources. The interaction is largely accomplished through a conglomeration of e-mail, newsgroups, dedicated forums, and scheduled chats. Study groups, remote access labs, exercises, and even telephone conferencing may also be incorporated.

To attend a virtual class, a student logs into the classroom to retrieve a lesson and related exercises. While online, she may participate in a discussion of the material by reading and posting on a class-specific message board. Instructor interaction is often accomplished via e-mail or message board. Unlike the multimedia courses, virtual classes often have specified start and end dates and lessons are presented on a fixed schedule, often weekly. Students can log in at any time during the week to complete the lesson, participate in discussions, and ask the instructor questions. A few virtual classrooms have specific meeting times and require all students to log on simultaneously and interact with the instructor in real time.

Hybrid courses mix self-paced, multimedia courseware with access to class-specific message boards, chat links, and other resources. Students proceed at their own pace and aren't obligated to comply with specific start and end dates, although there may be overall time limits. This means that one student may start the first module of a course at the same time as another student is finishing the fifth.

Most vendors permit you to sample a class before signing up. Use the opportunity to wander the virtual hallways and get a feel for the learning environment, because they vary widely. At Cyberstate University, for example, you'll encounter Professor Wire and

his smorgasbord of jokes and puns. You may enjoy his witty inter-
jections or find them incredibly irritating.

Online courses may be offered by commercial education centers, colleges, consulting groups, and private individuals. The format and content details of a particular online course vary considerably from vendor to vendor. Prices run all over the spectrum, as
do degree of instructor support, class quality, qualification for continuing education credits, and just about every other aspect you
can imagine.

Ziff-Davis University

Ziff-Davis Corporation, publisher of numerous industry magazines has jumped into the online training market with both feet.
They've created a virtual university and named it ZD Net University (ZDU). You'll find it at **www.zdu.com**.

ZDU structures itself this way: Individuals pay a fee (currently
$7.95/month or $69.95/year) to become members. While you're a
member, you can register for and attend as many classes as you
like. For each class, you log on at least once a week (at a time of
your choosing) to read the instructor-posted assignment and submit questions that are posted on the class message board. According to ZDU, the message board is managed by "the instructor,
teaching assistants, moderators, and other students." Classes
generally last four to eight weeks, and additional materials,
including books or downloadable files, may be required. Instructors stage live chat "office hours." Many self-paced tutorials are
available to subscribers as well.

QUICKTIP

As with college tuition, ZDU's subscription price does not cover course materials.
Typically, you will be required to purchase a companion text either directly from
ZDU or through the bookstore of your choice. Materials often cost $25–$50.

For a processing fee (currently $15), ZDU will submit your
information along with the course name and *recommended* number of continuing education units (CEUs), to the National Reg-
istry of Training Programs (NRTP) of the American Council on

Education (ACE). *If* the CEUs are granted, you'll receive a notice from ACE via mail.

As this book was being written, ZDU had just inaugurated its first Linux course, somewhat confusingly titled: Intro To UNIX. Despite its name, the course revolves around Red Hat Linux. The course description is shown in Figure 7.3.

FIGURE 7.3
ZDU offers Linux training on the Web

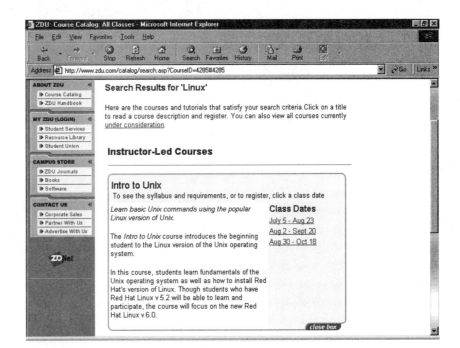

Magellan University

Magellan University, found at **magellan.edu**, offers instructor-led online sources, self-paced online courses with "tutor support," and online CBT. It is one of the first to offer a significant quantity of online Linux training (Figure 7.4). You can choose from introductory or more advanced level curricula. At press time the prices seem a bit on the high side for online training—$1,195 for the 8-week instructor-led sessions and $895 for the self-paced option. As with ZDU, some courses taken through Magellan are eligible for college credits, however, only through Pima Community College in Arizona.

FIGURE 7.4
Magellan University
Linux training on
the Web

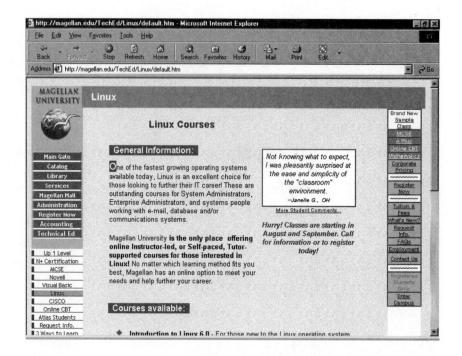

There are many more online instruction vendors besides those described above. Their course rosters may be limited to just a few classes or fill an extensive catalog. Their nature will vary considerably, too. Because this is an evolving business arena with exciting possibilities, you're likely to encounter an extensive variety of vendors, including colleges, individual entrepreneurs, technology businesses, and education companies. Table 7.3 outlines learning characteristics of online classes.

TABLE 7.3
Learning
characteristics of
online classes

Advantages	Disadvantages
Self-paced (within time limits)	No future value as a reference
Access to expert instructor	Requires computer and Internet connection
Interaction with other students	Price, format, and quality vary widely

Authorized Training Centers

Vendors of some Linux distributions offer training specific to their distribution and, when they have one, their certification.

Because they work in partnership with certification vendors, training partner center staff have the inside scoop on what it takes to pass particular tests, and what sort of practice is likely to pay off. You can get this same information elsewhere, but here it's likely to be delivered to you practically on a silver platter. Your instructors will be professional technical trainers, extremely well versed in the issues at hand.

Another big plus these centers offer is an appropriate computing environment. You'll get your hands on the real thing. And it will be free from the restrictions or potential for disaster that your employer's live network is likely to have.

The big downsides are cost and inconvenience. Intense authorized training can run up quite a tab. A single class can cost several thousand dollars. Of course, if your employer is willing to pay for it, cost won't be as big an issue.

Unlike other training that you can pursue at your own pace, you'll have to learn at a rate set by the rest of the class and the instructor. That rate may be slower or faster than you'd like. You'll have to adjust your work and leisure time to meet the training center's schedule, and if you miss a session, it may be difficult to catch up to the rest of the class.

Certification vendors that operate authorized instructor-led training networks include:

* Caldera Systems, which operates an international network of "Authorized Linux Education Centers." You can find the list of authorized centers on Caldera's Web site at: **http://www.calderasystems.com/education/**.

* Red Hat Inc., which holds RHCE certification training classes at its headquarters in Durham, North Carolina. They also offer additional classes across the United States through a partnership with Global Knowledge. You can use Global Knowledge's course locator (**db.globalknowledge.com/catalog/certdetail. asp?cat=RHCE**) shown in Figure 7.5 to find the training center closest to you.

* Sair has the Sair Linux and GNU Accredited Center for Education (SLG-ACE) program. This newly launched had a limited number of participating trainers as this book was going to press, but the list should expand rapidly. A list of SLG-ACE

participants can be found at **www.linuxcertification.com/seminarschedule.php3**.

Additional training networks may appear as Linux certification becomes more widespread.

Shop around and compare price, course format, instructor experience, lab equipment, and convenience factors. You may find considerable variation among training centers. Table 7.4 details learning characteristics of training center courses.

TABLE 7.4

Learning characteristics of training center courses

Advantages	Disadvantages
Interactive	No future value as a reference
Access to expert instructor	Most costly
Access to expensive technology	Often requires time in large blocks
Interaction with other students	Not self-paced
Easy to locate through sponsor	Compressed nature may reduce skill retention
Lots of training in a short time	May not be in convenient location

College Courses

Another way to fill in your knowledge gaps is to take one or more courses at a nearby college. The classes will be less condensed because they take place over the course of a semester and generally less expensive (especially if you utilize a community college). Because they extend over a full semester, you'll have more time to learn, study, and absorb information.

You typically don't have to matriculate and can sign up just for the course you want. If you wish, you can receive college credits. You may have the option to audit the class—i.e. attend but receive no grade—in exchange for an even lower tuition.

The institution you choose may or may not have a direct connection to your certification sponsor, but if it does, you can often obtain the exact same training curriculum you'd get at an authorized training center but at a lower price and spread out over a longer period of time. With Linux, there are also colleges with no official link to a certification program sponsor that still offer Linux training.

The first place to look is your local community and technical colleges. Check their Web sites or call the admissions offices and ask if they have Linux courses. You can also search the Web using the phrase "college AND linux" (without the quotes). Learning characteristics of college courses are listed in Table 7.5.

TABLE 7.5
Learning characteristics of college courses

Advantages	Disadvantages
Interactive	No future value as a reference
Access to experienced instructor	Trainer may be less qualified than at a training center
Interaction with other students	Not self-paced
Less costly than training center	Takes longer to complete course
Gentler learning pace	
Access to necessary equipment	
Often eligible for college credits	

Online Resources

An excellent way to augment any of these learning methods is to seek out additional information on the Internet. You can search for certification-specific resources or sites that contain the details of a particular aspect of Linux that you're studying. A vast storehouse of information about Linux products and technologies is available on the Internet. A major entry point to all of these goodies is at **www.cl.cam.ac.uk/users/iwj10/linux-faq/index.html** (shown in Figure 7.6). You'll find basic information to help you get started, along with more complete technical information and links to additional resources.

To locate useful Linux sites like this one, simply search using Yahoo! (**www.yahoo.com**), Infoseek (**www.infoseek.com**), or Excite (**www.excite.com**). Make your search as specific as possible. For example, to find Web pages relevant to partitioning a hard drive for use with Linux, try "Linux partition" (with the quotes).

Placing both words inside a set of quotes makes the search engine treat them as a phrase rather than separate keywords. This will return a list of links to pages that contain the exact phrase. To find documents relating to a particular certification, you could use the keywords Linux AND certification AND Sair. You'll get a list of pages containing all three of the keys, but they're allowed to be separated by other words not on your list. Because Linux certification is still very new, don't expect this list to be very long. The more specific you make your search words and phrases, the less trash you'll have to wade through to find the bits of treasure.

FIGURE 7.6
The mother lode
of Linux Frequently
Asked Questions
(FAQs)

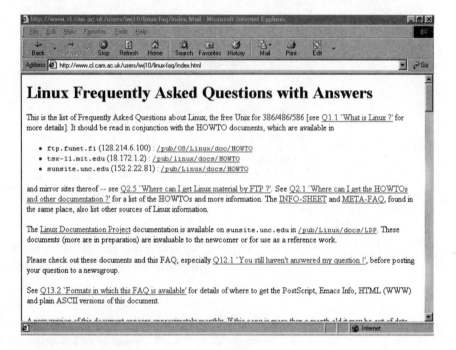

If you find that you're having little success, try a different search engine. Each search engine collects, indexes, and retrieves information in its own way. By executing an identical search on three different search engines, you'll come up with three different (albeit overlapping) sets of results.

What types of resources can you expect to uncover with these searches? Both commercial and noncommercial sites will turn up. Some will be hosted by businesses who want to sell you their related services, others by individuals with special interest in your search topic. The bounty you'll uncover is likely to include some of the following resources:

* Certification resource centers created by interested individuals
* Resource sites about a particular technology
* Exam-specific learning aids, such as quiz programs, books, and testing tips
* Unofficial (that is, not officially authorized) training programs and books
* Sponsor-authorized training venues
* Related discussion forums
* Home pages of individuals who hold a particular certification
* Articles and papers about the technology or certification
* Online versions of software and hardware manuals
* Related newsgroups and mailing lists you can join
* Study groups organized around your certification

You'll probably have to spend some time sorting through the results before you find the online resources that will prove most valuable to you. But one of the great things about online resources is that when you find one good page, it will often contain direct links to other sites of similar quality and content. Table 7.6 provides learning characteristics of online resources.

Remember to take what you find on the Internet with a grain of salt. Excellent, accurate, and in-depth resources are out there, along with slapped together, error-ridden pages. Most Web pages contain a link you can click on to contact the page's author. Don't hesitate to use it if only to get a feel for the person behind the information. You may well run across a kindred soul who is willing and able to serve as a fountain of knowledge about your certification program.

TABLE 7.6
Learning characteristics of online resources

Advantages	Disadvantages
Free	No guarantee of expertise
Usually contain many useful links	Information may be out of date, inaccurate, or incomplete
Tips and advice from certification veterans	May have to dig for the gold
Place to connect with other candidates	

Unofficial Training Programs

It's a consumer truism that generic goods are generally less expensive than the name brand version of the same item. That holds true for certification training, too. Entrepreneurs and others, who for one reason or another haven't obtained official sponsor approval, have established themselves in the training business. The lack of a certification sponsor's seal of approval doesn't automatically indicate poor quality or anything shady about the operation. It may simply be a business choice not to go the authorized route, and plenty of trainers have, for one reason or another, made that decision.

These "unauthorized" vendors offer seminars, workshops, CBT software, software-based study aids, video tapes, textbooks, and study guides, virtually the same mix of resources you can obtain through official channels. But as independent operators, they are free to develop their own curriculum and course format.

The good news is that unofficial vendors usually charge lower prices than their sponsor-authorized counterparts. Many are operated by skilled, knowledgeable professionals who know just what they're doing and how to best help you achieve certification. The bad news is that you can't count on the presence of either attribute. Table 7.7 enumerates learning characteristics of unofficial training vendors.

Before purchasing goods or services, check out any unfamiliar vendor as thoroughly as you can. Find out length of time in business, and if certification training is the product, inquire as to the exam success rate of graduates. Request the names and contact information of some past customers, then contact those people to find out the details of their experience with the vendor. Spend some time nosing around forums and Web sites for any bad press about the particular vendor. When people feel cheated, they generally aren't shy about sharing the details via an online site.

If a substantial amount of money is involved, it's worth it to call or write the Better Business Bureau in the vendor's home state and ask if there are any complaints on record against the company, and, if so, whether or not they have been satisfactorily resolved. Chances are that the vendor you're considering is running a quality operation, but it pays to be sure.

	Advantages	Disadvantages
TABLE 7.7 Learning characteristics of unofficial training vendors	Usually less expensive than authorized	No guarantee of expertise
	Not restricted to preapproved curriculum	Greater risk of inferior services and products
	May get more candid view of product	

Training Videos

If you prefer learning from an instructor but classroom instruction doesn't suit you for one reason or another, videos are an alternative that you may find appealing. Although you won't be able to interact with the instructor, you will be able to observe demonstrations of particular procedures. Voice, music, and visual stimulation will involve you, and, in many cases, animation, close-up shots, and virtual field trips will help to clarify concepts. Some videos apply a lead/follow approach. The video instructor demonstrates how to operate a particular piece of software, then you recreate the process using your own equipment. But many are passive affairs where you just sit and watch. Table 7.8 highlights learning characteristics of video tapes.

	Advantages	Disadvantages
TABLE 7.8 Learning characteristics of video tapes	Relatively low cost	Not interactive
	Self-paced sections	May contain excessive talking heads
	Can review as needed	Requires access to VCR equipment
	Opportunity to see techniques in action	

Training videos sometimes come with a support package that includes printed materials, review questions, and self-quizzes. They're significantly less expensive than other forms of instructor led training. In some cases, you may even be able to rent instead of purchase them, but if you do you won't have them on hand for future reference. There are already several Linux videos on the market. Check the reference section of this book for leads.

It's important to remember that although a particular training option may seem ideal to you, it may not be available for your certification program, in your area, or in your price range, or it may not be available for some other reason. If you can't obtain your first choice in training, there are probably several other options that will serve you nearly as well. There's also a lot of variation within categories, so be sure to shop around to get a clear understanding of what various training outlets have to offer.

Keep in mind that different certification requirements may best be met by different training alternatives. To learn how to physically connect and configure a series of routers, for example, you might prefer a hands-on workshop with tools, equipment, and an experienced technician on hand. But to understand the layers of the OSI model and how they interact, a video tape, audio cassette, or book may do the job as well or better.

In the next chapter, as part of developing your personal certification road map, you'll find out how to analyze your learning style and how to take the results into consideration when choosing a training alternative. You'll also determine just how much training you'll need and how to evaluate individual training outlets.

Chapter 8

Your Personal Training and Certification Road Map

Once you've decided which Linux certification to pursue, you're ready to lay out your plan for obtaining it. Is a detailed plan really necessary? Only if you want to save time, money, and frustration.

A certification plan is often referred to as a road map, and with good reason. The process of obtaining certification is very similar to the process of traveling from your home to a distant location. In both cases, there are many possible routes between your starting point and intended destination. Which route is best depends upon individual preferences. Is speed of the essence or do you prefer to see more along the way? Will you be camping out to save money or lodging at five-star hotels? Do you have the endurance and tenacity to undertake marathon drives or are shorter hops more to your liking?

The same issues apply to certification. Do you want to finish ASAP or delve more deeply into the elements? Are you aiming for minimal financial outlay or maximum comfort? Do you have the time and energy to immerse yourself for intense and extended training events or are shorter study and training sessions more to your liking?

Although it might be tempting to hop on the certification road as soon as possible and figure out each turn as it approaches, such impatience has a price. You're likely to spend more time and money than you have to and risk taking wrong turns along the way. By taking the time to understand your learning style and plot out which exams and courses you will take, in what order, and when, you'll be assured of meeting all the requirements and deadlines for your certification. You'll also be able to move smoothly from one requirement to the next without constantly needing to interrupt your progress to stop and figure out what to do next.

Your completed certification road map will list the requirements you need to meet, in the order you will need to accomplish them. It will also identify the methods you intend to use to prepare for each exam and include a timeline to keep you on target.

Creating your personal certification road map involves the following steps:

1. Select a track.
2. Record the requirements on your Personal Certification Plan.
3. Eliminate any requirements you can.

4. Decide how you'll meet the remaining requirements.
5. Set deadlines.

Your plan will be an evolving document. Expect to adjust and fine-tune it as you progress toward certification. You can even include long-term plans for additional certifications as well.

A Word on Tracks

Many certifications allow some amount of customization so you can closely match them with your needs.

These alternate paths are called tracks. They typically are organized in one of two ways:

* Around specific platforms and operating environments
* By job function

With Linux the choices are often related to the distribution vendor—there might be a Slackware track, a Red Hat track, a Debian track, and so on. You'll also encounter certification paths that differentiate between administrator and developer duties. Tracks are like the electives component of college degree programs where you get to choose what to minor in. Correspondingly, you can act as some college freshman do and choose the courses that are easiest to pass, or you can take advantage of this flexibility to follow a certification path that's tailored to your career goals.

The best way to choose your track is to read over the descriptions created by the sponsoring organization. Select the option that most closely matches the goals you intend to achieve through certification. For example, if you're planning to leverage your career at your current position, choose the track that most closely matches the operating environment you work in or that best describes the functions related to your job. If you're intending to use certification to move into a new area, look for the track that best bridges what you already know and what you'd like to know. Or if your goal is simply to advance your skills, select the track that best represents the skills you want to add or augment.

It's a good idea to discuss your options with other people who are familiar with the certification process and/or your goals. They can help you decide if a particular track or elective is "hot" or going out of style. There are several Internet venues for doing this, including Linux newsgroups such as **comp.os.linux.questions** and **earthweb.linux.general**.

Once you've settled on a certification track, begin filling in the Personal Certification Plan in Figure 8.1 by listing the requirements you'll need to meet, in the order that you intend to complete them. Be as detailed as possible. At this point, you should be able to list specific exams, experience requirements, applications to submit, fees you'll need to pay, and anything else that will be needed to obtain your certification. Write only in the requirements column for now. This is the "what" of your certification plan. The other columns, which will address "how" and "when," will follow shortly.

FIGURE 8.1
Personal
Certification Plan

Personal Certification Plan

Certification:_____

Target Completion Date:_____

X	Requirement	Target Date	Training/Study Method(s)	Notes

Deciding How to Prepare

Now that you've spelled out and pared down your requirements, it's time to determine how you will approach each of them. Depending upon your background and skills, some requirements will entail more preparation than others. That's why the next step of developing your Personal Certification Plan is to review each requirement and choose the study/training methods you will apply to achieve it.

Certification candidates have a rich array of learning alternatives to choose from—Chapter 7 explored them in detail. Deciding which method to apply toward a particular requirement is a highly individual process, and to make effective choices you first need to understand your personal learning style.

How Do You Learn?

People differ in how they perceive, understand, retain, and recall information. We all know individuals who can find their way anywhere providing they have a map to refer to, and others who are virtually guaranteed to get lost unless they're given oral directions. Give the map reader oral directions or the directions person a map and both will eventually reach their destinations, but their journeys will probably be longer and more stressful. Just like these travelers, learners have preferred methods of receiving and using information.

For an excellent (if extensive) discussion of many aspects of adult learning styles, read the Wave Technologies International white paper, *Learning: The Critical Technology*, which you can find at **www.wavetech.com/whtpaper/abttmwp.html**.

The people who study the science behind learning have identified and mapped these preferences in a number of different ways. By identifying and understanding your personal learning styles, you'll be able to select the training methods and tools that will work best for you. To help you do that, an exploration of two of the more widely accepted models follows. As you work to understand your learning preferences, keep two important things in mind:

✷ There is no "best" learning style.

✷ Sometimes options that cater to your learning preferences are unavailable or impractical. Although other learning styles may not be as ideal, they will still work.

One of the more common (and understandable) learning frameworks is organized around how we take in information. This theory identifies three basic learning styles based on human senses: visual (by sight), auditory (by sound), and tactile/kinesthetic (by touch and motion). Although most people can learn using any of these senses, most favor one over the others.

Visual learners take in information most easily by seeing it. If you prefer to look at pictures and images rather than listen to explanations, you may be a visual learner. The map reader mentioned above is a visual learner.

Readers are not necessarily visual learners. Many people "hear" the words in their head as they read them. For that reason, readers are considered auditory learners. Auditory learners understand ideas more quickly when they hear them spoken. If you learn more from a lecturer than from watching demonstrations on the same subject, then you may be an auditory learner. A tendency to "think out loud," is another indication that you learn through listening. In the earlier example of following directions, the person who prefers oral directions over a map is an auditory learner.

Tactile/kinesthetic learners prefer to touch and manipulate things. If you're one of those people who abhor reading directions and are happier diving right into whatever it is and figuring things out as you go along, you're likely to be a tactile/kinesthetic learner. A tactile/kinesthetic traveler typically has a good sense of direction and location and is less likely than the map reader or auditory traveler to get seriously lost.

The most effective instruction incorporates more than one learning style. The better teachers have been aware of this for some time and deliberately appeal to different learning styles. Kindergarten teachers, for example, often apply all of these perception styles when teaching the alphabet. When introducing a new letter, they show what the letter looks like (visual), say the letter out loud and have the students repeat it (auditory), and direct children to trace the shape of the letter with a finger or crayon (tactile/kinesthetic).

To determine whether you're more of a visual, auditory, or tactile/kinesthetic learner, take the online learning styles inventory at **www.howtolearn.com/ personal.html** (shown in Figure 8.2).

FIGURE 8.2
Discover your
learning style
online

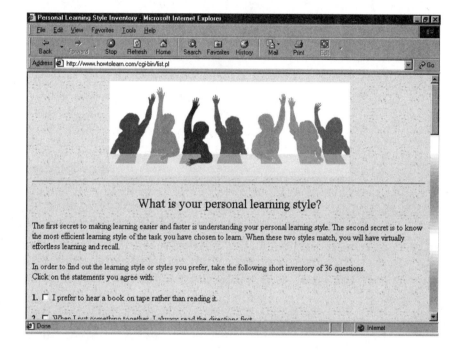

Peter Honey and Alan Mumford, building on the work of David Kolb, developed a second, widely referenced model. This framework is organized around how we think about things rather than around perceptive preferences. It identifies four types of learners: the activist, the pragmatist, the reflector, and the theorist. Once again, these categories aren't mutually exclusive. It's likely that you have traits linked to more than one of these learning styles, but you'll find one that describes you more accurately and completely than the others.

Individuals who fall under the first category—activists—are eager to dive right in and try out novel things. Do you enjoy new projects and frequently find yourself looking for the next project to tackle? Do you approach new ideas in an open-minded and enthusiastic fashion? Are you are always primed and ready for the next new experience? If so, then your learning style is probably activist.

Pragmatists are most interested in the application of what they learn. Do you return from a seminar filled with fresh ideas that you want to try out? Do you think of yourself as a practical person and like solving problems? Are you impatient with meetings that don't seem to be accomplishing a specific purpose? These are all signs of a pragmatist learner.

Reflectors are happiest when they can collect all the relevant information and study it carefully before reaching a conclusion. Do you prefer to make decisions at the last minute so that you can have as long as possible to consider potential ramifications? Do you enjoy collecting and analyzing data? Would you (or others close to you) describe yourself as a cautious person? If so, then you're probably a reflector.

Theorists like to understand how things fit together and what they mean. Do you prefer to analyze problems in an objective, step-by-step fashion? Do you look for the logic behind the ideas? Are uncertainty and ambiguity difficult for you to endure? These are all characteristics of a theorist learning style.

Once you have a good sense of your learning strengths, it's time to fill in some of the blanks in your Personal Certification Plan. For each requirement you have listed, fill in the training/study method(s) you want to use. Keep in mind which learning alternatives are best matched to the learning styles you've identified as your favorites. If you've determined that you're a tactile/kinesthetic person, for example, you'll find hands-on options more effective. If that's the case, consider interactive computer-based training (CBT) or instructor-led training (ILT) that includes lab work as your first choice. An auditory learner should turn to books and audio and video tapes, while a visual learner should seek out alternatives that include video tapes, print materials that include extensive illustrations, and instructor-led training.

A reflector may be happiest poring over the details found in product documentation, while a theorist will prefer a study guide that pays more attention to the why of things. An activist may be best served by getting his/her hands on the technology in question before worrying about the details of how it works. A pragmatist should look for methods that begin by explaining what something is good for. Printed materials and instructor-led training are likely options for a pragmatist.

You can expect to find a lot of variety among products within a single category. Though some CBT programs involve lots of interaction, others depend more heavily on reading from the screen. Some "talk to you" quite a bit. Others just settle for a beep and chirp now and again. Study guides can contain block after block of dense text or include diagrams, photos, and self-tests.

How Certification Candidates Study

As part of a 1998 Gartner Group study sponsored by Sylvan Prometric, Hewlett-Packard, Microsoft, Novell, and Sybase, more than 6,000 certification candidates were asked about their training methods. The results show which study methods candidates used most and which proved most useful.

Self-study was the primary method used by the majority (43 percent) of those surveyed. Twenty-seven percent of respondents reported using instructor-led training (ILT) as their predominant preparation tool. Less than 1% of those used Internet-based ILT as their primary study method. Figure 8.3 shows the breakdown of primary study methods reported.

Interestingly, the choice of a primary study method doesn't always correlate with the method that candidates identified as most useful. This is most apparent in on-the-job-training, which only 11.3 percent of candidates identified as their primary learning method, but 22.6 percent pegged as one of the most useful. Self-study methods were overwhelmingly designated useful (31.5 percent), and instructor-led training got the nod from just 18.7 percent. Figure 8.4 shows the study methods certification candidates found most useful.

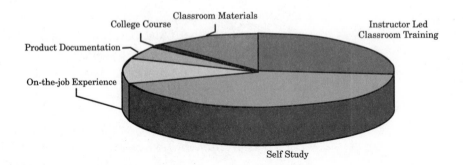

FIGURE 8.3
Primary study
method

Primary Certification Study Method
source: Gartner Group 1998

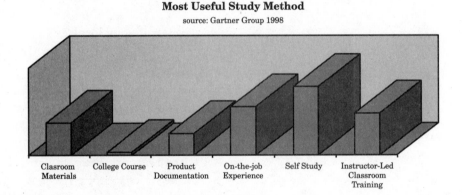

FIGURE 8.4
Most useful study
method

Most Useful Study Method
source: Gartner Group 1998

Finding Preparation Tools

Although there are many preparation tools available, you'll need to conduct a bit of a search to uncover a good selection. Places to check include:

✳ Your certification sponsor. If the company doesn't sell or provide preparation courses and materials, it can probably direct you to someone who does.

✳ Vendors listed in the resource section of this book.

✳ Internet search engines, such as Yahoo! and Infoseek, to uncover sites that include the name of your certification along with the word "preparation." You may have to look for general

Linux materials if none geared specifically toward your chosen certification area available.

✳ Web sites and forums uncovered while researching your certification or find in the resource section of this book; post a message asking for suggestions.

✳ Generic (non-certification specific) self-quiz programs that let you create your own practice tests. You can find them in shareware catalogs and on the Internet.

✳ Your local community colleges; inquire about computer technology offerings. These may not be officially authorized training, but may do the job.

✳ A nearby bookstore or one of the bookstores on the Web, such as Amazon Books (**www.amazon.com**), and search for titles related to your certification and/or study topic. Figure 8.5 shows an Amazon.com listing of popular Linux books.

✳ In the business pages of your local phone book under computers—training.

✳ The **comp.os.linux** Usenet newsgroup; brouse for suggestions.

FIGURE 8.5
Linux search results from Amazon.com

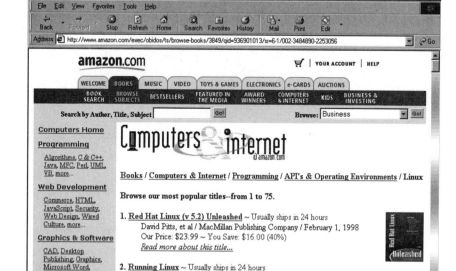

There are also a number of education clearinghouses on the Web. They include information on training companies and products and are searchable by geographic area and topic. Sites to visit include:

* Yahoo's computer training index (**yahoo.com/Business_ and_Economy/Companies/Computers/Services/ Training/**), this contains hundreds of links to trainers and training companies.
* Nerd World Media's computer training list (**www.nerdworld. com/nw190.html**), this is quite extensive.

Once you've added preparation methods for the requirements listed on your Personal Certification Plan, pull out your calendar and fill in a deadline for each requirement. Setting these target dates will help you keep on track and give you a picture of the time frame. When setting deadlines, remember to allow for vacations, holidays, business trips, and the like. Give yourself a little more time than the bare minimum you think is necessary. Then if something unexpected comes up and you fall a day or two behind, your schedule won't be thrown completely out of kilter. Finally, as mentioned before, remember that your plan isn't written in stone. You can change and adapt it to meet your needs along the way. But try to stick to the deadlines if you possibly can. Doing so will assure you make continued progress toward your goal of certification.

How to Evaluate a Training Center

There are two categories of training centers that you'll encounter: authorized and "other." Authorized training centers have an agreement with a Linux certification sponsor that specifies the details of their operations. The training partner agreements typically specify curriculum, course materials, facilities, equipment, and instructor qualifications. The theory behind authorized training centers is that you can obtain the same quality and level of training no matter which one you attend. However, the real world doesn't always conform neatly to plan. Instructors are individuals with varying classroom presence and skills. Equipment upkeep may be more meticulous at one center than another.

The "other" category encompasses all training firms and programs that lack the official seal of approval. This may be because they don't (or can't) meet sponsor requirements or because they simply want freedom from the complications of oversight and sponsor regulations.

Whichever type of facility interests you, it's important to evaluate how good a job it's likely to do of providing the services you want. The two most important aspects to investigate are the instructor and the classroom.

To assess the skill of the instructor, ask the training facility for the name of the instructor who will be teaching your class. Request a copy of the trainer's resume and copies of past course evaluations from classes that trainer led. Find out if the training facility is willing to direct you to students who've taken classes from the trainer in the past. Opinions from people who've taken past classes with an instructor are an excellent resource.

You may find the training center unwilling to provide such information. That may simply mean that they don't know who will be teaching the class; contract instructors are often brought in to teach courses. If that's the case, find out if the facility uses the same contractors again and again. If so, you can ask for information on each of the trainers who may teach your class. If the training company uses different trainers each time, they're taking a gamble with an unknown, and so are you. If that's the case, you may want to look elsewhere. Using new trainers each time may also mean that trainers have declined to come back for a return engagement, another potential warning sign.

The best way to assess a training facility's physical setup is to visit the classroom your course will be held in. If it's too far away, you'll have to do your best to find out the relevant information via telephone. Ask what kind of computers will be used in class. Is the hardware up to date? How much RAM does each computer have? What speed are the CPUs? Is there a router for each student, or will you be expected to share? Are the relevant hookups, such as network and Internet connections, present?

Don't overlook the layout of the classroom itself. Is there room to spread out your materials and move around or are desks crammed tightly together? What presentation devices, such as overhead projectors or whiteboards, will be used to display information to the entire class? Are they clearly visible from all seats? Are the chairs comfortable enough to spend hours in, or are they ergonomic nightmares?

Inquire about lunch arrangements, satisfaction guarantees, and whether you can come in before or after class to practice on your own. The ability to use the equipment after hours is a valuable option to have. Think about your past training experiences and what you liked and disliked about them. If specifics come to mind, find out if they will occur at the facility you're now considering.

If you feel uncomfortable poking and prodding like this, remember that you are considering spending a significant amount of time and money at the facility, and you have every right to know just what you'll be getting in return. Politely make your inquiries and jot down notes about what you discover. If the training facility has been in business for any time at all, they'll be used to it. And the time you spend checking out the center will be paid back tenfold if it saves you from enrolling somewhere that doesn't measure up. If you find a good center, you'll be able to return to it again and again.

Installing Linux on Your Home Computer

Although it may be possible to obtain Linux certification without hands-on practice, it certainly wouldn't be a good idea. There's nothing like interaction with the actual products to increase your understanding of the technology at hand. It's extremely unlikely you'll be able to pass any Linux certification exam without working with Linux. Besides, why would you want to? Even if you managed to pass, it would only come back to haunt you later. Although some Linux certification candidates have a working environment where they can get hands-on practice with the operating system, many do not. For that reason it's common practice to install Linux on a computer at home. This also gives you valuable experience with the installation process, something you may not have even if you work with Linux at your place of employment.

QUICKTIP

One of the handiest ways to install Linux without disrupting your current operating system is to create a dual-boot system. A computer set up this way gives the user a choice at startup of which operating system to use.

To get Linux up and running on your home computer, all you really need is a copy of the operating system. Use the Linux distribution most closely related to the certification you have chosen. You can often obtain a copy at no charge from a vendor's Web site, although often you have to hunt around a bit to find the free version. Downloads are currently available from the following sources, among others:

* Caldera OpenLinux **www.calderasystems.com/openstore/**
* Debian Linux **www.debian.org/distrib/**
* Red Hat Linux **www.redhat.com/download/**
* Slackware Linux **ftp.cdrom.com/pub/linux/slackware**
* SuSE Linux **www.suse.com**

Distributions contain a rather extensive collection of software, and can take quite a long time to download successfully from the Internet. It's often worthwhile to pay a few dollars to have a CD-ROM containing the software shipped to you. Another option is to buy a Linux "how-to" book that comes with the operating system on a companion CD-ROM. This gives you printed materials to refer to, including installation instructions. If you go the book route, make certain the included software is a recent version.

Although distribution typically comes with some sort of automated installation program, loading Linux onto your computer can still be a little complex. In fact, difficulty of installation is one of the main complaints voiced about Linux. This is largely, although not entirely, due to the need to create specially formatted Linux partitions on your hard drive.

Whenever you mess with partitions on your hard drive, you can accidentally and irretrievably lose data without trying very hard. Be sure to back up critical data before attempting to install Linux! Also seriously consider purchasing and using a handy utility program called PartitionMagic from PowerQuest. This program has a graphical interface that allows you resize, move, and create partitions with relative ease and safety and without destroying data. It works with FAT, FAT32, NTFS, HPFS, and Linux ext2 file systems. Its companion program, BootMagic, works well too. PartitionMagic costs about $70. It can be purchased and downloaded directly from the PowerQuest Web site at www.powerquest.com or through most software outlets.

Whichever distribution you choose, you'll find plenty of installation help available to you in the form of free online documentation and FAQs. Some of the best sources are:

* The Linux Getting Started and Installation Guide from the Linux Documentation Project (**www.linuxdoc.org/index.html#guide**)
* LinuxCare's Linux Setup Forum (**lc.experts-exchange.com/Computers/Operating_Systems/Linux/Setup/**)
* The **comp.os.linux**.setup newsgroup (shown in Figure 8.6)

You might also consider hooking up with a local Linux User's Group (LUG). An index of such groups can be found on the Linux-HQ Web site at: **www.linuxhq.com/users/index.html**.

FIGURE 8.6
Linux installation help on the Web

Subject	From	Date
Monster Fusion and XF86 Information for you all !	Mark Thompson	31 Aug 1999
NEWBIE:how to set up a cluster	"Santiago Rodriguez Llorente"	1 Sep 1999
Re: DHCP troubles	leomania@my-deja.com	01 Sep 1999
Re: IE for linux	"M. Smith"	31 Aug 1999
Re: How do i get my Herculese Stringray 128/3d working with *	"Brent Willcox"	30 Aug 1999
Re: Save my 486... Linux and HDD controller board	roscoe@troll.dhis.org	31 Aug 1999
Swap over NFS on kernel 2.2	Mohd-Hanafiah Abdullah	1 Sep 1999
Re: Corrupted Partition Table	ghelbig	31 Aug 1999
Re: Optimal Linux RAID Support? Questions.	leomania@my-deja.com	01 Sep 1999
Installing RPMs from CD	"Bill Smith"	31 Aug 1999
-> Re: Installing RPMs from CD	ghelbig	31 Aug 1999
Re: can't print after kernel upgrade	John Soltow	31 Aug 1999
Re: new user?	Assad Khan	31 Aug 1999

By using these resources and following the advice contained within them, you'll have Linux up and running and ready to play with in no time. This hands-on practice is really an irreplaceable part of earning a Linux certification.

Following Your Plan

As you step through the requirements in your Personal Certification Plan, it helps to take a methodical approach. Your process should go something like this:

1. Read objectives for that exam.
2. Read the sponsor's information on how to prepare for that exam.
3. Complete any study/training classes and materials.
4. Get hands-on experience.
5. Review/practice.
6. Register for the exam.
7. Take the exam.

Don't hesitate to modify these steps to suit your personality and needs. Some people prefer to schedule their exam first and use the exam date as motivation to keep on track. You'll also find that, for some requirements, your existing knowledge and experience will make it possible for you to skip steps and still perform just fine on the exam.

Once you've completed the preparation of your plan, store it somewhere close at hand so that you can refer to it at will. Whenever you complete a requirement, mark an X in the column provided for that purpose. Those Xs will accumulate into a tower of accomplishment, and before you know it, you'll reach your goal and become a Linux-certified computer professional.

Chapter 9

Study Secrets

Is it possible to graduate from high school, college, or even graduate school without mastering effective study skills? In a word, yes. Learning how to learn rarely receives the attention it should in our system of education. It sometimes seems to be assumed that this is something everyone knows instinctively, like putting your hands out to catch yourself when you stumble.

In fact, extending your arms to cushion a fall isn't instinctive, it just feels that way because you've been doing it for so long that it's become second nature. If you observe young children who've just begun to walk, you'll notice that they stumble a lot. And when they stumble, they fall, usually face first. It's only after repeatedly banging their foreheads or noses that they begin to catch themselves with their hands.

At first glance, studying might also seem like an inherent skill that you either do or don't have. But like putting your hands out when you trip, it's a learned behavior. Similarly, once you've mastered effective techniques, you'll be able to apply them again and again throughout your life. At first this will require deliberate effort, but with time and practice, it, too, can become second nature.

You already know how to study, you say? If you're really fortunate, then you do. More likely, you know just enough to get by. When study skills are lacking, an increase in effort can sometimes compensate for lack of ability. But studying doesn't have to be a mind-numbing feat of endurance, and exams don't have to tie your stomach in knots. Nor should you feel embarrassed if your study skills are weak; it's not that difficult to fix them. Once you do, you'll find the act of learning can become downright pleasurable.

As an adult learner, your educational circumstances are significantly different from what they were when you were in high school or college. It's likely that you have more demands competing for your time, including a full-time job and possibly a family. But you have an advantage over your counterparts in a very important way—motivation. You're studying because you've identified a goal you want to obtain (Linux certification). You have a concrete vision of how achieving your goal will benefit you. You're placing at least some of your own money on the line. Getting down to business will be easier this time around.

Learning to study effectively means gaining control and understanding in three main areas: environment, methods, and motivation. The skills you already have in these areas can be strengthened and augmented with new techniques. First, let's look at a few myths about studying.

You Might Have Heard That...

Smart People Don't Have to Study

This is one of the most widely held misconceptions about studying. Everyone knows an individual who appears to glide through academics with little effort, always getting excellent scores on exams yet never seeming to crack a book. How can this be?

It simply isn't true. Some people need less study time than others, but that often can be linked to efficient and effective techniques rather than to a high I.Q. score. Consider reading speed. One student may read at a rate of 250 words a minute and will take about six hours to read a 90,000-word book. A faster reader, cruising along at 500 words per minute, will finish that same book in only three hours. Is the slower reader not as smart? Not necessarily. He's just not as skilled a reader.

The other contributing factor to the myth that smart people don't have to study has to do with where they study. Rather than trying to concentrate in the midst of a crowded cafeteria, for example, they hit the books in a private (and quieter) environment. Only those who live with them see them studying. And if word starts to circulate that they're so smart that they don't have to study, why deny it?

Cramming Is a Good Way to Remember Things

No. Cramming is the way to forget things! Think back to a time when you applied this technique yourself, probably out of desperation over an exam looming the next day. You may have achieved a decent score on that test, but what do you remember of the material now? Or even just a week after the test? If you're like most people, the facts quickly evaporated from your mind.

The human brain strengthens the connections between bits of information through repetition. Although cramming may stuff enough facts into short-term memory to pass an exam, short-term memory is just that, here today and gone tomorrow. Storing information in long-term memory requires repetition and sustained effort. Certainly, last-minute studying does have its place: as a review tool. But its true effectiveness is as a supplement to a more sustained kind of learning that will place information at your service today, next week, and next year.

The More You Study, the More You Learn

Longer study periods covering greater quantities of material may, in fact, be detrimental to your ability to recall the information. Your attention span isn't unlimited. Everyone reaches a saturation point where information seems to flow into one brain cell and then proceed directly out of another. It's as if your brain is saying "give me a break!" In fact, that may be just what is happening. Recent research suggests that the human brain requires time for new information or skills to become "hard wired," and that introducing a second skill or batch of information right on the heels of the first interferes with that process. Essentially, the brain needs time to process what it has just received.

Think about learning two phone numbers. If you work on both simultaneously, you'll probably exchange digits between them and take more time to be able to recall either one correctly. However, if you take them one at a time, and get the first down cold before taking on the next, such confusion is unlikely to occur. More studying is not automatically better.

Background Noise Can Help You Concentrate

Studying with the television running may feel like less work, but it's also working less. When part of your mind is occupied filtering and interpreting background noise, it's not available to focus on the information you're studying. Background music also interferes with your ability to concentrate, although music without lyrics is significantly less distracting than music with them. For best results, focus your full attention on your task. You'll finish sooner and can then fully enjoy your music or television show.

Studying Requires Substantial, Uninterrupted Blocks of Time

Ideally, you should have at least some interrupted periods. But not having them doesn't preclude study opportunities. Squeezing "study snacks" into the margins of your daily life can be very beneficial. Consider the times you find yourself waiting: for the bus, for an elevator, for the next available bank teller, or for a take-out lunch. If you carry notes, in some form, in your pocket, you can whip them out at these times and grab a few minutes of power studying. Over the course of a week, these "study snacks" can add up to a significant meal of information.

When to Study

You don't have to be a time-management expert to recognize that most people cram an incredible array of activities into the course of a week. If you're one of them, you may be wondering how you're going to squeeze study time into an already crowded schedule. Although small amounts of study time can prove quite valuable, longer, uninterrupted blocks are necessary. Finding them can be a challenge. Fortunately, it's one that you can conquer.

Every week contains 168 hours. That's more than 10,000 minutes. A basic 8:00–5:00 job, with no overtime and a half hour commute each way, cuts 50 hours off the top. Allocate another 45 minutes to shower, dress, and eat breakfast before leaving the house, and that's another 3 3/4 hours gone. What about sleep? At eight hours a night you're snoozing away 56 hours each week. Take another half hour a day to microwave and eat dinner and the total reaches 113 hours. That's 6,795 of your precious allotment of minutes expended on basic living, without even getting to sleep in on Saturday morning.

That's the bad news. The good news is that the above barebones regimen still leaves another 55 hours or so (specifically, 3,285 minutes) in your time bank. It's up to you to spend it wisely.

Granted, much, if not all, of that time is already spoken for. Some of it's devoted to activities you won't want to give up. But if you examine your use of time closely, chances are you'll be able to massage your schedule and slide study time into your life fairly painlessly.

If the time slots open to studying aren't obvious, a time usage chart will reveal them. To make one, mark 15 minute time increments along the left side of a piece of paper. Create seven columns across the top, one for each day of the week. During the next week, record what you do throughout the day by listing the activity and blocking off the amount of time used. Figure 9.1 shows a partially completed time usage chart.

FIGURE 9.1
Sample time usage chart

		Monday	Tuesday	Wednesday	Thursday	Friday	Saturday	Sunday
	7:00	Rise &						
	7:15	Bkfst						
	7:30	Commute						
	7:45	to-work						
	8:00	Work						
	8:15							
	8:30							
	8:45							
	9:00							
	9:15							
	9:30							
	9:45							
	10:00	Break						
	10:15	Work						
	10:30							
	10:45							
	11:00							
	11:15							
	11:30							
	11:45							
	12:00	Find-Keys						
	12:15	Lunch						

At the end of the week, add the total amount of time you spent on each activity. Analyze your chart to determine:

* On which activities you spend the most time? Is the amount of time you devote to them reasonable? If not, think about how you can cut back.
* Which are the biggest time wasters? Does your time chart show hours of television watching, excessive phone calls, or frequent nights out? Looking for misplaced items is a frequent time waster that probably won't even make it onto your chart.
* What can you cut back or eliminate to make room for studying? The time wasters are prime candidates for the ax. You can let the answering machine take phone calls, become more

organized so you don't spend as much time finding things, and/or turn off your television. You also might identify commitments, such as volunteer work or league sports, that you can reduce while you're working toward certification.

This isn't to say that you should completely cut out your social life and leisure activities. In fact, those are things you should be careful to include in your schedule. To succeed as a learner, you also need time away from the books so you can relax and maintain your health.

When choosing study times, keep the following principles in mind:

* Schedule study time during those times of day that you feel best. If you're a morning person, consider getting up early so you can get in a half hour before work. Are you a night person? Then skip the evening news and work on your certification program instead. You'll absorb material quickly and more easily when you are fully alert.

* Learn to say no. During this time, try to avoid taking on extra work. Some people find it hard to refuse any request, especially those that come from coworkers or charities. But a simple reply like: "I'd love to be able to do that for you, but right now my schedule is booked solid. Maybe another time?" will protect your study time without hurting feelings. If you're someone who finds it difficult to say no, practice in front a mirror until the words just flow from your lips.

* Build a cushion into your time estimates. Avoid the temptation to schedule things to the minute. Inevitably, something unexpected will occur. If you haven't allowed time for it, you'll end up chasing your schedule for days afterward.

* Study the worst first. If you are dreading a particular study unit or practice material, take it on first. Chances are you'll discover it isn't nearly as onerous as you expected, and with the hardest part out of the way the remaining materials will be a cake walk.

Where to Study

Where you choose to study affects how successful you will be at learning and remembering the information you cover. Although it's possible to study on the subway, a park bench, or at the kitchen table, your best study space is likely to be elsewhere. What makes a study area ideal? The perfect study environment is one where you can work in distraction-free comfort. It's physically and psychologically conducive to the work at hand, without being so comfortable it puts you to sleep.

Selecting a regular study place has another advantage: mental conditioning. Think of Pavlov's famous dogs. Each time the animals were to be fed, Pavlov rang a bell. Soon, the dogs began to salivate at the sound of the bell alone. They developed a physical response to the expectation of food. They were conditioned to respond to the bell.

Similarly, you can condition yourself to study. If you use the same study spot again and again, you will begin to associate it with studying. Over time, your mind and body will become conditioned to learn whenever you enter your study area. Sitting down and getting to work will become more automatic.

Your chosen space should have adequate lighting; bright, but not glaring. It should provide a chair and desk or table. The chair should be a standard desk chair, or one you might find in a conference room or classroom. Don't study in a cushy arm chair. You'll end up slouching and holding your study materials at an awkward angle, both of which can interfere with your ability to concentrate and cause muscle soreness. If you're lying back in a soft chair, especially in a warm room, you may doze off.

The work surface can be a desk or table. Whichever it is, there should be plenty of space to spread out your study materials. It should be at a comfortable height so you can study for extended periods without strain. The surrounding environment should be quiet and free from distractions and interruptions. That means the television and radio should be off, and, if you're at home, let the answering machine answer the phone. Don't park yourself in front of a picture window either; a blank wall will be less distracting. Instruct family members and coworkers not to interrupt you. Have all your study materials—calculator, notebook, extra pens, and so on—at hand so you won't have to get up to fetch something.

Schedule regular study times. It will help you get into the habit of studying and will aid the conditioning process mentioned above. Choose a time of day when you usually feel alert. Consider eating a high-protein snack beforehand so you don't get hungry.

Study sessions don't have to be marathon events. If you need a break, take one. Get up, stretch, and wander down the hall for a few minutes. Try to limit breaks to ten minutes or less. Four one-hour study sessions will prove more beneficial than one four-hour session.

Common study locations include a library, an empty conference room, or a kitchen table. Lack of the perfect study area shouldn't keep you from the task at hand. Though a comfortable, well-lit, and distraction-free environment is best, reality may dictate other circumstances. Do your best to schedule study periods following these ideal conditions, but when it comes down to it, if life interferes, study where and when you can.

How to Study

Once you've nailed down the when and where of your study plan, it's time to focus on study techniques. By making effective use of your study time, you can cut down the amount of time needed while simultaneously increasing your comprehension, recall, test scores, and self-confidence.

Study skills are best organized by task. Thanks to the perennial fountain of students and teachers, methods have been developed for getting the most out of a textbook, taking effective notes, tricks to improve your memory, test preparation, and more. Although there are also tips and tricks for writing papers, you're not likely to need to do that in the course of certification training, so it isn't covered in this book.

The key to all these methods is your involvement. To be an effective learner, you need to be an active learner. The information that comes your way via self-study and classroom activities won't stick with you just because it passes by your eyes or ears. But if you operate with the intention of making it stick by using methods that have been proven to work, you will learn and remember.

How to Read a Textbook

One of the most effective and most widely taught textbook study methods has been around since the 1940s, when it was first developed by Dr. Francis Robinson. It's called SQ3R. The acronym is derived from the five steps of the system: Survey, Question, Read, Recite, and Review. Following them will greatly increase your comprehension and recall of textbook material. They can be applied to an entire book, to a single chapter, or to any reading assignment. Let's go over the steps in order.

Survey

The first step is to survey the reading material. Just as a construction surveyor determines the lay of the land, your goal is to determine the overall shape of the book. Read the title, preface, introduction, and table of contents. Then flip through the rest of the book (or chapter), reading only the boldface headings and subheadings. Scan any illustrations to see what they are about. Surveying an entire book should take less than a half hour. When you're finished, you'll have a good feel for what the book is about and how it's organized.

Question

The next step, signified by the Q in SQ3R, is to question. This very important step transforms you from a passive reader to an active one. Instead of expecting the book to feed you information, you'll be able to work to extract it by focusing on learning the answers to questions you develop in advance. To develop your questions, scan back through the reading material, again focusing on the headings and subheadings. This time, rephrase them as questions. Table 9.1 shows headings from a book chapter about Linux, along with questions that could be derived from them.

TABLE 9.1

Headings and
questions from a
Linux text

Section Heading	Question
How to Manage Your Files	What methods are available for managing files?
How to Manage Your Users	How are users added, deleted, and configured?
How to Manage Your Software with lisa	What is lisa and how does it work?
How to Manage Your Services	What services are available and how do I manage them?

Read

The third step (the first R) is to read each section keeping in mind the questions you formulated in the previous step. Pay especially close attention to the first and last sentences of each paragraph. The first sentence, called the *topic sentence*, will reveal the main idea of the paragraph. The last sentence typically brings discussion of that particular idea to a conclusion.

The first time through new material, leave your highlighter pens on the desk. Otherwise you will tend to underline too much and the wrong things. Save highlighting for a later read-through, when you'll be better able to identify key points.

Recite

The second of the three Rs in SQ3R stands for recite. After you read each section, *without consulting your notes or the text*, do your best to recite the questions you developed and their answers. You can do this silently or out loud. Out loud is better because it applies an additional sense, your hearing, to enhance your learning. If you can't answer the questions from memory, look back through the text and try again. When you can answer the questions from memory, go on to the next section.

Review

The final R stands for review. This is where you begin seriously building your memory of the information. Go back over all the questions you created for all of the sections you read. Try to answer them again. To add kinesthetic (touch/movement) learning, write out the questions and their answers. If you jot them down on index cards, you can then review the information pretty much anywhere, any time you have a few spare minutes. Repetition will help solidify the information in your mind.

That's all there is to it. Next time you open a textbook remember the acronym SQ3R. Then do it. After you (S)urvey, (Q)uestion, (R)ead, (R)ecite, and (R)eview, you'll know a lot more than if you had simply read the book.

How to Get the Most From a Class

Just as you can get more from a textbook by becoming an active reader, you can boost your classroom comprehension by becoming an active listener. To become an active listener in a classroom setting, you'll need to prepare, pay attention, participate, and take notes.

Before Class

What you do before class dramatically affects how much you learn during class. If you prepare properly, the actual class time will be almost a review, reinforcing information you've already learned. You won't be struggling to keep up because you will have developed a good idea of what's coming and familiarized yourself with the concepts and language that are likely to arise.

* Preview the material to be covered. Before the first meeting of a new course, obtain a course outline from the professor, along with a set of objectives. Read over it to find out what will be covered. Determine exactly what you will be expected to know when the class is complete. If a textbook accompanies the course, scan through it ahead of time, using the survey method described above.

* Prior to each class session, check over the course outline to see what material is due to be covered. If you have a textbook with corresponding chapters, read it using the SQ3R method *before* class.

* Arrive early. The first few minutes of class time are often very important. During this time the instructor is likely to introduce

the topic at hand and sketch the shape of the material to come. If you're busy opening your notebook and greeting your neighbor, you won't be paying attention, you'll miss out on this important information, and you'll be a step behind for the remainder of the class session. It's much wiser to arrive 10 or 15 minutes beforehand to get yourself organized and mentally in gear.

During Class

* Pay attention. You can't remember what you haven't learned in the first place.
* Take notes. Research has shown that students who take notes during class remember more than those who don't, *even if they never look at those notes again*. The process of taking notes forces you to pay attention and to organize your thoughts.
* Participate in discussions. Again, this forces you to be an active listener. Besides that, you'll also have the opportunity to clarify any points you find confusing. By speaking, you'll also reinforce your learning by verbalizing some of what you've read and heard.

After Class

* Stay late. At least a few minutes late. It can be tough to pay attention when others around you are packing up their books, but those last few minutes of class are as important (if not more) than the first few. Your instructor may use them to summarize what was covered, or, if he/she has run short on time, may cram 15 minutes of material into the last five. The end of class is also when you're likely to find out what will be covered next session and what you should do to prepare.
* Review your notes immediately after class and fill in any gaps. This will take just five or ten minutes and could save you hours later on. That's because although you'll remember most of the lecture/material for a short time, by the next day, unless you've reinforced it mentally, much of what you heard will slip away.
* In conjunction with reviewing your notes (or in lieu of, if time doesn't permit you to sit down with them immediately after

class), conduct a mental review of the class session. You can do this in the car on your way home or in the cafeteria. Recall what the main points of the session were and why they are important.

Note Taking 101

Taking good notes isn't a hit-or-miss proposition, it's a learned skill. Effective note taking will help you focus on what is being said, understand it, and recall the material later on. You can gain all of this without requiring a minute more than you'll spend sitting in class anyway.

Although taking notes isn't as simple as pulling out a piece of paper and recording what the instructor says, it's not much more difficult either. To begin, start each class with a fresh piece of paper and record the date and lecture title (if there is one) at the top. Then draw a vertical line about two inches from the left edge of the page, dividing it into two columns. Most of your notes will go into the second, wider column. The first column is for comments, words, and other marks that will enable you to quickly identify key sections of your notes. Little or nothing will go there until you review your notes later.

When class begins, start writing your notes. Don't try to record every word the instructor utters. Instead, aim to capture key points and subtopics, using a structure similar to outlining. Distinguish between major and minor points by indenting or underlining. Write in your own words, not the instructor's. By rephrasing what is said, you'll deepen your understanding of it. The exception to this guideline is if the material is a definition, formula, or rule. In those cases, it's best to record exactly what the instructor says, to ensure accuracy.

For expediency in note recording and review, use descriptive words and phrases instead of whole sentences. You can save additional time by developing your own shorthand. To do so, substitute symbols and abbreviations for words or parts of words that appear frequently (see sidebar for shorthand suggestions). Add new shortcuts gradually, so you don't find yourself with a page of jumbled shortcuts that you can't decode easily. Remember, your personal shorthand is intended to save you time, not add confusion. Let it develop over time.

Shorthand Substitutions

Replace *ing* with *g*: *configurg* instead of *configuring*

w/ for with: *w/ program loaded* instead of *with program loaded*

w/o for without: *w/o reformat* instead of *without reformat*

R for are, *U* for you: *U R here* instead of *you are here*

+ for and: *compile + bind first* instead of *compile and bind first*

Use digits instead for numbers: *4 principles* instead of *four principles*

< for less than or lower: *< cost* instead of *lower cost*

> for greater than or more: *> flexibility* instead of *greater flexibility*

= for is the same as: *time = money* instead of *time is money*

leave out vowels that aren't critical: *prgrm* for *program*

Deciding what to include or exclude can be challenging at first, but once you develop your skills and grow familiar with your instructor's style, it will become second nature. Try to capture the main ideas and their subtopics. Listen for key phrases that indicate important information will follow, such as:

* "The four principles are"
* "Most importantly"
* "The most frequent mistake is"
* "Always remember"
* "In conclusion"
* And of course, "will be on the test"

Through voice and body language, the instructor may give cues that key points are imminent. Watch for increased animation or a change in the pitch of the speaker's voice, which should alert you that important points are forthcoming. Pay close attention to anything that is emphasized through use of the chalkboard. If you miss something, leave a blank space in your notes so that you can fill it in later.

Review your notes as soon as possible after class. This is the time for that left-hand column. Use it to highlight especially key points and to serve as a quick index to your notes. For example, you might mark ! next to an important point and ? next to something you need to clarify. Identify sections of your notes with key words describing the topic, so that you can locate them easily. Figure 9.2 shows a sample page of notes from a class about the OSI reference model.

Make sure you record your name and phone number on the inside of the front cover of your notebook. Then, if you accidentally leave it somewhere, you may get it back; otherwise a moment of inattention may cost you all of your notes.

FIGURE 9.2
Sample lecture
notes

5/20/99
OSI·ref·mod

	7·lyrs:·Phys,·dta·lnk,·ntwrk,·trans,·sess,·present,·app
*	Pls·Do·Not·Throw·Sausage·Pizza·Away·(PDNTSPA)
1	phys=bits
2	data·lnk·=·LLC·+·MAC MAC·=·phys·addrssng Data·in2·frames
3	Ntwrk·lyr·=·logical·addrsng --IP·here --routers·opr8·here

How to Remember

Do you have a good memory or a bad memory? Although the ability to recall information does vary between individuals, it's another study skill (and life skill) that you can significantly improve.

In *Learn To Be A Master Student* authors Robert Rooney and Anthony Lipuma identify three basic functions of memory: labeling information as you learn it, storing it in your brain, and recalling it. You can improve two of these functions. The third, storing, doesn't need enhancement. Your brain already has more storage capacity than you can possibly use in your lifetime, no matter how much information you stuff in there. Don't you wish your computer's hard drive were like that?

The labeling part of the memory process involves deliberately identifying information as you learn it. This can be accomplished through linking new information with other things you already know or by organizing it in a way that makes it easier to remember. There are several tricks you can use to improve your labeling skills, including mnemonics and memory mapping. Both will be described shortly.

Your ability to recall information improves with practice. Every time you remember a particular piece of data, your brain becomes better at retrieving it. The brain path to where it is stored becomes more clearly delineated and more deeply entrenched. The process can be compared to finding your way to a new place of employment for the first time versus finding your way there for the twenty-first time. That initial trip requires considerable attention and maybe a wrong turn or two. By the time you've worked there three weeks, you can practically drive there in your sleep (and some mornings it probably feels like you do).

You can also create more than one pathway to a particular piece of information. Doing so enables you to do what you would have to if you encountered a road closure on the way to work—take an alternate route. The more routes you have to work (and the more pathways you create to the information stored in your brain), the less likely it becomes that you'll get stranded without reaching your destination.

GRASP

The word grasp means to lay hold of with the mind. Here's how to GRASP what you want to learn.

* **(G)**et it the first time. If you're not paying attention, you won't learn, and you can't remember what you haven't learned.

* **(R)**emember to remember. Learn with the intention of remembering information for a long time (not just until the next exam).
* **(A)**ssociate new information with something you already know, or arrange it in a pattern that's easy to remember.
* **(S)**tudy the same information different ways to create more than one path to retrieving it.
* **(P)**ractice remembering. The more you recall a piece of information, the easier it will become.

Mnemonics

Remember SQ3R? That's right, it stands for Study, Question, Read, Recite, Review. Because you have linked the acronym to the process of reading a textbook, you can more easily remember the individual steps. SQ3R and GRASP are examples of mnemonic devices—memory cues that help you label and recall information. Other mnemonics you've probably encountered include: Every Good Boy Does Fine, which helps you remember the notes (EGBDF) associated with the lines of the treble clef; and ROY G. BIV for the colors of the rainbow (red, orange, yellow, green, blue, indigo, violet). Remember the verse "Thirty days hath September"? That's a mnemonic, too.

Mnemonics are powerful tools that make memorizing easier, more interesting, and even fun. They also enable you to remember longer. How many years has it been since you first met good, old ROY G. BIV?

You can create your own mnemonics. Acronyms are a form of mnemonics that the computer world is awash in already. Consider WAN (Wide Area Network), RAM (Random Access Memory), IOS (Internetworking Operating System), PROM (Programmable Read Only Memory), and ISDN (Integrated Services Digital Network), just to name a few.

To create your own acronyms, consider the items you need to memorize. Can you rearrange them so that the first letters form an acronym you can remember? What if you needed to memorize the stages of the systems development process, in order? They are:

1. Requirements Stage
2. Evaluation Stage
3. Design Stage
4. Implementation Stage

How handy that the first letters form the acronym REDI! Just remember that to develop a new Linux-based application, you have to get REDI first. In this example, the items needed to be recalled in order. But when they don't, feel free to play with them, rearranging them to see what you can come up with.

Another powerful type of mnemonic is rhyme. Putting information into rhyme format or to the tune of a familiar song creates a fun association that makes it easier to recall.

Another helpful memory trick is to count. For example, if you know that there are seven layers in the OSI network model, you'll know to keep trying if only six come to mind at first.

The Power of Pictures

Consider using pictures to help you remember, especially if you are a visual learner (Chapter 8 explained how to determine your learning style). Visualize or actually draw a picture that illustrates a concept you want to remember. You can put yourself in the picture or not. If you can conjure up a humorous scenario, so much the better.

For example, if you study communication, you'll discover that communication requires: a sender, a receiver, a message, a channel to convey the message, and feedback that informs the sender if or how the message was received. The sender transmits the message over the channel to the receiver. Anything that disrupts the smooth operation of any of the elements is called noise.

How might you turn this information into a memorable image? Here's just one of the infinite possibilities: Picture a husband and wife talking to each other across the living room. The husband is trying to tell the wife that they've been invited to a party. In this example the husband is the sender, the wife is the receiver, the channel is the air in the living room, and the message is the news of the invitation. Now picture a four-year-old and a seven-year-old sprawled on the floor somewhere between couple. Suddenly they begin to squabble loudly over a red crayon. Can you guess which element they represent? The feedback, in this case, might be the wife shaking her head in frustration and pointing at the noisy children.

Another way you can capitalize on the power of pictures is through a technique called *memory mapping*. Don't worry, it doesn't require a class in cartography or any artistic ability. If you can draw basic shapes and lines, you can create a memory map.

Memory maps are similar to other tools you may be familiar with—data flow diagrams and structure charts. All these tools provide a way to organize information in a logical fashion by arranging it as parts of a diagram. The act of creating them helps you organize your thoughts and forces you to identify how the pieces of whatever you're mapping fit together.

To create a memory map, begin by drawing a shape of your choice, such as a circle, square, diamond, or star, in the center of a blank page. Inside the shape, write a word describing what you're mapping. For each main idea associated with the topic, draw a line extending outward from the shape. Add additional lines branching off of the main ones for associated ideas and topics. Figure 9.3 shows a memory map for the GRASP system.

FIGURE 9.3
GRASP
memory map

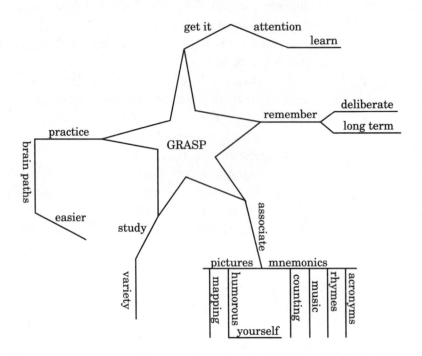

No two memory maps will look alike. Each is unique to the topic and to the person who created it. Illustrating and organizing information this way utilizes both motion and sight (visualization) to help you remember it later on.

Study Groups

Contrary to popular assumption, a study group isn't a place to learn new information; it's a place to practice and reinforce what you've already learned. Depending on other group members to provide you with an introduction to something you haven't studied yet is risky—it may be presented inaccurately, and once you learn something the wrong way, learning it correctly is more difficult. It's wiser to get the facts down first, then use a study group setting to reinforce them.

Study groups are good for increasing your understanding of a topic. Because no two people see things exactly the same way, another participant may be crystal clear on a concept that you're struggling with and can guide you through it. You can return the favor for a different concept. You can also compare interpretations. The process of discussing subject matter will clarify material and solidify it in your mind.

Study group members can also drill each other with flash cards or exchange essay questions. This sort of interaction is very valuable when preparing for tests.

You may be able to join an existing study group, but, more likely, you'll have to form your own. Look for two or three individuals working on the same material (or certification) as yourself. You may find them online or through a class you're participating in.

Set regular meeting times—once a week is a common interval—and choose a site conducive to your purpose. A library may not be a good option unless there's a room you can use so that your discussions won't disrupt others. An empty classroom or someone's dining room table are also possibilities. Limit meetings to about an hour per session; any longer and the extra time is likely to be spent on socializing rather than studying.

If you're preparing for certification through self-study, your best bet for forming a study group is likely to be via the Internet. Prowl forums and newsgroups devoted to the topic(s) in which you're interested, and consider posting a message seeking individuals interested in forming a virtual study group. You can also use the Web search engines to seek out such groups. Use the name of your certification and the phrase "study group" as search keys.

Self-Quizzing

One of the simplest ways to practice recalling information is via the self-quiz. Talk about versatility and convenience—you can self-quiz almost anywhere. You can do it with spiffy software, audio tape, or cheap 3 x 5 index cards. You can time yourself, or not. And how often do you get the chance to make up your own questions for a test?

Depending upon your choice of certification and how deep your pockets are, you can purchase quizzes that other people have made specifically for your certification.

Linux certification was so new as this book was being written, that no practice exam software had yet become available, however, such software has appeared for most other popular certifications so its availability is only a matter of time. To give you an idea of what such software looks like, Figure 9.4 shows a screen from BeachFront Quizzer's preparation package for Cisco certification.

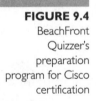

FIGURE 9.4
BeachFront
Quizzer's
preparation
program for Cisco
certification

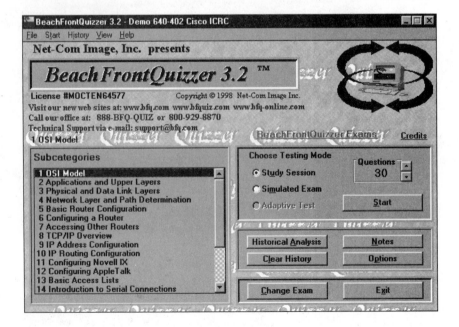

Many of these prepackaged quizzes are available in software format. Others come in workbooks. This book's resource section includes contact information that will help you find Linux certification preparation software and books.

Besides certification-specific software, there are a number of shareware programs that allow you to create quizzes on any topic of your choice. These can be especially useful if commercial programs are too expensive or unavailable for the material you wish to practice. Figure 9.5 shows WinFlash, by Open Window (**www.openwindow.com**). A free trial version is available on the company's Web site.

FIGURE 9.5
WinFlash self-quizzing software

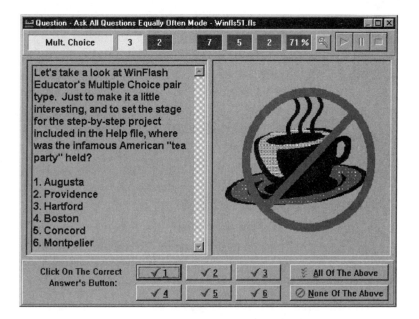

If you prefer to go low tech, you can create a set of flash cards using 3 x 5 index cards. Write the question on the front of the card and the correct answer on the back. If you keep a deck of these cards on hand, you can sneak in practice whenever it's convenient to do so. When you think you have one set of cards down cold, put them aside and start another. Come back to the first set later, and see how much you remember.

Books on tape are becoming popular with people on the go. You can create a quiz on tape to listen to during your daily commute or during exercise workouts. To do so, prepare a list of questions and answers. Then insert a fresh tape into your tape recorder and press record. Read a question aloud, let the tape roll for a few seconds (however long you want to allow yourself to answer the question you just read), then read the answer aloud. Repeat the procedure for each question on your list. When you play back the quiz later, try to answer the questions before the recorded answer plays. Before you record an entire quiz, run a test batch of a few questions to verify that the tape recorder is set up and operating properly.

Taking Tests

If you asked learners to choose the aspect of the educational process that causes them the most anxiety, the overwhelming majority would cite tests. Why? Because a test presents an opportunity for failure, and nobody likes to fail. In fact, fear of failure sometimes leads people who know the material cold to blank out on test day, and just what they feared most would happen, does.

Consider what will happen to you if you do fail a test. Will your coworkers burst into laughter when you return to the office? Will your spouse or lover leave you? Will you lose your job and, as a result, be unable to pay your mortgage, which will then cause you to lose your house and end up lying penniless, in a gutter and alone some cold night? Of course not.

So, putting first things first, don't blow this test thing out of proportion. If you don't pass the test, you'll probably have to take it again. Big deal. It might not be your idea of a good time, but it's hardly life-shattering. And the fact is, if you prepare effectively, you're infinitely more likely to succeed than fail.

Before the Test

What constitutes effective preparation? Most importantly, it doesn't begin the night before the exam. As discussed earlier in this chapter, cramming is an ineffective learning tool and only marginally successful as a last-minute act of desperation. Pull an all-nighter and your mind may be stuffed with facts, but they will be shrouded in a fatigue-induced fog. When the fog dissipates, the facts are likely to go with it.

If, on the other hand, you've been studying throughout a course, you're already halfway prepared for the final exam. That's because you've GRASPed the majority of the information and only have to review and practice recalling it the way the test will ask you to.

The first step is to find out as much as possible about the format and content of the exam. Questions to answer include:

* What will you be expected to know?
* Which question format will be utilized—multiple choice, essay questions, or true-false? Currently most computer certification tests are multiple choice.
* How long will you have to complete the test?
* Will you be able to return to questions later if you skip over them?
* Will points be subtracted for wrong answers?

You should be able to obtain the answers to these questions from your certification sponsor, instructor, and/or testing center. Many of these questions are also answered in Chapter 10 of this book. Once you've identified the characteristics of the particular test, you can tailor your review methods accordingly.

Review the material that you've identified as likely to be on the test. Try to guess what questions will appear on the test, then practice answering them. You can practice by reciting aloud, creating written or recorded self-tests, or using commercially available self-testing software and certification preparation guides. If you belong to a study group, quiz each other and discuss your answers.

QUICKTIP

Pay special attention to vocabulary and terminology. Make certain you know exactly what they mean. If you don't understand a question, you won't be able to answer it.

Develop an overall test strategy, depending on the type of exam. The following advice focuses on multiple-choice exams, the most common format of current certification test questions. These exams count an unanswered question the same way as an incorrect answer. If you won't be penalized for wrong answers (as opposed to skipping the question entirely) then it pays to guess when you don't know the correct answer.

On some exams you will be able to mark questions to return to later. When this is the case, be sure to *mark* the questions or you will *not* be able to return to them. Answer the questions you're certain of first, marking the more challenging ones, and then return to the marked questions when you've finished the easy ones. This strategy enables you to answer a larger percentage of the questions and to answer the easiest ones right away.

The night before, do a brief review and remind yourself that you've prepared and are as ready as you're going to be. Don't stress yourself out poring over your notes again and again. Instead, spend the evening in some pleasant, relaxing way, then get a good night's sleep so you'll be rested and ready to excel.

The Day of the Test

On the day of the test, allow yourself plenty of time to arrive at the test site. Would you rather arrive at the last minute, adrenaline pumping from the stress of too many red lights, or 10 or 15 minutes early, time you can easily fill with a final review of your note cards or trip to the restroom?

Make certain to bring several forms of identification, including a photo ID, and, of course, if you haven't already provided it, payment.

If you feel tense or anxious, apply a few relaxation techniques. One of the most basic is breathing. Take a deep breath, filling not just your chest, but every nook and cranny of your insides all the way down to your abdomen. Inhale from your navel, like a baby does. Exhale slowly, and feel your muscles relaxing as you your breath carries the tension out of your body. Repeat the breathing several times.

When the test begins, follow your preplanned strategy.

* If the test format is suitable, remember to go through and answer the easy questions first.
* Pay close attention to instructions. Are you supposed to select just one answer or all answers that apply?

* Read each question carefully, and twice. It's easy to misread a question and end up with the wrong answer as a result. It's also a waste and something you can avoid.
* Be alert for modifiers like *always*, *never*, *not*, and *except* that can radically affect the meaning of the question.
* Mentally answer the question *before* reading the answer choices. Then look for the choice that most accurately reflects your answer. This can spare you unnecessary confusion created by the test itself.
* If you don't know the answer, make an educated guess (see sidebar).
* If you finish before the time limit, and the software permits it (which isn't always the case), go back over the test and verify your answers. But *don't* change an answer unless you have good reason to believe it's wrong. Research indicates that our first guess is usually our best.

If other people are taking the exam at the same time, don't pay any attention to when they finish. Just because others are done before you doesn't mean that they will end up with a better score. Correspondingly, if you finish first, it doesn't mean you must have missed something. Take your time, keep an eye on the exam clock if there's a time limit, and concentrate on regurgitating what you've learned. If you've prepared using effective techniques, such as the ones detailed in this chapter, you have nothing to worry about.

Making an Educated Guess

If you find yourself facing a question you just don't know the answer to, consider guessing. If there are four possible choices, you automatically have a 25 percent chance of randomly selecting the correct answer. Apply some guessing techniques, and the odds shoot upward in your favor.

Successful guessing relies heavily on the process of elimination. For that reason, the first step is to eliminate any choices that are clearly wrong. If you have four answers to choose from, and you can discard two of them as incorrect, you've gone from a one in four chance of picking the right answer to a one in two chance.

Unless your exam format allows more than one answer choice for each question "all of the above" is basically equivalent to "more than one of the above." If "all of the above" is an option, and you can see at least two correct answers, then choose it.

Sometimes you'll find that, in the course of presenting the question and answers, one test item will provide hints that can help you answer another. Be alert for these and use them when you find them.

Many test-taking experts advise that if you have no idea which choice is correct, and "all of the above" is an option, you should choose "all of the above." By the same token, if you can't decide between two similar answers, choose the one that gives the most complete information.

A Half Dozen Ways to Beat Procrastination—Today

Effective study techniques are powerful productivity boosters—if you use them. But if the procrastinator's mantra—"I'll do it tomorrow"—starts playing in your head, it can wreak havoc on your certification plans. Procrastination often masquerades as some other, ostensibly legitimate, demand for your time. Only on close examination is the disguise pierced. The following are examples of what you can do to the keep the procrastination beast on a leash.

Study 15 Minutes a Day

For some unfathomable reason, when it's time to study, the laundry in the corner suddenly becomes more urgent than the new material. So does mowing the lawn. Anything that delays the dreaded moment of sitting down and beginning becomes more attractive than work.

But getting started doesn't have to be so difficult. Set yourself a daily deadline by which you must sit down and commence 15 minutes of studying. That's right, a mere 15 minutes. When that deadline arrives, force yourself into your study space and work until the time is up. The method's magic is that once you get going, you won't want to stop! You're virtually guaranteed to continue long beyond 15 minutes and accomplish plenty.

Put Procrastination to Work for You

Make procrastination your slave instead of your master. When you're reluctant to begin a particular project, consider other study tasks you could be doing instead. Is your Personal Certification Plan current? Have you reviewed your vocabulary list lately? Why not go back and draw a memory map for that concept you covered last week? Even if you don't get to the project you really ought to be doing today, other valuable tasks will be completed: there really is nothing like procrastination for getting things done. And once you begin, you just might find yourself picking up the work you're avoiding and completing that as well.

Quell Household Distractions

People who study at home know what it's like: the nearby refrigerator seems to call your name. Friends and family telephone to chat just as you settle in to study. You're wearing your last pair of underwear and really should run the laundry through.

Although it's certainly the prerogative (and even pleasure) of someone who studies at home to tend to a chore during a break, don't let this "can" become a "should." As in I should do this chore or I ought to do that one because I'm right here and it needs to be done.

During study hours you are not at home—you are at work. If the refrigerator is a problem, weaken its pull by stocking it with lettuce and fruit instead of high-fat treats. When callers disrupt your concentration, let the answering machine pick up or simply offer to return calls later. If tasks such as piled-up dishes beg attention, imagine how you would respond if your study space were uptown at the library instead of upstairs. Would you drive home and suds up or leave them for later? Save your chores and errands for after study time. They won't go anywhere.

Respect What You're Doing

Frequently, adult learners give their educational efforts a back seat to everything else and consequently get little done. The logic goes something like this: It isn't that important; after all, I do it out of choice, and I already have a job.

The person who lets this thought pattern continue is placing serious limits on his/her success. Your certification goals are meaningful and valuable. You are just fortunate (and clever) enough to be in charge of your own future. Education and professional advancement are something you've decided to go after. Don't let insecurity stop you!

It may help to review your accomplishments. Go over your Personal Certification Plan and review what you've already achieved. Revisit your reasons for pursuing Linux certification in the first place. Count your successes and see how you can build on them.

When you interact with others, don't be afraid to talk about your educational accomplishments and struggles or that troublesome exam. To become a confident and successful student, you must act and feel like one.

Get Regular

Although a flexible schedule is overtly a plus, a regular routine will ensure productivity. Identify certain hours to study every week. You can pick how many and which ones, but decide on a core set of hours, with others you can add or omit as needed. Instruct members of your household not to interrupt you during those times unless there is blood or fire involved.

Have a designated study space and go there during your study time; your equipment and supplies will be at hand and you'll become conditioned to work when you're in that space. If you have children, arrange child care during your scheduled hours or plan to study when they're in bed or at school. Alternatively, study at work, the library, or another site away from home.

Entering the Zone

Imagine an ideal performance state, a "zone of productivity" where your learning flows unimpeded as if from a greased mechanism. It's a lofty aspiration, but you can certainly make strides in that direction, starting today. After all, it will only take 15 minutes.

Putting It All Together

Keep in mind that there are many study methods available. The methods you've read about here are solid, specific approaches to common learning tasks. Nonetheless, they are by no means the only solutions available. If you want to learn additional study methods, check out your local bookstore and library for books about studying.

Thanks to the many colleges and universities connected to the Internet, you can also access study tips via the Web. Educational institutions around the world have put study advice online for your free, 24-hour perusal. Virginia Polytechnic Institute (**www.ucc.vt.edu/stdysk/stdyhlp.html**); University of California, Berkeley (**128.32.89.153/CalRENHP.html**); the University of Texas (**www.utexas.edu/student/lsc/handouts/stutips. html**); and Dartmouth (**www.dartmouth.edu/admin/acskills/ index.html#study**) are good places to start. Figure 9.6 shows Virginia Tech's Web-based study skills resource center.

At first it may feel like the effort that it takes to be an active learner requires more time and energy than it's worth. But once you get into the swing of it, you'll find that the time you put into learning how to learn will be paid back ten times over; you'll be able to remember more and maybe even study less.

FIGURE 9.6
Virginia Polytechnic
offers study advice
via the Web

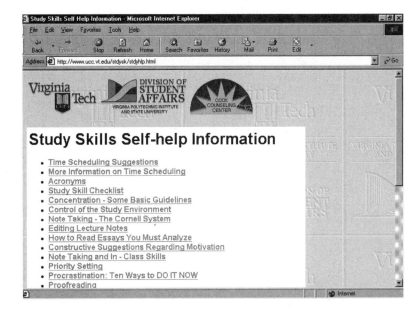

Chapter 10

All About
Linux Tests

Linux certification tests, like those for other certifications, are primarily administered through Sylvan Prometric testing centers. There are approximately 2000 of these centers serving more than 80 countries worldwide. Sylvan Prometric provides testing services for many of the best-known certification programs. If you've taken a certification test before, you probably taken it at a Sylvan testing center.

Red Hat testing is different in that it's primarily offered in conjunction with the associated preparation class. Because Red Hat has recently partnered with Global Knowledge to increase the availability of this class, the class/exam combination is available in a wide number of US locations. If you choose to take the exam without the class, you'll have to visit Red Hat offices in Durham, North Carolina, or Stockley Park, Uxbridge, England.

A few Linux certification exams are delivered in the most convenient format of all—online. Brainbench supplies exams this way, and Digital Metrics used to do so before merging efforts with the Linux Professional Institute. Many certification sponsors avoid online delivery because of security concerns.

Hands-on lab exams are much less widely available than online exams or those delivered through outlets such as Sylvan Prometric. You'll often have to take them at the sponsor's facilities, although in some cases other locations are available. Table 10.1 shows which testing outlet each Linux certification vendor uses.

TABLE 10.1
Linux certification
exam outlets

Sponsor	Testing Outlet	To Register
CyberTech	own network	888-357-5200
Linux Professional Institute	Sylvan (planned)	pending
Prosoft Training	Sylvan	877-795-6871
Red Hat	Red Hat & Global Knowledge	919-547-0012 ext 241
Sair	Sylvan	888-895-6717
Brainbench	Online	www.brainbench.com

Registering for an Exam with Sylvan Prometric

When you're ready to register for exam, there are two ways you can reserve your spot. The first is to call Sylvan Prometric's testing phone number associated with your certification vendor (see Table 10.1). The listed numbers work in the United States and Canada. Phone numbers from outside the United States are listed on Sylvan Prometric's Web site at **www.2test.com**. If you prefer, you can choose to register online through **www.2test.com** (shown in Figure 10.1). In addition to allowing online registration, this Web site incorporates a test center locator that lets you find the test site most convenient to you.

Whichever way you register, you will be asked for a personal ID number. This number will be used each time you register for any certification exam, whether or not it's related to Linux. In the United States a testing candidate's social security number is usually used. However, Sylvan can assign you a different ID number if you request one. Take care to use that same ID number every time you register for an exam. Use care when providing your address information as well, as that is what your certification sponsor will use to contact you, send you welcome kits, and so on. If you register via telephone, have the clerk read your information back to you to guarantee that it's correct.

There is no required waiting period between registering for a certification exam and taking it. However, testing center seats do fill up, so it's a good idea to reserve your spot several weeks in advance. It's also a good idea to verify the accuracy of the reservation several days after you make it. Confirm that you are registered for the test you intend to take, and at the time you specified.

The test center will download your exam the night before your scheduled appointment. On exam day, you can call the test center as soon as they open to verify that your exam has been downloaded and is ready for you. Although download failures are rare, this can save you travelling to the center only to find no test awaiting once you arrive.

Bring two forms of identification, one of which must be a photo ID, to the testing center with you. You will be provided with a small wipe-off board, like a white board, along with a marker to use for notes and calculations during the exam. Until recently you could ask for paper and pencil instead, but that's no longer allowed. You will be required to return the board before leaving the testing center.

Certification exams are almost always closed book. No notes or other resources, including a calculator, can be taken into the exam room with you. You will also need to leave any last-minute study materials with the receptionist. To avoid forgetting them when you leave, consider leaving your car keys/bus pass as well. This will make it impossible to get away without your other belongings.

continued on next page

You will take the test in a room dedicated to that purpose. There may be other people taking different tests in the same room. Exam rooms are typically monitored via video camera to deter cheating. When you sit down in front of the computer containing your exam, the test administrator will log you in using your unique Sylvan testing ID.

Before taking the certification exam, you'll have the option of completing a practice test to familiarize yourself with the testing software. This is really only necessary if you haven't used practice tests as part of your preparation, or if you feel uncomfortable with computer-based testing.

When you finish the exam, your score will appear on the screen. Do not continue past that point until you have your official score sheet in hand. Although it's extremely unlikely that your score will be lost, better safe than sorry.

After your exam, Sylvan Prometric transmits your results to your certification's sponsor where they are entered into your candidate record. Your records may be updated within a few hours or it may take up to several days.

FIGURE 10.1

Sylvan Prometric's Registration Web site

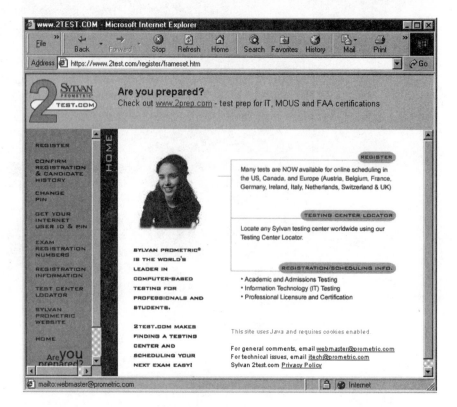

Exam and Question Formats

All certification exams (other than lab exams) are administered via computer. Each test has a specific number of questions, time limit, and passing score (see tables). These change from time to time as vendors update their exams, so don't count on information you receive from previous candidates being 100% accurate. You will be reminded of the parameters for your particular exam at the beginning of your session.

There are several types of questions you may encounter:

* Multiple choice with a single answer
* Multiple choice with multiple answers
* Freeform response
* Scenario-based

Single-answer multiple choice questions are very straightforward—read the question and choose the best answer from the list of possible answers. If you don't know the answer to a question of this type, eliminate the choices you know are wrong, and choose from what's left.

QUICK TIP

Just prior to taking an exam, brush up on exam strategies by reviewing the "Taking Tests" section in Chapter 9: Study Secrets.

Multiple-answer multiple choice questions are a bit trickier since you won't have the benefit of knowing how many of the answers should be picked. Instead, you will be directed to "mark all correct answers." Again, use the process of elimination. For example, if you see that all of the above is a choice, and one of the other options is definitely wrong, you can eliminate two of the possible choices right away. To keep track of your progress use your marker board to write down a shorthand version of each answer. As you consider each answer option, cross it out if it's wrong, or put a check mark next to it if it's correct. This makes it possible to jump around in the list of answers without missing any or losing track of choices you've already made. Read these questions carefully! Sometimes you will be given the number of answers you should select as part of the question, such as "which three statements about the GNU General Public License are correct"?

Freeform response questions are usually used to test your knowledge of command syntax. You might be asked to type in the command to accomplish a particular task, such as to change permissions on a particular file or directory. When answering this type of question, be very careful to avoid typos and to spell the command and its parameters correctly. Misspelling the command will cause the question to be scored as wrong.

Scenario questions attempt to add a level of real-world complexity to exam questions. A typical scenario question will present you with a paragraph or two about a specific networking situation, followed by a series of questions related to that scenario. Often the scenario will be accompanied by an exhibit—a diagram of a network configuration, for example. The questions that are based on a particular scenario may be in any of the previously described formats.

Sample Exam Questions

Question 1. Which type of file partition is needed for Linux?
  a. ext2
  b. dos
  c. bash
  d. ntfs
  e. lin
Answer: a

Question 2. Basic Linux shell commands such as ls and mv are contained in which directory?
  a. /bin
  b. /boot
  c. /sys
  d. /lib
  e. /linux
Answer: a

continued on next page

> **Question 3.** The pwd command is used to change a password.
> a. true
> b. false
> Answer: b. false: the pwd command tells you the directory you are currently in. The password command is passwd.
>
> **Question 4.** Type the command to display the names of files in a directory, along with their permissions.
> Answer: ls -l

Exam Details and Objectives

Each certification exam is accompanied by an associated list of objectives. This list can be found on the vendor's Web site and should be the backbone of your study plan. Objective lists ensure that you study the material that will appear on the test, and save you from devoting extra time to items that won't be. Read the objectives when you first begin preparing for a particular exam and review them periodically to confirm that you're covering the required material. Look for tasks you must be able to perform as well as knowledge you will be expected to display.

These objective lists range from exceptionally terse to very informational. Some will simply list topic areas while others name specific tasks and knowledge items. If your exam is paired with one of the latter, you've got it easy. When you feel ready to take the exam, sit down and go through the objective list one item at a time. When you can answer every question and perform each task on the list you're ready to take the real exam.

CyberTech Exams

CyberTech's Linux Certification exam is multiple choice and contains 100 questions. Passing is 70% or better. If you score 90% or above, you'll receive the "master" designation. You may retake the exam as many times as you wish, but you'll have to pay the $95 fee each time. The CyberTech registration fee includes access to study materials and practice tests. You'll also find an outline of covered material on the CyberTech Web site at: **www.getcertified. com/coi/describ1.asp?Subject=LNX131&**.

LPI Exams

As you know, LPIC (Linux Professional Institute Certification) comes in three levels and each level requires passing multiple exams. All these exams were still in the planning stages as this book was going to press. Only the objectives for the first-level one exam were close to completion at that time. They can be found on the LPI Web site at **www.lpi.org/objectives/1.html**.

All LPIC exams will be closed-book and last from one to two hours. They will probably be administered through Sylvan Prometric, but it's possible another outlet will be used instead. Check the Linux Professional Institute Web site (**www.lpi.org**) for the latest details.

ProsoftTraining.com Exams

The ProsoftTraining.com Linux Certified Administrator exam costs $100 and is delivered through Sylvan Prometric outlets. To register, call 877-795-6871 or 612-820-5871 or visit **www.2test.com**. The test ID number is LCO-610. The exam is multiple-choice. To pass you'll need to score 75% overall, and no less than 70% on individual test sections. There are a few sample questions, without answers, online at: **www.prosofttraining.com/certification/ tests/610.htm** (see Figure 10.2).

Red Hat Exams

Red Hat's RHCE exam consists of three components, which are all completed in a single, day-long session lasting six to seven hours. The first component is a written test that lasts one to two hours. Next comes a two-hour hands-on lab which focuses on Red Hat Linux installation and network services configuration. The final section is another hands-on lab exam, this time covering diagnostics and troubleshooting. It spans three hours. According to Red Hat, both lab exam sections "present realistic problems that require

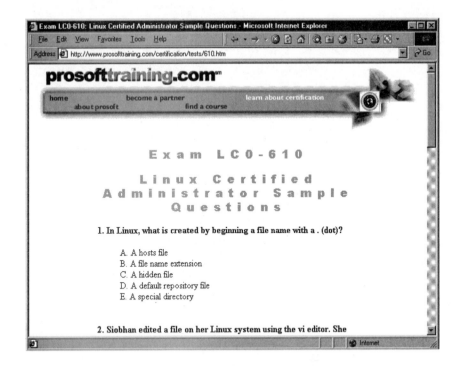

FIGURE 10.2
Online sample
questions

planning, diagnosis, and development of complete solution." The questions and problems may relate to anything covered in the four-day RHCE training curriculum or listed in the RHCE prerequisites. That curriculum is available on the Red Hat Web site at: **www.redhat.com/products/training_course.html**. It's a good idea to review the prerequisites as well. A prerequisites outline can be found at **www.redhat.com/products/training_prereq.html**.

The Red Hat Certified Examiner (RHCX) test is administered at Red Hat's Durham, North Carolina location and in Stockely Park, Uxbridge, England. It is only offered in conjunction with a Red Hat's Train-the-Trainer class and cannot be taken separately. To become an RHCX you must be an RHCE as well. To facilitate this, the RHCE exam is administered on the first day of the five day trainer class at the North Carolina location. Candidates attending the shorter, three-day training in England must already have the RHCE. Information on the RHCX course (which cost $2,498 in the US and £990 + VAT in England as this book went to press) can be found on Red Hat's Web site at: **www.redhat.com/products/training_rh310.html**.

The RHCX exam itself covers:

* Downloading the RHCE exam kit
* Setting up and configuring the training machines and network for the RHCE exam
* Testing the training network and RHCE exam prior to administration
* Administering and procotoring the RHCE exam
* Evaluating, grading, and uploading results to Red Hat

Beta Exams

When a certification sponsor is getting ready to introduce a new exam, it often does so by making a preliminary version available. These are called *beta exams*. They are available through the standard outlets and typically are free, or, on occasion half-price. Candidates who do not want to wait for the final version, or who want to cut their certification costs, often find beta exams attractive.

Beta exams have their downside. For starters, you'll have to wait substantially longer to receive your test results—six to eight weeks or even more. It's not unusual for score reports to arrive even later than originally anticipated by the certification sponsor. Second, the exam will usually be longer, sometimes much longer. This is because the sponsor is trying out as many questions as possible on each candidate in order to assess the validity and difficulty of each question. This can add substantially to your time commitment and stress level.

Although beta exams may differ from the final version of the exam, passing one still counts toward certification. If you take a beta exam, you will not receive a score printout immediately following the exam—you'll have to wait for one to be mailed to you. Beta exams are available for a limited time, typically a month or less. Certification beta exams are announced on certification sponsor Web sites.

Sair Exams

As described in Chapter 4, each Sair certification requires passing four exams—one each for Linux installation, network connectivity, system administration, and security, ethics and privacy. Sair exams are administered through Sylvan Prometric and cost $99 each. Call Sylvan at 888-895-6717 to register. Each exam contains about 50 multiple choice questions. Passing requires a score of 74% or better.

In the future, during what Sair calls "phase two," a level-four test that incorporates written essay questions, hands-on demonstrations, and an oral exam will be launched. Sair estimates that the fee for this in-depth exam will be approximately $400.

Detailed objectives for the currently available exams are posted on the Sair Web site at **www.linuxcertification.org/study.php3**. Sair also provides several brief sample tests (see Figure 10.3), which you can try online at **www.linuxcertification.org/sampletestindex.php3**. To give you an idea of the format of Sair's outlines, the objectives for the Level One Installation & Configuration exam are:

The student will answer the questions or perform the following skills:

Theory of Operation

* State the definition, origins, cost, and tradeoff of free software.
* Compare proprietary versus open source software licenses.
* List the GNU public license (GPL) principles.
* Describe how to sell free software.
* Describe the structural components of Linux.
* Contrast multi-user multi-tasking versus single-sequential user multi-tasking.
* Contrast command-line interpreters versus graphical user interfaces with tradeoffs.
* List PC system architecture configuration issues.
* Describe hard-disk partitioning strategies.
* Contrast video adapter versus monitor capabilities.
* List the network configuration parameters.

Base System

* List and give the tradeoff of installation media.
* Explain the Linux device driver lag and give examples.
* List the installation steps common to all distributions.
* Contrast high-volume Linux distributions and give tradeoffs.
* Install four Linux distributions.
* Describe the configuration tools COAS, Linuxconf, and Yast.

* List the boot up sequence, log-in, and shut-down sequence.
* Define "package" and describe how to use it.
* Describe basic file system principles.
* Explain the use of mounting versus the use of "mtools" for removable media.
* List and describe the role of common directories.
* List and describe the use of basic system navigation programs ps, kill, w, etc.
* Describe the use and misuse of the superuser account.
* List the steps in creating a user account.
* Install, configure, and navigate two X11 window managers.

Shells and Commands

* Describe shell configuration files.
* Compare and contrast environmental versus shell variables.
* Use commands that pass special characters among programs.
* Use commands that allow programs to communicate.
* Manipulate files and directories.
* Use the shell for multitasking.
* Describe common shell editing commands.
* Use the following commands in isolation or in combination with each other: ls, cd, more, less, cp, mv, mkdir, rm, rmdir, ln, head, tail, file, grep, du, df, and zcat.
* Use the following vi commands: i, ZZ, :w, :w! :q!, dd, x, D, J.

System Services

* List and describe seven tools that provide information on other tools.
* Describe and use LILO.
* Install run-time device drivers.
* Configure a printer capabilities file.
* Configure a printer filter.
* Use lpr, lpq, lprm, and lpc to control file printing.
* List the sections of the X server configuration file.
* Configure the X server video hardware.
* Contrast xf86config, XF86Setup, Xconfiguator, and SaX.
* Describe five components of the X Window system architecture.

* List and give the tradeoffs of Afterstep, KDE, Window Maker, FVWM95, Enlightenment, and Blackbox.

Applications

* Describe the general control of X11 desktops.
* Describe Netscape functions, FTP functions, Telnet functions, and mail functions.
* Contrast WYSIWYG versus mark-up word processing.
* Contrast ApplixWare, WordPerfect, and StarOffice.
* Contrast GIMP, X-Fig, and ImageMagick.

Troubleshooting

* Describe the cause and solution to read errors.
* Explain why FTP keeps missing certain files in group transfers.
* Explain the problem and solution when LILO says LI.
* Define rescue disk and describe three reasons for using it.
* Explain how to get around a locked-up program.
* List eight steps to resolve an unresponsive printer.
* Explain why Linux may report the wrong time and describe how to fix the problem.
* Describe how to reset the console screen, the keyboard repeat rate, and the Num Lock key.
* Describe the role of system logging and how to use it for troubleshooting.

Brainbench Exams

Brainbench exams are administered via the Web. When you're ready to take an exam, point your Web browser to **www.brainbench.com**, where you will be able to complete the registration process. Once you've registered you'll be given an identification code. The code can be used to take the test immediately, or you can return to the site at a later time.

QUICKTIP

Brainbench exams use computer adaptive testing (CAT) technology, which means that rather than having a set sequence of questions, each question is selected based on your answers to previous questions.

FIGURE 10.3
Online certification
exam

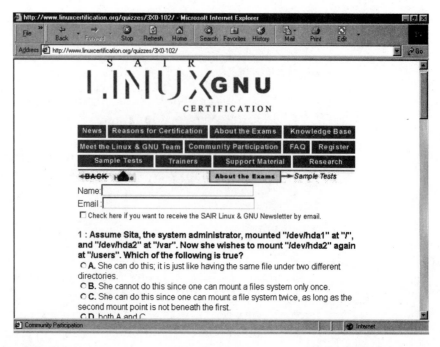

Brainbench exams contain between 24 and 40 multiple-choice questions. The questions are drawn from a database containing hundreds of questions. Each question has five possible answers and you have to pick the best one. Some questions may include additional information, such as a code snippet or diagram. Figure 10.4 shows a sample screen from a Brainbench exam.

You'll have 3 minutes (180 seconds) to answer a question. A timer displayed in the status bar of your browser will keep track of time for you. If you don't select an answer to the question within the allotted time, the question will be marked incorrect and you'll automatically move on to the next question. Once time is up on a question, you can't change the answer. Unlike other certification exams, this one is open-book. You're allowed to look things up, as long as you can do so *very* quickly, which means you have to be an ace with Linux documentation pages.

To pass the exam you'll need to score 2.75 out of a possible 5.0. If you score 4.0 or better, you'll earn the Master Linux Administrator designation. On average, 60% of candidates taking the Administrator exam pass, and 12% obtain the Master certification. You can retake this exam as many times as you'd like, with no waiting period.

FIGURE 10.4
Online certification
exam

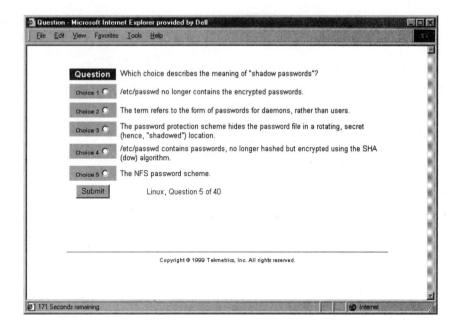

The content of the Brainbench Certified Linux Administrator exam encompasses the following areas:

Configuration and Administration

* Daemons
* Run levels
* File systems
* Users
* Shells
* X-servers & clients
* X-starting and using

General Issues

* History and culture
* Open-source issues

Installation

* Boot, multi-boot
* Deciding on setup
* Hardware—drives and peripherals
* Partitioning
* System Installation

Networking

* Internetworking (Samba)
* Local and remote printing
* Mail, HTTP, NFS, DNS
* Proxy Services
* Setup and Routing
* Troubleshooting

Sys Admin and Security

* Firewalls and NAT
* Network Security
* Password Management (NIS, Yp)
* Quotas and Logging

* SUID, SGID, "nobody" processes
* Wrappers, PAM

It can't be stressed enough that you must get lots of hands-on practice if you hope to pass this exam. If you don't have a Linux environment to practice on at work, you'll have to set one up at home (see Chapter 8) or find another way to gain access to the operating system.

When taking any of these exams, keep the big picture in perspective. Your goal is to obtain a particular Linux certification. Part of that may well require taking one or more exams more than once. If you fail an exam, instead of berating yourself, turn it into a learning experience that will help you pass next time. Immediately upon leaving the testing room, sit down with pen and paper and write down everything you remember about the exam, particularly the areas you were weak in. As soon as possible, review these areas using your study materials. If the materials you have don't adequately cover the topics, get some additional materials that do. Then, reschedule the exam, and take it again. Keep your goal of certification in mind and persist until you've accomplished it. If you're determined and stick with it, you will achieve your goal of becoming certified in Linux.

Part 3

Utilize Your Certification to the Max

Chapter 11

Advertising Your New Status

You've planned, studied, passed the tests, filed your application, signed whatever you needed to sign, and been granted the Linux certification you chose. Give yourself a well-deserved pat on the back, but don't rest on your laurels. Choosing the right certification and obtaining it is 80 percent of the job. The other 20 percent is making the effort to capitalize on what you've already accomplished. Many professionals before you have discovered ways to put their certifications to work. By following what others have done, and perhaps adding a few inventive flourishes of your own, you can maximize the positive effect certification can have on your career.

Looking Good in Print

Most Linux certification sponsors have created a logo that uniquely identifies individuals that have completed their program. These logos are professionally designed, and they're often heavily marketed by the certification sponsor to promote understanding of the logo's significance to your potential customers, to employers, and to others throughout the computer industry. This creates brand recognition, something marketing organizations across industries work to achieve. By utilizing these logos to promote yourself, you can benefit from the effort and financing that have gone into the sponsor's logo program. This is one of the easiest ways to advertise your status as a certified professional, and can help inspire the confidence of potential clients and employers.

Certification logos can be used on your business cards, resume, marketing materials, Web site, e-mail signature, and almost anywhere else you can think of. To prevent misuse and abuse of these logos, you'll receive guidelines for proper usage. Although such control over your use of the logos may feel annoying, it's really for your benefit as much as for the certification vendor's. By assuring that these logos are used in a professional and consistent manner, the vendor is protecting and building their value.

Logos generally are provided in several formats. This makes it easier for you to utilize them for various purposes, and you end up with a more professional result. It's possible to convert files between graphical file formats using special utility file conversion programs, but some resolution may be lost, which is one reason certification sponsors generally offer logos in various formats. Electronic formats, such as GIF, JPG, EPS, and TIF, can be imported into word processing, desktop publishing, graphics (such as Web design), and other computer programs. Typically the menu command to use will be some variation of **Insert | Picture** or **Import | Image**.

Camera-ready logos, another format for logo distribution, are, as the name implies, suitable for photographing, with good results. They're provided in a high-resolution, sharply printed format and can be physically pasted directly onto originals before reproduction. These are most often used on promotional materials, such as brochures, that are run off in quantity by a printer.

Commercial printers sometimes prefer to receive graphics in a particular format—the one that works best with their system. If you're having the logo included on your business card or on other commercially printed materials, ask the printing company which format will produce the best results. They may prefer camera-ready art or a particular file type.

Besides incorporating a certification logo on your personal materials, consider the marketing potential it offers your employer. If you're the first person at your company to obtain Linux certification, by doing so you've added value to the company's service offerings. Linux resellers need multiple certified individuals on staff to qualify for various reseller levels, and thus will benefit substantially from your certification. Your company may well want to advertise your new status for its own benefit.

Consider a company specializing in building Linux-based servers that can claim "Linux Certified Administrator on staff," or "Red Hat Certified Engineer (RHCE) on staff." Such announcements would, of course, be accompanied by reproductions of the relevant logo. This type of employer marketing of your certification is a win-win situation. The employer wins through gaining increased credibility, which may well lead to added revenue, and you gain by boosting your value to your employer and earning a reputation for yourself as an expert.

Marketing Magic Via the Internet

More than a few publications rave about the potential of the Internet and World Wide Web as marketing tools, and most of the claims are true. The Web is a versatile medium. It's affordable, accessible, and for most computer professionals, a do-it-yourself opportunity, especially for computer-related services and products, such as your services as a computer professional. It provides access to an incredible number of interested potential customers/employers, and recruiters and employers use it as a tool to uncover talent and fill positions. You can use it to market yourself as a computer professional, to establish a professional reputation, and to display your talent to those who might be interested in compensating you handsomely for it.

The potential of the Web as a marketing medium to advertise your certified status is limited only by the extent of your creativity. To begin with, you can use it to:

* Communicate with your clients via electronic mailings
* Draw interested clients and employers to you by creating a Web site
* Make professional networking a pleasure
* Establish name recognition and expert status for yourself

Information on posting your resumé online is included in Chapter 13, which covers how to use certification to land a new job.

You can do all of this with minimum financial outlay and a bit of your time. Best of all, the Web is an enjoyable medium to work with, and even though you'll be using it for professional purposes, the process can be as much (or more) fun as it is work.

Internet Connection Resources

This list includes some of the Internet access providers available to you. Online services will often send you free software and offer a free trial period. ISPs rarely provide the free trial and sometimes charge a one-time set up fee.

Popular Online Services

America Online (AOL); 800-827-6364; **www.aol.com**

CompuServe (CSi); 800-848-8990; **www.compuserve.com**

Microsoft Network (MSN); 800-228-7007; **www.msn.com**

Internet Service Providers (ISPs)

Finding an ISP with a local phone number can be a challenge. It's a good idea to inquire at a local computer store or ask friends which provider they use. There are many ISPs that serve a limited geographical area—usually right around their office. These often offer more personalized service and support than do their nationwide counterparts. ISPs that serve every state in the USA include:

ActiveNation; 888-477-4968; www.activenation.com

Big Planet; 801-345-7000; **www.bigplanet.com**

City Online; 888-4-CITYOL; **www.citycom.com**

Connect America; 800-941-3108; **www.coninternet.com**

EarthLink Network; 800-395-8425; **www.earthlink.com**

Epoch Internet; 888-77-EPOCH; **www.eni.net**

GTE; 888-GTE-SURF; **www.gte.net**

IBM; 800-455-5056; **www.ibm.net**

MCI; 800-888-0800; **www.mci.com**

Prodigy Internet; 914-448-8000; **www.prodigy.com**

If you can access the Internet, search for a new provider by area code, using The List, at thelist.internet.com (shown in Figure 11.1). It contains information on over 7,800 ISPs, including service and pricing information. It's worth a trip to the local public library to view this list—libraries often provide free Internet access for patrons.

FIGURE 11.1
The List—A
searchable index to
help you find the
perfect ISP

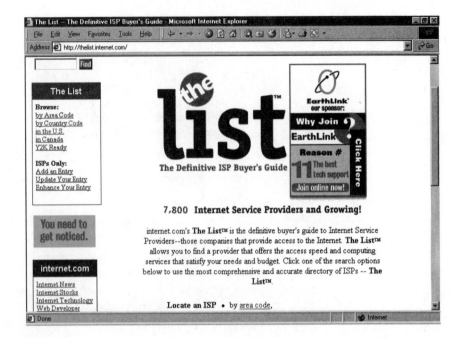

Direct E-mail

Whichever Internet access you have, chances are it comes with
unlimited e-mail access. This means that you have free access to
one of the more effective forms of advertising: direct mail marketing. The trick with e-mail, even more so than with the earth-
bound variety, is to target your recipients carefully. In cyberspace,
junk mail is very poorly received. If you are perceived as a junk e-
mailer (also called a *spammer*), you will do your image more harm
than good. Word travels fast on the Internet, whether or not the
message is positive.

So how can you make appropriate use of e-mail to advertise
your status as a Linux certified professional? One method is to
send an FYI update to your past and present clients (and/or your
employer's), reminding them of your skills, availability, and, of
course, certified status. Keep such messages short and to the
point. For example:

ABC company is pleased to announce the we now have
a Master Sair/Linux GNU Certified Engineer (MLCE)

on staff. This certification, granted only by Sair, signifies the attainment of the highest standards in design, installation, and management of complex Linux environments.

This would be followed by another paragraph or two about the services ABC company currently offers and a call to action, such as: "To boost your Network performance, call ABC," along with contact information.

If any companies or recruiters have your resume on file, you would then send them a variation of the above message, along with an updated version of your resume.

Your Cyber Billboard

Whether you obtain Internet access through an online service or ISP, your account will usually include space on the provider's server for your personal Web pages. You are paying for this as part of your basic subscription fee, so don't let it go to waste. ISPs, in particular, may charge extra for Web page storage, but usually the fee for a basic personal site will be nominal. Some Web sites will even host your home page for free, without your having to be a subscriber to a particular service. Yahoo! maintains an index of such sites at **www.yahoo.com/Business_and_Economy/Companies/ Internet_Services/Web_Services/Hosting/Free_Web_Pages/**.

Creating a Web site that will showcase your talents doesn't require a degree in graphics design. The site can be a straightforward, one-page affair, or a multi-part masterpiece, depending on your goals, aspirations, and how much time you're willing to devote to the project. Thanks to the plentiful supply of Web design software packages available today, you don't even have to learn HTML (hypertext markup language), which is used to hard-code Web pages. Instead, you can point, click, and highlight, inserting pictures, text, and links where you'd like them. As you paint the screen with images and text, the design program translates the results into HTML for you. Figure 11.2 shows one such program.

You can find these Web design tools (sometimes called HTML editors) at your local software outlet or download them from Web sites on the Internet. The AOLPress program, for example, can be found at **www.aolpress.com**. You can jump to reviews of various HTML software programs and find out how to obtain them from Yahoo!'s index of HTML editors at **www.yahoo.com/Computers_and_Internet/Software/Internet/World_Wide_Web/HTML_Editors**.

FIGURE 11.2
Using Microsoft's
FrontPage2000 to
design a Web site

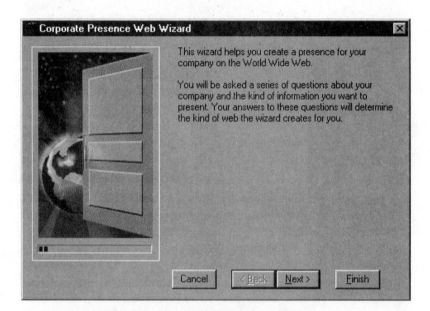

An endless supply of available HTML tutorials will provide you with step-by-step advice on the creation of your Web site. You can find Web design books in the computer section of your local bookstore or order them from one of the online bookstores, such **amazon.com** and **fatbrain.com**. You can also find plenty of free advice, much of it pretty good, on various Web sites. For starters, check out:

✳ The NCSA (National Center for Supercomputing Applications) Beginner's Guide to HTML (**www.ncsa.uiuc.edu/General/Internet/WWW/HTMLPrimer.html**) is an excellent place to get the basics on HTML, its various components, and how to put it to work for you. You can also download this file to print out or read using Adobe Acrobat Reader, which can be obtained free at **www.adobe.com**.

✳ If you already have HTML basics down cold, you might want to learn the ins and outs of more advanced techniques, including floating frames, marquees, meta tags, and more. You can read about all of these at **www.htmlgoodies.com**, Joe Burns's extensive HTML site (shown in Figure 11.3).

FIGURE 11.3
The HTML goodies Web site

What To Put On Your Pages

Give some thought to what you want to include on your Web pages. It's good to develop an overall plan before beginning, so your site will have a cohesive feel. You don't have to create the whole thing all at once. Start with a main page (this will be your home page), and add to it over time. Strive to make your site interesting by providing a variety of content.

Check out what other computer professionals are doing with their Web pages to see what works and what doesn't. You can jump to many of them from Yahoo!'s high-tech resumes index at **www.yahoo.com/Computers_and_Internet/ Employment/Resumes/Individual_Resumes/**.

Think of your main page as a table of contents for your site. Your contact information should be there, along with a brief introduction so visitors know what they are looking at and who created the site. You'll also need links to other pages in your site, accompanied by descriptions so visitors can choose whether or not to view them.

Web Site Design Tips

Go easy on the graphics. Pictures take longer to download than text, and visitors may jump to another site rather than wait for a page full of graphics, no matter how amazing, to download.

Make navigation between pages simple. Visitors should be able to return to the main page with a single mouse click.

Don't get too fancy. Web pages with purple lettering on black backgrounds, or other jarring combinations, prove nearly impossible to read. When in doubt, it's best to be conservative with the use of color. For similar reasons, stick to one or two fonts in various sizes.

Don't incorporate large blocks of text that span the width of a monitor. Narrow columns with wide margins will be easier on the eyes.

If you use a background texture or image, make sure it doesn't obscure the clarity of the text that overlies it.

If you include links to other sites, check them periodically to ensure they still work. There are many free programs to automate this task. FrontPage does it as well.

Include an e-mail link to your electronic mailbox, and display the address too. Sometimes people may not have the mail portion of their Web browser working properly, and they'll want to know your e-mail address to respond using another mail program.

Don't put personal information you don't want the whole world to know on your Web site. This may include pictures of your children or your home phone number.

Verify that your page appears properly to individuals viewing it with different Web browsers. At the very least, try it out with both Netscape and Internet Explorer.

Possible pages include: your resumé; links and/or reviews of Web resources that are linked to your area of professional expertise; reviews of products you work with; links to the Web sites of clients who maintain an online presence; examples of your work; testimonials from satisfied customers (get their permission first); or a tutorial on something you're qualified to teach about. Make it a goal to create a page that will prove useful to people who stop by.

Ideally, you should make your Web site a resource that visitors come back to again and again. To accomplish this, it's important to add new material periodically. It's a good idea to build this task into your schedule, otherwise it will fall by the wayside and before you know it your Web site will be full of outdated material and broken links—transforming it from a positive career tool to a potentially negative one.

QUICKTIP

Few interesting Web sites begin with the author's resumé, so create a separate page for yours and link to it from the main page.

You'll also want to build what are called *keywords* into your site, especially on the main page. Keywords are words and phrases individuals searching through the Net are likely to use. The trick is to figure out which words the users you want to draw to your site are likely to be using. Think about words that are common to your field of expertise and to your goals. Include both the acronyms and the spelled out words. For example, you might work in the words internetwork, networking, and independent consultant.

QUICKTIP

It's possible to embed hidden keywords within a Web page by rendering the keyword in the same color as the background, thus making it invisible to the human eye, but readily available to computer search engines. Unscrupulous individuals have been known to incorporate the word sex in this way, to draw unsuspecting visitors to their Web site. A visitor who arrives finds no sexual content and has no clue why he/she has ended up at your page. This kind of trickery is not likely to enhance the professional image you'd like to present and is best avoided.

When you're ready to present your Web site to the world, you'll need to upload it to your access provider's computer. Typically, this is accomplished using a special file transfer program, and your provider should supply you with instructions on how to do so.

If You Build It, Will They Come?

Creating a Web site and launching it into cyberspace doesn't automatically generate a readership. A few people will stumble across it, for sure, but your goal is to achieve much more than that. One measure of a Web site's success is the number of accesses (called *traffic* or *hits*) it receives. To build up traffic to your Web site, you'll need to spend a little time promoting it, but doing so won't take long.

To advertise your Web site, add the URL to your print materials, including your business card and marketing brochures. It should become a standard part of your contact information and be included in your e-mail messages as well.

A second, arguably more powerful way to promote it, is via the Internet. You need to get your site included by the search engines (Yahoo!, Infoseek, AltaVista, and so on). To do this, you can visit the site of each search engine and follow the individual instructions. Or you can use one of the free tools, such as Promotion World's submission tool. (**www.promotionworld.com/tools/submit/index.html**), that lets you submit your URL(s) to more than 30 search engines without having to visit each one independently. The tool is shown in Figure 11.4.

If your time is in short supply, consider signing up with a submission service. For a fee, these services will submit your Web site information to a specified number of search engines. To locate one, visit Yahoo!'s index of Web site announcement and promotion services (shown in Figure 11.5), at **yahoo.com/Computers_and_Internet/Internet/World_Wide_Web/Information_and_Documentation/Site_Announcement_and_Promotion/**.

For the interested Web site promoter, many additional methods for increasing traffic to your site exist. Read about them in some of the excellent articles that have been written on the subject. You'll find plenty of them at the following sites:

FIGURE 11.4
Free automated
URL submission

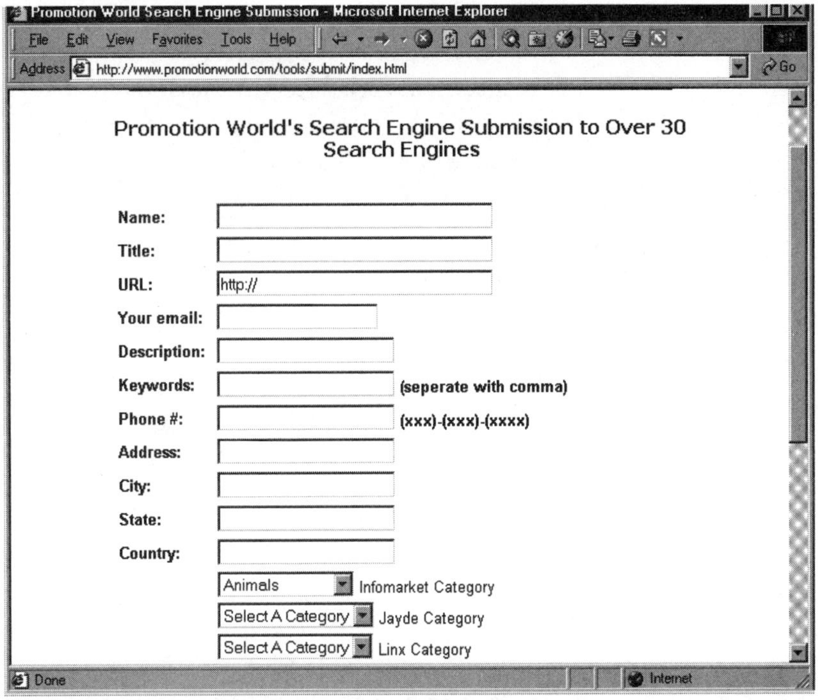

FIGURE 11.5
Plenty of site
promotion help
available

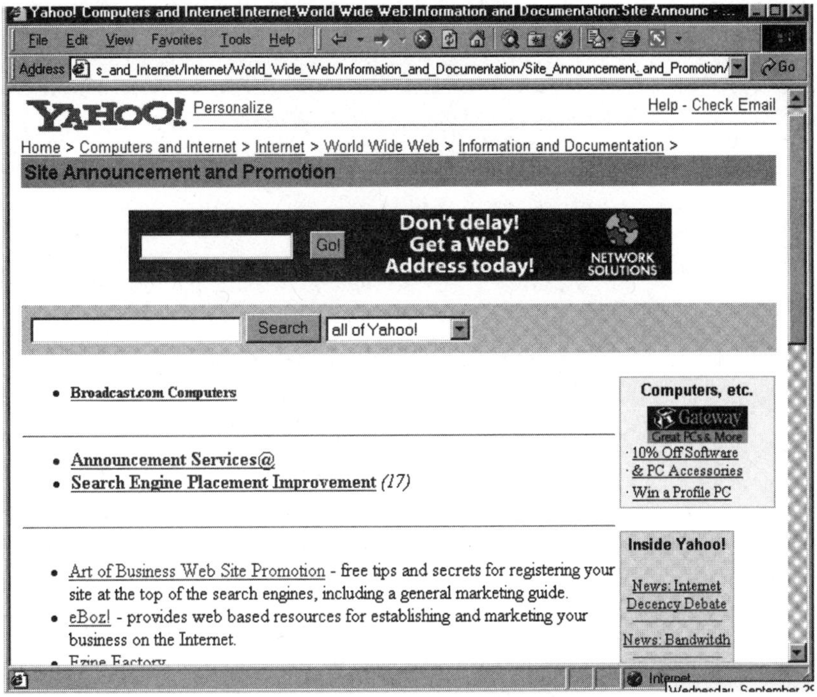

* The Website Promoters Resource Center (**www.wprc.com**) is an excellent and robust site that contains tools and advice related to Web site promotion via targeted e-mail, banner advertising, URL submissions, and press releases. If you want a consultant to assist you with your promotion efforts, you can find him or her here, too.
* ClickZ (**www.clickz.com**) contains loads of tips, resources, and articles related to online marketing. You can also elect to receive a free electronic subscription to the ClickZ newsletter.
* Promotion World (**www.promotionworld.com**) explains how to promote your Web site and build up traffic, all for free. You can also subscribe to The Promotion World Informer, a weekly electronic newsletter packed full of tips and tricks for promoting your Web site.

You might also want to pick up one of several excellent, currently available books about Web site promotion, such as *Poor Richard's Internet Marketing and Promotions: How to Promote Yourself, Your Business, Your Ideas Online* by Peter Kent and Tara Calishain (Top Floor Publishing 1999).

Clearly the Internet is not only a natural ally for the computer professional, it's also an easy-to-learn, low-cost marketing tool. Your potential employers and clients are out there trolling for experts like yourself. Why not make it easy for them to find you?

Networking and Lurking

In the career sense, networking means getting the word out about who you are and what you do. It means getting to know the people who may prove beneficial to your career at some point in the future. Perhaps they'll introduce you to the hiring manager of a company you want to work for, or maybe end up needing your professional services themselves. How do you know which people those are? You don't. It's impossible to predict who'll remember your name and pass it on when a need arises. Fortunately, the Internet provides an efficient networking medium, and you won't even have to endure any boring speeches or attend distant professional dinners to connect with clients and peers. You can do it all from your personal computer.

One of the strengths of the Internet is its power to bring people together. Individuals whose paths would never cross in a different environment can meet online and exchange information that will benefit one another. Part of the nature of the Internet community is that people are interested in helping each other out. Perhaps it's related to the age-old urge to offer advice, or maybe it's just a special, cyber brand of goodwill. Either way, professionals online typically expect to receive help and advice and to offer it. By jumping into this community give and take, you can tap into the power of networking without leaving your desk. You can use this environment to promote your professional abilities.

The primary places in which such networking occurs are forums and newsgroups. The two have much in common, and the terms are sometimes used interchangeably, but they are actually quite different. Both are repositories of discussion and information related to a particular topic. However, a forum is part of the World Wide Web, and as such, can be accessed using a Web browser. It will bear a name such as "The Client/Server Forum." Newsgroups, on the other hand, are a part of the Internet called Usenet. They are accessed using a program called a *newsreader*. Often the terms forum and newsgroup are used interchangeably. Newsgroup names follow a standard format that indicates the subject matter at hand. Abbreviations or word fractions, separated by dots, are strung together to identify the topic. A newsgroup titled comp.os.linux.hardware, for example, is clearly identified as a place for messages about Linux hardware issues. Table 11.1 lists common newsgroup abbreviations and their meanings.

TABLE 11.1
Newsgroup abbreviations

Abbreviation	Meaning	Example
alt	Alternative	alt.fan.linus-torvalds
biz	Business	biz.marketplace.services.computers
comp	Computer	comp.jobs
misc	Miscellaneous	misc.jobs.wanted
rec	Recreational	rec.games.computer.quake.playing

continued on next page

TABLE 11.1
continued

Abbreviation	Meaning	Example
sci	Science	sci.physics.research
soc	Society	soc.activism
sys	Systems	comp.dcom.sys.cisco
os	Operating System	comp.os.linux.network
lang	Language	comp.lang.c

A forum is associated with a particular Web site or online service. Forums generally serve a smaller readership than newsgroups. They may be sponsored by a company with related products and services or by an interested individual. When you post a message to a forum, you may have the option to hide it from everyone but the person you are replying to. Although this is sometimes a good option to use, many times a reply will be of potential interest to others who follow the messages, so you won't want to conceal it. A forum is more likely (although not guaranteed) to be moderated, which means less off-topic ranting and raving.

Messages posted to a newsgroup are visible to all and anybody who wishes to read and respond to them can do so. They are more likely to include a high number of junk postings—off topic, often off-the-wall rantings. They also boast a greater number of readers and messages. In both forums and newsgroups, you can read messages, respond to them, and post questions of your own. However, neither is a place to post advertisements for yourself or your services, and doing so will get you an e-mail box full of angry complaints (a.k.a. *flames*).

Using newsgroups and forums to network and promote yourself is really very simple: all you have to do is share your expertise. The self-promotion is incidental to the advice you are offering and, thus, is acceptable according to the rules of Internet good conduct (sometimes called *netiquette*). It's also a powerful way to put your name and affiliations in front of many people, as well as demonstrate your expertise. To make this work, you'll need to do two things: create a signature and identify appropriate newsgroups and forums.

Your Signature

A signature is the closing section that will end each e-mail and posting you create. Think of it as your electronic letterhead. Your signature should include your name; business title; e-mail address; phone number; phrases conveying additional information about you; and, sometimes, a personal slogan. Depending on the nature of your message and where you post it, you may choose to include your physical address, or exclude your phone number. Some e-mail software will allow you to include a graphic, such as a certification logo, in your e-mail, but if you do so, consider that not all recipients will be able to view it properly.

The promotional parts of the signature are your business title and slogan. The business title conveys what kind of professional you are. The slogan can be a quote you feel is representative of yourself or you think is funny and can be included or excluded as you prefer. Any slogan should always be succinct—preferably one line. Figure 11.6 shows a signature that a Linux-certified professional might use. It's a good idea to create several variations of your signature so that you have several to choose from and can select the signature that is most appropriate for the environment to which you're posting.

FIGURE 11.6
Example of a personal signature

Prowling the Net

Once you've created your signature, it's time to identify target newsgroups and forums. There are thousands of them out there. Obviously, it's impossible to peruse them all. Although you can probably find some automated program to post your message to all of them, that would be a big mistake (remember netiquette?). Besides, in this case quality is more important than quantity. So pick a few newsgroups or forums that you'll want to visit regularly. How many depends on how much time you're willing to devote. Two is a manageable number to start with.

You're going to have to do a bit of exploring to uncover outlets that match your professional interests. Don't limit yourself to computer-specific sites; if you're interested in a particular industry or technology, seek out forums and newsgroups related to it. Businesses and individuals in those industries may have need of your expertise as well. Here are a few possibilities to get you started:

* **comp.os.linux.admin** (Usenet)
* **comp.linux.misc** (Usenet)
* **discussions.earthweb.com** (IT discussion forums and Usenet gateway)
* **searchlinux.com/**

The first thing to do when you discover a promising newsgroup or forum is lurk. In Internet lingo, lurkers are individuals who are present but don't participate. In your case, that means read and pay attention, but don't post anything. This will enable you to get a solid feel for what material is discussed in the forum and what doesn't belong. It will also protect you from inadvertently posting something inappropriate that will generate ill will and start you off on the wrong foot. After several visits as a lurker, you'll be able to decide if the outlet is one you'd like to participate in, and if so, what type of participation is most appropriate.

When you've found a forum or newsgroup that appeals to you and you've lurked enough to be certain of the content and format, you're ready to make your premiere appearance. Watch for a question that you can answer with authority. When one appears, create a thoughtful, grammatically correct, spell-checked posting that addresses the issue at hand and concludes with the signature you've developed. Every time you do this, you're advertising your professional expertise, and, if you've done your signature file right, your credentials. Over time you'll become known to the people in the forum as a thoughtful, experienced professional. When they need just such a person, or know someone who does, your name will come to mind.

Chapter **12**

Moving Up

Career advancement can follow many paths, and enhancing your professional credentials through earning a Linux certification opens more of them to you. Now you're faced with the enviable (if somewhat daunting) task of deciding which route to pursue; you've come to an intersection on your career path, and you get to choose in which direction to proceed.

Straight ahead lies the path of least resistance—continuing as you are in the same job with the same responsibilities. You might choose to keep on straight ahead if you're very content with your current position and/or have too much going on in other, non-work areas of your life, to devote mental energy to choosing one of the turns. Taking one of the turns, on the other hand, will require a bit of energy and effort, as they both involve upward movement. Turn one way to move up within your current organization, or the other to advance by moving on to a different employer (possibly even yourself). This career intersection is fast approaching, and you've earned yourself a green light through certification. It's time to step on the gas.

Up or Out?

Before you press the career accelerator too hard, you'll need to decide which way you're going to turn at this intersection. Because you've already made the choice to undertake certification, you're probably not completely satisfied with the status quo. That eliminates proceeding straight ahead, and leaves you with deciding whether you'd like to advance within your current company, or look elsewhere. If your current workplace isn't meeting many or all of the needs you defined as important, and isn't likely to, then moving on may be your best option. Chapter 13 includes advice and hints on choosing that direction. If, on the other hand, your current employment has a lot going for it, and has the potential to meet most or all of the needs you defined as important, then moving up within your current organization is your logical choice, and this chapter will help speed you on your way.

There are two basic moves you can make to advance your career at your current place of employment: up or over. Moving up means increasing your responsibilities and place within the hierarchy of the organization without straying far from your current areas of expertise and/or department. Moving up makes you a more senior member of the organization. It should always come with a raise. Moving up can also mean staying where you are but going after a raise to reflect your increased value now that you've become certified.

A lateral move, on the other hand, may bring no raise or even a reduction in pay, but will provide you with something else of value instead. That something else may be a bridge into a new part of the company that offers potential for greater advancement in the long run. Or it may be sliding into a new technical specialty that has attracted your interest.

Laying the Groundwork

Whether you're after a promotion or a raise, careful planning will maximize your likelihood of success. Before actually reaching the moment when you utter the words describing what you want, you need to do a little advance work to solidify your position. The goal of this work is to remind your employer just how fantastic an asset to the organization you are, and how valuable. This isn't something you can do in a single day, at least not without hampering your chances of success. What you want to do, instead, is parade your value in front of the decision maker(s) in subtle and not-so-subtle ways, over a period of time. What you don't want to do is come across as pushy. That's more likely to work against you than for you. Instead, your goal should be to strike a balance, going far enough to keep your accomplishments visible, without becoming annoying. You should be doing this the whole time you're working toward your certification—don't wait until you've passed your final Linux exam—that's when you'll make your move, capitalizing on the groundwork you've put in place along the way.

Understand Your Manager

When planning your advancement campaign it's important to distinguish between what you feel is important and what your boss thinks is important. You can't give yourself a raise or promotion, the boss can. If you don't already know his or her opinions of what makes an employee outstanding, do a little detective work. Are technical skills highly valued? Independent work? Fast work? Teamwork? Skillful interaction with customers? Does the boss notice whether you arrive at 7:50 or 8:01? Everyone has opinions and pet peeves; do your best to scope out those of your boss. If you've received employee evaluations in the past, go back over them for clues. Has anyone in your department been promoted lately? Try to determine the basis for that move. Once you've identified what matters to those in control of granting your raise or promotion, you can describe your accomplishments in ways that cater to them.

Share the Good News

By now you've notified your manager that you've successfully obtained a Linux certification, but have you explained just what that means to the company? One way to do this is to pass on the results of research studies that have investigated the issue. Several studies have been conducted, some by certifying organizations and others by independent research organizations. The results quantify the value of certification to employers. You can obtain some of these studies free, via the Internet, and pass them on to your boss with a note that says something to the effect of "thought you might find this interesting." Because the data comes from someone other than you, it will seem less like your tooting your own horn. Unfortunately there are no such studies done specifically on Linux certification, so you'll have to extrapolate and encourage your employer to do the same. Resources you can view and download from the net include:

✳ **www.ibm.com/Education/certify/news/proidc.phtml** is an IDC study titled: "Benefits And Productivity Gains Realized Through Certification." This study was sponsored by IBM, Lotus, Microsoft, Sybase, and Sylvan Prometric. It begins: "IT certification has a significant positive effect on IS productivity and network uptime," and continues with graphs and data that back up and expand up on that claim (see Figure 12.1). This oft-quoted white paper is beginning to be a bit dated, but is still a decent resource for your purposes.

✳ **www.itaa.org/workforce/studies/hw98.htm**—Visit this site for details on how to obtain the Information Technology Association of America (ITAA) IT Workforce Study, which identifies a shortage of IT workers in the United States, stating that at many companies 10% of IT positions go unfilled due to a lack of qualified applicants. This study is repeated annually, and the report from 1997 is available as well. It wouldn't hurt for your boss to be aware of some of these statistics, like the one in the 1997 study that states "Sixty-eight percent of IT companies cite a lack of skilled/trained workers as a barrier to their companies' future ability to grow."

FIGURE 12.1
Certification
white paper

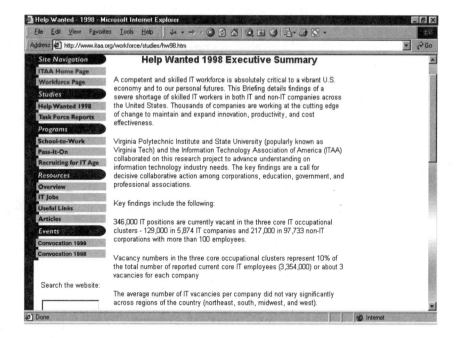

Magazine articles touting the value of Linux certification and certification in general are also worth passing across your boss's desk. You can find quite a few online or in your local library's periodical room. The following references will get you started:

 * "Certification Pays for Networking Pros" (*Information Week*, 6/7/99)
 * "Linux Certification for the Software Professional" (*Linux Journal* 4/99)
 * "When Certification Pays" (*Smart Reseller* 3/22/99)
 * "Certification Sense" (*Smart Reseller News* 11/20/98)

Be a (Visible) Problem Solver

Whether you're after a raise or a promotion, you can help your position considerably if you can create a reputation for yourself as a problem solver. This is a step that will require extra time, since you'll need to do this without compromising your current responsibilities. However, companies love problem solvers, and if you can manage to become one, advancement within the organization will come more easily.

To solve problems, you first have to identify them. It's easiest to start with your personal area of authority. Examine quantifiable aspects of your daily activities, such as number of support incidents handled, system downtime, turnaround time for various tasks, or the incidence of software bugs. For each topic you examine, ask yourself:

1. Is this number the best it can be?
2. If not, why not?
3. What can realistically be done to change this?
4. How much will it cost to change this?
5. What will changing this accomplish for my organization?
6. Considering the answers to 4 and 5, is this a worthwhile change to implement?

You are looking for items that will improve the company's bottom line in a quantifiable way. Likely areas include heightening customer satisfaction (and thus retention), cutting costs, speeding production, or increasing quality. You may run across numbers that could be improved, but with methods that aren't cost effective. Those are worth a second look—to seek a creative approach that would be cost effective.

Look for problems that are widely visible, so that your solutions will have an impact that's widely apparent too.

If you're fortunate and talented enough to already have your own bailiwick operating like a well-greased machine, then expand your problem search outside it. What do your coworkers complain about? Your customers? Or, best of all, your boss? The next time you hear them complain, instead of just empathizing, probe a bit for details and make a mental note to brainstorm potential solutions.

You may think that you'll have trouble identifying problems and coming up with ways to solve them, but any company has processes that can be improved. Most employees are quite busy coping with the day-to-day tasks that make up their job responsibilities, and expend little if any time and energy on analyzing and problem solving. You'll find that once you develop a problem-solving mindset, potential areas for improvement will practically jump out at you, and the difficulty won't be in picking them out, but in deciding which ones you have the time, energy, and interest to pursue.

Becoming a company problem solver has additional benefits. Coworkers will appreciate you (though maybe with a bit of envy attached) because you make their jobs easier by solving their problems. In addition, witnessing your personal efforts' having a positive impact on the day to day operations of the organization can be quite satisfying. Of course, it will also enhance your image with the company execs.

If you're not already keeping a log of your accomplishments, you should be. Remembering everything you've done over the course of a year without one is practically impossible. Your log doesn't have to be anything fancy—a simple notebook or computer file will do. When you get or finish an assignment, record the date and a brief summary (a sentence or two should do) describing the task and possibly its consequences. If your boss praises you for something, jot that down too. Your entries don't need to go into intricate detail, but serve instead to jog your memory. If you make do lists, you can hold on to those as well (or instead) as evidence of what you've accomplished.

Be Part of the Team (Better Yet, Be the Captain)

Shining through your own work is important, but add a reputation for teamwork and/or leadership and you'll have an especially winning combination. The ability to work with others is valuable precisely because teamwork is not always easy. How can you demonstrate your people skills?

* Join a company-wide task force.
* Play on the company softball team.
* Organize the company picnic or holiday party.
* Volunteer your time to a company-sponsored charity activity.

Each of these has the added bonus of increasing your visibility both inside and outside your current department. You look good *and* your boss looks good because your activities will reflect on him/her as well. These activities also provide you with an opportunity to hone leadership skills in a lower-pressure environment.

Although organizing the company picnic might not be your idea of a good time, find a way to be enthusiastic. If your heart isn't in the project/activity, don't sign on or your efforts may well backfire.

Asking for a Raise

If a coworker walked up to you in the lunch room and asked what your paycheck was last week, you'd probably be speechless for a moment or two. Whether for better or worse, it's just not a question you go around asking—individual compensation details are very personal, and often cloaked in secrecy. Talking about them is practically taboo, and asking for a raise can feel quite intimidating.

This environment of secrecy benefits employers, because it provides them with an edge when it comes to negotiating compensation; they know what every other person in the office makes—you can usually only guess and estimate. But if negotiating a raise is rather a game of wits, employers don't hold all the cards. There are plenty of steps you can take to load the deck in your favor. Assuming you've already begun laying the groundwork as described above, here's a step-by-step guide to going after that raise:

1. Figure out what you're worth.
2. Study the organizational pay structure.
3. Bone up on the organization's performance data.
4. Prepare your case detailing why you're worth more.
5. Choose your moment.
6. Ask for the raise.

What Are You Worth?

To receive a raise, you'll need to prove that your value to the organization justifies one. You can do this by:

* Proving you're being paid at below market rate, or
* Proving that you're worth more than the market rate because of the contributions you make to the company's bottom line—often because of special skills or experience.

In either case you'll need figures to support your position. Developing them isn't very difficult, although it does involve a bit of homework.

Salary Surveys

Salary surveys are a good place to find out the going rate for your type of position. Fortunately, surveys covering computer professions are plentiful and easy to obtain. The fastest way to get additional IT salary information is available is via the Internet.

The JobStar salary survey site (**jobstar.org/tools/salary/sal-comp.htm**) is a great place to start. There you'll find a collection of links to salary information specifically relevant to computer professionals. Figure 12.2 shows the JobStar Computer and Engineering Salary Information page.

To find additional salary resources, use one of the major search engines such as Infoseek (**www.infoseek.com**) or Yahoo! (**www.yahoo.com**) to ferret them out. Search using the phrases "salary survey" AND "computer." Pay attention to the dates and source of the information, to make sure that it is both current and credible.

You can also get salary surveys from professional organizations and societies. Trade publications such as *InformationWeek* and

Computerworld carry them periodically. Research and consulting companies in the computer field often publish salary surveys too. Romac International (which incorporated Source Services in an April 1998 merger), for example, prints an annual survey that's free to anyone who requests a copy.

FIGURE 12.2
JobStar salary
center

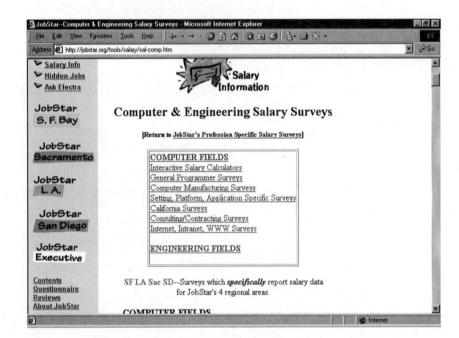

When using a salary survey to determine the going rate for your position, you need to match your job responsibilities and organization type as closely as possible. Don't go by the job title alone, as the same job can go by different names. Instead, focus on the description of duties. Some surveys break down pay rates by employer size, which will enable you to narrow your research even further.

Depending on the area of the country (or world) you're in, pay rates will vary. A programmer in New York City, for example, will typically receive a higher salary than one in Lima, Ohio. Of course, they'll have higher living expenses, too. Look for a salary survey that provides regional information so you can determine the relevant pay rates for your geographical area. You can also check with recruiting and employment agencies in your area.

They may have job listings similar to yours, and will have a good sense of going rates.

Salary calculators let you enter your skills, years of experience, and other qualifications and provide a custom estimation of your salary worth. Keep in mind that there are probably variables for which these tools don't account—such as special additional skills and so on—but they can still be a good place to start. Figure 12.3 shows a Web-based salary calculator.

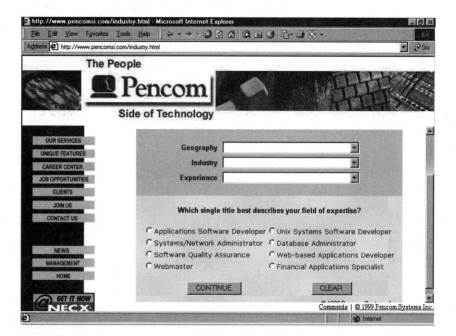

FIGURE 12.3
Pencom's interactive salary calculator

Internet Sources of Salary Surveys

www.dice.com/ratesurvey contains the results of the 1999 IT salary survey conducted by Contract Professional magazine and dice.com.

www.currents.net/resources/iwantanewjob/calculate/index.html contains an interactive salary survey calculator from Computer Currents and iwantanewjob.com.

www.experienceondemand.com is the place to find Romac International's online national salary snapshot.

continued on next page

www.datamasters.com/survey.html contains current US regional salary information from DataMasters.

http://www.computerworld.com/home/print.nsf/all/990906BFA6 contains statistics and analysis from *Computerworld*'s 1999 Salary Survey.

www.jdresources.com/salaryf.html is the Web site for J & D Resources' IT salary survey, and provides national rate ranges by job title. Historical salary information is included.

www.realrates.com/survey.htm is the Web page for The Real Rate Survey of rates received by computer contractors and consultants.

www.jobfactory.com/salary.htm contains a salary comparison calculator that you can use to translate salary information for one geographic location into equivalent information for a different location.

How Does Your Employer Pay?

The next thing to investigate is the compensation structure used by your employer. It's important to understand that you are much more likely to obtain a raise by working within the organization's pay structure than by ignoring or trying to circumvent it.

Many companies will provide job descriptions and pay ranges if you ask. You may also be able to find out the amount of the maximum raise given. It's also important to ask how your performance is evaluated, and how raises are determined. There may be a formula in place that you should know about. For example, if you're already at the top of the pay scale allowed for your current position, then your efforts would be better spent on pursuing a promotion than a raise.

Find out if raises are given at a particular time (often following an annual performance review), but don't assume that such guidelines are carved in stone. If you can provide evidence that you deserve an increase even though it hasn't been a year since your last one, go ahead and ask for it.

This information should be available through your human resources department, and possibly on the company intranet. If it is not, ask coworkers or your supervisor if they know where you can obtain copies of the current policies.

How Has Your Organization Been Performing Lately?

You may have a sense of how your organization has done during the last few years, in terms of growth and profits. Taking the time to bone up on the details will enable you to bargain from a position of knowledge. If your boss says "we can't give you a raise—the company has been running in the red for the last two years," you won't be taken by surprise. On the other hand, if your employer's profits have been climbing, you can incorporate that fact into your case for a salary increase.

By the way, poor organizational earnings are not a bona fide, iron clad reason to turn down your request for a raise. It's a factor to take into consideration when making your request, and definitely something of which you should be aware, but it doesn't mean you should cancel your plans for advancement. Even if your company is operating in the red, if you're doing an excellent job, or have increased your value to the company through certification, you still have legitimate qualities to take to the salary bargaining table.

To find out your company's financial standing, read the annual reports for the past few years. You may also be able to look up the information online, through a business database resource such as *Hoover's* (**www.hoovers.com**). Look at historical information and future projections as well as snapshot of the firm's current financial health. It also wouldn't hurt to do research for newspaper and magazine articles about your company and its products and services.

Preparing Your Case

When you've completed the first three steps, you're halfway there. Now you'll use the information you've gathered to make your case for why you should be given a raise. First compare your current compensation to the figures you obtained through your salary research. If yours is at or off the low end of the scale, you're in a good position to argue that you're not being paid at market value for your work. Don't forget to point out that you're actually worth more than the market average, because you've continued your professional development and obtained certification. Use the certification-related research and statistics you uncovered earlier to bolster your position.

If you're going to use the market rate approach, be prepared to identify the functions you perform, and provide the survey data that will support your claims of below-average compensation. Multiple survey sources will be greeted with more credibility than a single source, and make your position very strong.

If you discover that your compensation ranks in the upper portion of the range for your area, skills, and responsibilities, then the going rate argument won't do you much good. The good news is that if you're at the top of the scale, you can feel reassured that the organization values you and your work; the bad news is, you may have to work harder to make your case for a raise. But it certainly can be done. On the other hand, that should also suggest that you look into a promotion to a higher-level job, with increased responsibilities and correspondingly higher pay.

To justify a raise when your compensation is already at or above the ranges uncovered by your research, you'll need to show why you are especially valuable to the company, and therefore worth compensating at a higher rate than average. The best way to do that is to translate your activities into dollars. If you've followed the earlier advice about becoming a problem solver, you can start there. How much money have you added to the company's bottom line through your efforts? Did you train coworkers in a technology? Find out what the going rates are for such training if it had been obtained from an outside source. Have you become more efficient at performing particular tasks? If you can complete a job that took you 50 hours last year in only 40 hours this year (perhaps due to your certification-related training), that's a 25 percent increase in productivity. If you do the math for other activities where your efficiency has increased, you'll be able to translate those into quantifiable savings for the company, too.

If you want to carry your calculations a step further, figure out your hourly pay rate (don't forget to include the dollar value of your benefits) and multiply it by the number of hours of work you've saved the organization. The result will be a dollar savings you've provided your employer. Using the above example, you've saved the organization 10 hours of your time (which you were able to devote to other tasks thanks to your new efficiency). If you determine that your hourly rate is $25 then you save your employer $250 each time you complete the task. If you do it once a quarter, that's $1,000 per year in savings that you've personally generated. When you analyze your other improvements in a similar way, the dollar amounts may add up quickly.

Don't forget to consider whether your certification qualifies your employer to become a Linux distribution reseller, or to become a higher-level reseller. If you are the only Linux-certified individual on staff, or one of only a few, you may be especially valuable to your employer.

Once you have your approach figured out, practice your pitch in private or in front of someone you trust, like a spouse. You can also use a tape recorder or video camera to record your practice session, and review it until you are satisfied with your performance. Your presentation will come out much more smoothly if you've run through it a few times in advance. You'll also be able to relax a bit more, once you know you can state your case effectively.

Timing

When your boss has just returned from receiving a chewing out in a meeting, it's the wrong time to ask for your raise. When he/she returns from an annual meeting that included announcements of the organization's staggering gain in market share, led by a product produced by your division, that's a great time. Chances are that your range of timing opportunities will fall somewhere between these two extremes. Pay attention to the atmosphere in your workplace, and choose a time that seems favorable.

Raise Day

When your homework is complete and the time seems ripe, broach the subject of your raise. Something simple like "I'd like to speak to you about a raise. Can we schedule a time to talk?" will do nicely. Although it's unlikely that you'll be offered a meeting on the spot, be prepared just in case. If you get put off for a week or more, do your best to be patient, and use the delay as an excuse to get in a few more practice sessions and to further prove your worthiness.

When your meeting time arrives, follow these dos and don'ts:

* Do dress and groom yourself to business perfection the day of the meeting. Not only will it improve the image you present, but it will relieve you of any worry about your physical appearance.
* Don't say that you *need* a raise. Need isn't the issue here. What the company *owes* you isn't exactly relevant either. What matters is that you can prove that your increased value justifies the raise.
* Do provide documentation that details your accomplishments. Your boss won't be able to remember everything and will be able to use your documentation to make your case to higher-ups, if necessary.
* Do provide figures and be prepared to produce evidence that backs them up on the spot.
* Don't be confrontational. This is more like a sales meeting than a boxing match, and hostility won't sell anyone anything. Make eye contact, but don't engage in the stare down.

Above all, relax. You know you've prepared your case as best as can be done. You've practice and know what you will say. You're as ready as a person can be. And whether you get the raise or not, stand up, shake hands, and thank your boss for taking the time to meet with you. Remember, post-certification isn't the only time you can ask for a raise, it's just an especially good one.

Securing a Promotion

Shortly after you've earned certification can be a good time to make a play for a career move upwards, through a promotion. This is especially true if you chose your certification with an eye toward moving into a new specialty.

Begin by laying the groundwork for career advancement, as described above. Pay special attention to increasing your visibility within the organization. Once that's under way, follow these steps to go after your promotion:

1. Identify a target position.
2. Research the position.
3. Get an interview with the right person.
4. Prepare for the interview.
5. Interview for the position.
6. Follow up.

Promotion to What?

To gain a promotion, you'll first need to identify a target position. Tell your boss you're interested in getting a promotion. Ask what the next step up is and what the requirements are. If the position one up from yours isn't likely to be open any time soon, or doesn't interest you, look around for other options. Many organizations have an in-house job posting system, either on a bulletin board somewhere or accessible via the company network. Some organizations collect such postings in a notebook in the human resources department, and you'll have to go there and leaf through them.

When examining your alternatives, pay special attention to transition positions that will open the door to further advancement. For example, if many of the organizations managers came from a particular department or a particular position, you should focus on jobs in those areas first. To find this out, you can ask your boss or other "higher-ups" how they came to hold their current position within the company. Most will be flattered that you're interested, and happy to share with you the story of their advancement. If you're lucky, you might even land a career mentor this way.

It's not necessary, or even desirable, to limit yourself to positions that seem easily within reach. Don't be afraid to stretch a little, and pursue jobs that you have only some of the qualifications for. You might just land one of them.

Homing In on Your Target

Once you've identified a target position, find out everything you can about it. Is it a newly created position or a recently vacated one? If the job isn't new, why did the person who previously held it leave? If the person is still at the company, or fairly nearby, consider a lunch invitation and ask about the details of the job and reasons for leaving it. You might find out that the boss is difficult to work for, which could lead you to reconsider your choice. At the very least you'll gain an understanding of what duties and responsibilities the position really entails. Be sure to ask what the person liked most and least about working in that position.

If the individual who previously held the position is inaccessible to you, you'll have to dig up details in other ways. Study the functions of the department the job falls under. Take someone from that area to lunch and pump him/her (nicely, of course) for information. It's fine to explain to them why you're asking. You might even gain an edge if he/she happens to like you.

One way to learn more about a particular position is to volunteer to take on some of the tasks it includes. This will involve extra work, since you'll still have to complete your own job functions, but is an approach that has several things going for it. First of all, you'll gain first-hand experience by test-driving part of the job. Second, you'll be demonstrating your ability to perform the functions, and to do them well. Third, you'll show your initiative and willingness to go the extra mile by extending yourself in this way.

Get On the Schedule

After you've chosen a position to pursue, find out who will be conducting interviews for the position, and who will be making the hiring decision. This may not be the same person. Approach the appropriate contact and state that you are interested in pursuing the position, and would like to schedule a meeting to discuss your candidacy. When choosing a date, allow yourself time to adequately prepare, but don't set it so far into the future that your anxiety builds over the delay.

Preparing for the Interview

Unlike asking for a raise, for which you get to create and present a case that proves your position, an interview for a promotion to a new position will be structured and directed by the person doing the interviewing. Learn everything you can about that person. How did he/she advance to the position he now holds? Are there particular peeves and preferences of which you should be aware? If you can turn up someone else who's been interviewed by the same person, ask what the interview was like, what questions were asked, and overall how it went.

Once you've researched the position and the interviewer, begin planning your approach. How will you demonstrate that you hold the skills and qualifications needed for the position? Create a list that records each requirement and how you fulfill it. Don't forget to mention your ongoing technical training, but don't limit yourself to technical qualifications. Pay attention to human relations, leadership skills, and personal work habits too; these can be very important as you advance within the organization. This process will help solidify your qualifications in your own mind, so that they will flow smoothly from your lips during your interview.

Prepare a few questions to ask the interviewer. They might be about some of the technical details of the position or cover other issues. If you can phrase the questions in a way that demonstrates the knowledge you've gained through researching the position, so much the better. For example, you could say, "I know the sales department runs a token ring LAN with 52 workstations. How many of those are expected to begin running Linux over the next year?" The point is to show that you are interested, informed, and thoughtful. You may not get to use all your questions, but prepare several to have in mind.

Consider reading a "how to interview" book to refresh your memory on successful answers and body language. *Ace the Technical Interview* by Michael Rothstein (McGraw-Hill 1998) is written specifically for IT job candidates. You'll find it and many additional titles, in the career center of your local library or bookstore.

The Interview

Knowing that you are fully prepared will enable you to complete the interview process in a confident, relaxed manner. You may well feel stress from the pressure of the interview, but stress can be good as well as bad—it keeps you on your toes. Keep the following tips in mind:

* As always, dress for success. Choose attire that corresponds to the dress code of the position you are applying for, not the one you already hold.
* Be on time and pay attention to your body language. The interviewer will be taking cues from how you act as well as what you say.
* Maintain friendly eye contact and speak with sincerity.
* Do your best to avoid fidgeting. If you're a fidgeter by nature, direct your restlessness to a covert site: you can always jiggle your toes inside your shoes and the interviewer will never know.
* If you find yourself in a stressful situation, or unexpectedly challenged by the interviewer, remember that there's a good chance that you're probably being tested for your reaction to the situation. Keep your cool, and maintain your position if challenged on something (although it's certainly good to acknowledge another's point of view).
* Avoid discussing salary. Let the interviewer bring it up, if it comes up at all during the session.
* Bring extra copies of your resume in case they're needed.

As the interview gets under way, work to be an active rather than passive part of the process. Listen carefully. Ask questions to clarify just what the interviewer would like to know. When answering, draw from your prepared material. Work in information that shows how you are suited to fill the position. Don't forget to ask some of the questions you prepared earlier. You may be interviewed by more than one person—either in sequence or all at once. Be prepared for this and take notes on interviewer names and titles.

At the conclusion of the interview, shake the interviewer's hand and thank him/her for her time. Restate that you want the position, and are looking forward to hearing from him/her.

Follow Up

Interview follow-up is an often neglected part of the process. By making sure you don't overlook this step, you'll put yourself ahead of many of your competitors. If an agency arranged the interview for you, telephone your agency contact as soon as possible after the interview to let that person know how the process went and whether or not you want the position.

Also as soon as possible after the interview, write a letter thanking the interviewer for his/her time. Summarize the nature of your meeting, and reiterate your qualifications for the position. If you met with several individuals in the course of the interview, remember to thank them as well. Include a fresh copy of your resume.

If you don't hear within a few days, it's okay to call and ask when a decision will be made about the position. Just don't make a pest of yourself with numerous calls or messages.

If you don't get the job, don't take it too personally. There are often many candidates competing for a position, and you may have to repeat this process several times before you obtain a promotion. Ask the interviewer why you weren't chosen. It might be easier for both of you if you phrase the question in a way that explores why the other candidate was better suited to the position instead of asking for a list of your shortcomings. Consider whether you can augment your qualifications to strengthen your candidacy next time around.

Increasing Consulting Rates

If you're an independent consultant, you can't really seek a promotion, but you can boost your rates to reflect your increased value as a certified professional. At the same time, you need to be careful not to price yourself out of the market.

The best way to determine the rates you can reasonably charge is to find out what other consultants who provide the same services bill. There are several places you can turn to for this information. One is the placement firms who connect professionals like yourself with potential employers. A firm in your area should be able to give you an idea of the local rates.

Contracting opportunities posted on the Internet are another source of rate information. You can search computer job boards for contracts that utilize skills like your own, and look for postings that contain rate information. A good place to look is DICE at **www.dice.com**. Another excellent Internet source is author Janet Ruhl's real rates survey (**www.realrates.com**), which collects rate information from consultants who visit the site and makes it available to anyone who's interested. The results of a Linux-related search of Real Rates site is shown in Figure 12.4.

Another possibility is to frequent forums and mailing lists where other Linux-certified individuals congregate, and connect with other consultants like yourself. E-mail them privately, and inquire if they're willing to share information on their billing rates or pay on previous contracts.

Use your rate research to determine a range for your services and skills. Remember to take into account your experience level and any special qualifications, such as level of Linux certification and other certifications you hold. If previous clients question your new rates, explain that you have simply revised them to reflect current market rates for services like your own.

FIGURE 12.4
Linux fee reports on Janet Ruhl's Real Rates Survey Web site

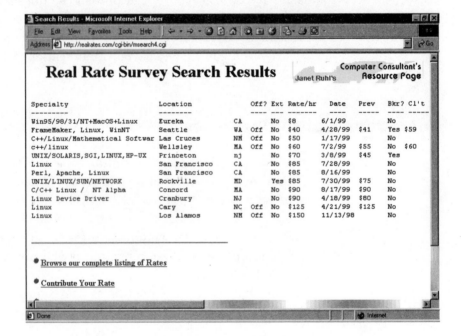

Specialty	Location	Off?	Ext	Rate/hr	Date	Prev	Bkr?	Cl't
Win95/98/31/NT+MacOS+Linux	Eureka	CA		No	$8	6/1/99		No	
FrameMaker, Linux, WinNT	Seattle	WA	Off	No	$40	4/28/99	$41	Yes	$59
C++/Linux/Mathematical Softwar	Las Cruces	NM	Off	No	$50	1/17/99		No	
c++/linux	Wellsley	MA	Off	No	$60	7/2/99	$55	No	$60
UNIX/SOLARIS,SGI,LINUX,HP-UX	Princeton	nj		No	$70	3/8/99	$45	Yes	
Linux	San Francisco	CA		No	$85	7/28/99		No	
Perl, Apache, Linux	San Francisco	CA		No	$85	8/16/99		No	
UNIX/LINUX/SUN/NETWORK	Rockville	MD		Yes	$85	7/30/99	$75	No	
C/C++ Linux / NT Alpha	Concord	MA		No	$90	8/17/99	$90	No	
Linux Device Driver	Cranbury	NJ		No	$90	4/18/99	$80	No	
Linux	Cary	NC	Off	No	$125	4/21/99	$125	No	
Linux	Los Alamos	NM	Off	No	$150	11/13/98		No	

Real Rate Survey Search Results   Janet Ruhl's   Computer Consultant's Resource Page

* Browse our complete listing of Rates
* Contribute Your Rate

What to Do If Your Efforts Don't Work

Taking a planned, organized approach to career advancement will usually bring prompt results. This is especially true in the current IT industry environment, where demand for skilled technical people continues to outpace supply, and demand for certified individuals is especially strong. However, your first or second attempts may still be unsuccessful. Persistence is an important factor in career advancement, in any profession. If your first efforts at moving up don't come to fruition, analyze the reasons why, take aim at a new goal, and try again. Whether or not your efforts result in immediate advancement, keep a professional attitude. Things to keep in mind include:

* **Have a graceful fallback plan.** If the boss says no to your raise or promotion, or your clients balk at your rate increase, what will you do? Have your response planned in advance so that it can roll off your tongue, despite your disappointment. Remember, you can always try again.

* **Don't burn bridges is a trite saying but wise advice.** You never know if the person you aggravate today will be your boss or coworker at some time in the future. Make every effort to be considerate and professional. Don't let anger or hostility cloud your judgment (and potentially your future advancement).

* **Don't make a pest of yourself.** Persistence is important, but it should not become annoyance. Constantly reminding your boss that you want a raise or a promotion will make you an irritation and work against you. Work to demonstrate your value and monitor yourself to prevent this problem.

Finding Career Advancement Advice on the Web

Although most Internet career sites focus on finding a job rather than moving up within your current organization, there are several useful advancement resources you might want to visit.

careerplanning.miningco.com is the About.com's career advancement site. It features articles, links, and a forum where you can post your questions and advice for others. The site is shown in Figure 12.5.

continued on next page

www.hardatwork.com/Escalator/career1.html is the Web site of the Hard@Work Career Escalator. It contains an ongoing discussion of career advancement topics, articles on promotions, raises, and career breakpoints, and interview help.

FIGURE 12.5

Career advice from About.com

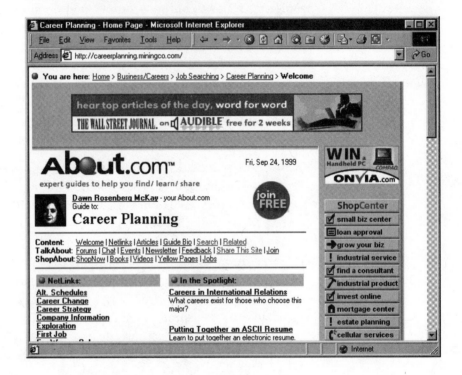

By preparing carefully, you'll boost yourself to the front of the queue for raises and promotions. You'll also be able to move upward more swiftly than coworkers who wait for advancement to come to them instead of going after it. Throughout your career, you should work to keep your skills current with workplace needs. That will require constant reassessment and planning for where you want to go next. Although career advancement requires strategizing and effort to succeed, the payoff will be well worth it.

Chapter 13

Moving On

Because earning a Linux certification gives your marketability a sudden boost, it's often used as a springboard to a new position. In fact, many professionals pursue certification with the primary intention of using it to land a new job. A 1998 survey of certification candidates revealed that 17 percent of them expect certification to be a deciding factor in helping them secure a new job. That's up 2 percent from 1997. More than half of respondents are pursuing certification as a means to advance in their profession.

Although Linux certification can also help you move up through the ranks at your current place of employment, for one reason or another, many professionals prefer to move on to an entirely new job situation. If you're ready to move on, or simply want to explore the possibilities, you first need to develop a profile of the type of job you'd like to obtain. Next, you'll need to dust off your resumé and update it to reflect your certified status. Then, dive into the job market and begin exploring your options. There are loads of jobs out there, and one of them is bound to be just right for you.

Before You Start Your Search

Before diving into a job search, take the time to define exactly what you want to accomplish by finding a new position. As a starting point, examine your current job and identify its shortcomings and strengths. Rate it on items such as amount of responsibility, on-call duties, compensation, potential for advancement, access to technologies you're interested in working with, and your general overall satisfaction with the work environment. By identifying where your current employer falls short, you can increase your chances that the new position you find will prove a step up. Sometimes an assessment like this has a surprise result: you find out your current appointment is actually providing you with most of which you want. If that's the case, consider an upward or lateral move at your current place of employment.

As you prepare to enter the job market, remember that it can be a stressful place. You're going to encounter rejection, especially if you go for positions at the upper range of your qualifications. Don't take it personally. Rejection isn't an indication of your personal worth. Rather, it signifies that there wasn't a match between yourself, the position, and the hiring manager. If you don't collect a few (or even many) of those "we regret to inform you" letters, then you're probably not aiming high enough.

Another stress factor to consider is the wait. It's unlikely your first resumé will hit the optimum target. Patience is necessary, as is persistence. Don't expect immediate success or you'll almost certainly be disappointed. You may have to dig into vacation time to attend interviews and devote some of your leisure hours to researching positions and companies and performing other marketing tasks.

On the up side, remember why you started the certification process in the first place—to advance your career. Whether you're after higher pay, a position with greater responsibilities, entrance into a new area of expertise, or any other positive career move, changing jobs is a powerful way to put your certification to work for you.

A Resumé Tune-up

Once you've clarified the type of position you're after and reminded yourself of the nature of job searches, it's time to sharpen your resumé, which will of course include information on your new Linux certification(s). Later on you may create unique versions, tailored to a particular job opening, but first, you'll need a starting resumé; one that's as strong as you can make it.

Resumés can be as individual as the person who creates them and may be classified into a half dozen formats. For a comprehensive discussion of resumé formats and wording, visit your local bookstore or library for a resumé writing guide. You can also try one of these handy online resumé aids:

* **content.monster.com/resume/** contains numerous sample resumés and cover letters, as well as articles to help you hone a perfect resumé of your own.

* **www.his.com/~rockport/resumes.htm** "How to Write an Exceptional Resumé" is an excellent, in-depth presentation on-resumé writing goals and practices. Figure 13.1 shows this Web site.

✳ **www.bio.com/hr/search/ResumeRocket.html** The article,
"Resumé Rocket Science" puts resumé writing in perspective
and will help you make yours the best it can be.

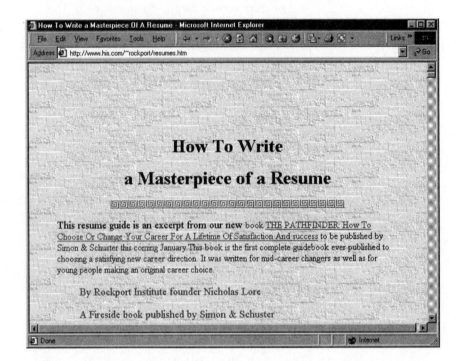

FIGURE 13.1
Exceptional
resumé advice
Web site

Meanwhile, here's a resumé refresher, which may be all you
need. The two most widely used resumé styles are chronological
and functional. Any format you choose should lead off with your
name, address, telephone number, and e-mail address. An
employment objective often follows, such as:

Professional Objective: A position managing Web servers in
a corporate environment.

Because specific technical skills are of critical importance in
the hiring of computer professionals, they are listed prominently.
Depending on the diversity of your experience, you may decide to
lump them under a single heading, such as technical skills, or
break them out by category. This is one possible place to list your
certifications.

Software/OS:	Linux, Novell Netware, MS-DOS, Windows/NT, Solaris, FreeBSD, UNIX
Hardware:	Sun Sparc, Pentium multi-processors, IBM-compatible microcomputers, NCR Tower
Certifications:	MLCE, CNE

Work history or education follows next, depending on which you think is strongest. The work history section is where the chronological and functional styles diverge. Chronological resumés organize work history by employer, starting with the most recent (usually current) and working backwards. They work well to emphasize continuous growth in a single profession. Each entry includes dates, employer, location, and job title, followed by a succinct description of duties and accomplishments. For example:

1997–Present   Associate Systems Analyst, ABC Corporation, Hartford, CT

Responsible for software and hardware installation and maintenance of 200-node network with Internet link. Prepared and presented training seminars and materials at the data center and the customer site. Developed PC applications in C. Performed technical support activities for local intranet.

Resumés organized in the functional style highlight work experience by job function rather than by date and employer. This format is especially useful when you are changing professions or if you want to emphasize the scope of your experience over the continuity. For example:

Project Leadership: Directed development of in-house customer support workstation from design phase through implementation. Supervised and coordinated team of four programmer-analysts. Delivered projects on time and under budget.

In the Education section, achievements should be listed from most recent to least recent. That means your certifications should be first. If you have a college degree, don't bother to list your high school diploma.

Your resumé should also list professional affiliations, honors and awards, publications, and any additional qualifications you hold. *Don't* include personal information such as family/marital status, age, race, religion, health information, or a physical description of yourself. Such information is irrelevant to your qualifications for employment.

No matter how perfect your resumé is, it's not going to get you the job; you'll have to do that in person through one or more interviews. What your resumé will do is get you that interview that will allow you to compete for the position in the first place. For that reason, it's important to make it as perfect as you can and to emphasize your strengths.

You may be able to create a powerful resumé on your own, especially if you have an existing resumé to work from, but take advantage of one or more of the how-to books available to guide you through the process. If you don't feel satisfied with the result, consider utilizing a resumé preparation service. You can also obtain resumé help from the career resource office of a school you have attended.

Books To Help

Knock 'Em Dead 1999: The Ultimate Job Seeker's Handbook by Martin John Yate (William Mulvey, 1998)

The $100,000 Resume by Craig Scott Rice (McGraw-Hill, 1998)

The Overnight Resume by Donald Asher (Ten Speed Press, 1999)

Winning Resumes for Computer Personnel, 2nd ed by Anne Hart (Barrons, 1998)

Resumé Magic: Trade Secrets of a Professional Resume Writer by Susan Britton Whitcomb (Jist Works 1998)

But Is It Computer Friendly?

Resumé layout has long been a challenge to those who aren't desktop publishing wizards. It can take a dozen reprints to get the margins just right; settle on sharp, decent-sized fonts; and otherwise manipulate your resumé so that it looks appealing.

Today that's only half the job. You also need a resumé that's appealing to computers.

If you submit your beautifully designed masterpiece electronically, as is often required these days, it may arrive at the other end looking scrambled. Unless you're Picasso, that's not going to work in your favor. To get around this problem, you need a version of your resumé that's computer readable.

The safest bet when transmitting resumés electronically is to use ASCII format. ASCII (American Standard Code for Information Interchange) can be read by many different kinds of computers. Saving your resumé in ASCII format will keep the text, tabs, and spacing but lose all other formatting, such as indents, special fonts, bold print, and underlining. But once you've created a reasonable ASCII resumé, you'll be able to transmit it electronically and have it arrive looking the same as when you sent it.

To create an ASCII version of your resumé, use your word processor and select a font that *isn't* proportionally spaced. Courier is a good choice. Don't apply any formatting as you input your resumé information. You can still make it appear clean and appealing through the use of spaces and tabs to line things up. No line should be longer than 69 characters, or it may wrap in funny places on the recipient's screen.

To save your ASCII resumé, chose **File | Save As** from your word processor's menu. Then look for one of the following options: DOS Text, Text Only, or ASCII. Select the option and save your file.

Before shipping your resumé off to a potential employer, e-mail it to yourself and see what shape it arrives in.

QUICK TIP

Another request you may encounter is for a scannable resumé. The employer will feed your resumé through a scanner and convert it using OCR (optical character recognition) software into a text file for storage in a database. Although any resumé can be scanned, results vary widely and illegible results are common. If you design your resumé with scanning in mind, you can maximize the chances that yours will scan beautifully. To make your resumé scanner friendly, follow these guidelines:

- ✳ Keep the format simple, standard, and free of borders.
- ✳ Avoid graphics.
- ✳ Use basic, sans serif fonts (such as Arial) that won't confuse scanning software.
- ✳ Select a font size between 10 and 14 point.
- ✳ Use light colored paper; white is best.
- ✳ Send an original. Photocopies may not be high enough quality.
- ✳ Send it in a flat 9 × 12 envelope so it arrives without folds or creases.

As you can see, you may need to create more than one version of your resumé to meet employer requirements. But because the differences will be in formatting rather than in content, doing so shouldn't be excessively time consuming. And the beauty of electronic resumés lies in their accessibility. They can be searched and called up anytime from anywhere.

QUICKTIP

Rebecca Smith's eResumés & Resources (**www.eresumes.com**) is the *only* site you'll need to find out everything about electronic resumés. This wonderful resource covers everything from how to put your resumé into formats that computers can handle to creating an online resumé and finding places to post it. You can also browse a gallery of resumés that show how others are marketing themselves online, read loads of useful articles, and even grab a few laughs.

Keeping It Hush-Hush

There are many reasons why you might wish to keep your job search plans to yourself, the foremost being that if your search ends without turning up a superior offer, the relationship with your current employer hasn't been damaged. But discretion has its price; you won't be able to network as extensively for fear of word getting back to your employer. Word of mouth can be a powerful job search tool, and giving it up can cramp your style considerably. You'll have to weigh the factors on both sides to decide whether a clandestine job search or a public one will serve you best.

If you do want to keep your plans to yourself, or at least be reasonably discreet, employ the following practices:

* Put only your home phone number on your resumé, not your work number. Install an answering machine and check it daily to make sure it's operating properly. Call it throughout the day to check for messages so you can respond promptly.

* Don't return calls from your desk. Return calls from an empty conference room or, better yet, a phone away from your place of work.

* Don't use your employer's materials in your job search. Supply your own paper, and get your copies made at a copy shop.

* If you require the use of a fax machine, use one that's public (or one that belongs to a friend). Some libraries have a fax machine available, as do copy shops.

* Don't use your business e-mail address for job search communications. Whether it's morally acceptable or not, it's legal for your boss to read your electronic mail.

* Make every effort to conduct your job search without impinging on your work hours. Utilize breaks, your lunch hour, and before and after hours options as frequently as possible.

If, despite your efforts, your boss discovers your job search, make the best of it. Explain why you were looking and that you were doing so on your own time. Reassure your employer that you will not leave him/her in the lurch and even offer to help find/train your replacement.

What if your current employer offers incentives to keep you from leaving? Consider carefully before accepting. You've already made up your mind to leave, and now that your boss knows that, the question of your dedication and loyalty will linger throughout your career with this employer. It may be best to not accept the inducements to stay and instead stick with your original plan to land that new job. On the other hand, if you're offered the plum you were looking for, take it.

How to Find Job Openings

A primary activity of the job search is to find suitable job postings. Professionals in the computer field are currently enjoying a bountiful time, with more jobs than there are qualified people to fill them. This gap is projected to widen.

An study conducted annually since 1997 by the Information Technology Association of America (ITAA) warns that the need for IT workers exceeds supply and will continue to do so until growth slows in both IT and non-IT industries.

According to the ITAA 1998 study, there are approximately 346,000 unfilled programmer, systems analyst, and computer scientist/engineer jobs in America today. This number actually understates the overall demand for such workers, because it only accounts for specifically defined computer positions. Broaden the definition to include other job titles/functions such as project manager or team leader that involve computers, and the number jumps to over half a million. The study also found that both IT and non-IT companies are finding it very difficult to hire and retain qualified personnel.

All this indicates that it's an IT worker's market out there, and you have plenty of opportunities to choose from. All you have to do is find the right ones. Thanks to the information technology boom, locating potential employment is easier than ever. You can connect with companies searching for skilled technology workers in many different ways, including through:

* Linux distribution vendor and service company Web sites
* Headhunters and recruiting companies
* Print advertisements in newspapers and magazines
* Job fairs
* Internet and Web job banks
* Networking opportunities

To find your optimum position, you'll want to explore multiple avenues. Don't overlook opportunities to advance at your current place of employment. See Chapter 12 for help and advice on using your certification to get ahead right where you are.

Linux Vendors and Service Company Web Sites

If you're looking for a Linux-focused job, why not go straight to the source? Just as with other IT companies, Linux distribution vendors usually have a help-wanted sign hanging out. Due to the decentralized nature of Linux, there are also a number of companies devoted to Linux support. These are also prime sources of employment opportunities.

One of the easiest ways to explore job openings at such vendors is by visiting their Web sites and looking for an employment link. Most have them. An example employment page is shown in Figure 13.2. To save you some time, here are a few company employment sites to get you started:

✳ SuSE—**www.suse.com/jobs.html**
✳ Caldera Systems—**www.calderasystems.com/jobs/**
✳ Red Hat—**www.redhat.com/about/careers.html**
✳ LinuxCare—**www.linuxcare.com/company/employment/ index.epl**
✳ VA LiNUX Systems—**www.varesearch.com/jobs/**

FIGURE 13.2
Job openings at
LinuxCare

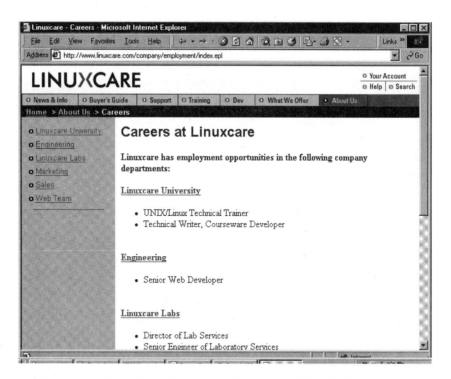

When you run through those, check out Yahoo!'s Linux companies page at: **yahoo.com/Business_and_Economy/Companies/ Computers/Business_to_Business/Software/Operating_ Systems/Linux/** (shown in Figure 13.3).

FIGURE 13.3
Linux companies =
Linux job
opportunities

Headhunters

Headhunters (also known as *recruiters*) are individuals who find people to fill jobs. Headhunters are hungry. They're always looking for resumés because without resumés they can't fill positions. And they're always looking for positions to fill because they can't place people without jobs to put them in. Like sharks, they are always on the hunt. Like sharks, they've been known to bite the hand that feeds them.

Bad headhunters may send you on as many interviews as possible without performing adequate screening first, with the goal of getting you placed somewhere, anywhere, so they can get paid their fees. They've even been suspected, on occasion, of sending a candidate to a position that's a poor match because they want to get someone out there to look like they're doing something for the client company. Firms that practice these tactics are sometimes called *body shops*.

Working through a middleman has additional drawbacks. When communication has to pass through an additional layer, it's more likely to get muddled. When you work with a headhunter, communication between you and the potential employer passes through that extra layer.

Sometimes headhunters will conceal the identity of the company behind a job opening until after they have your resumé and have interviewed you. They do this for fear you'll go straight to the company yourself. Of course, if you did go to the company yourself, it might not do you much good because, in a large company, you'd have no idea who the hiring manger for the position in question was, and your resumé might never reach the right person.

Although headhunters are much maligned, often with good reason, a good one can prove very valuable. Headhunters know the jobs that are out there. They have connections at corporations and relationships with hiring managers. Because of their relationships with hiring companies, headhunters are often aware of jobs that haven't been advertised. They can put you in for an excellent job you otherwise wouldn't have known existed; and they can negotiate money for you. That can be a big plus if you find negotiating compensation packages about as appealing as a severe case of stomach flu. Because the headhunter's payoff is a percentage of your first year's salary, he/she has a strong incentive to get you the biggest paycheck possible.

Given that headhunters can do so much for you, you may well decide to work with one or more. You'll find an extensive array of them on the World Wide Web. You'll find a huge directory of them on Yahoo! at **yahoo.com/Business_and_Economy/Companies/ Computers/Employment/Recruiting_and_Placement/**. They can also be found by looking for names at the bottom of job postings or use one of the other search engines. Ask friends who they deal with; they may be able to point you toward quality recruiters.

Before submitting your resumé to a recruiter, find out as much as you can. Inquire about procedures and insist that your resumé not be submitted anywhere, for any reason, without your prior approval. It's a small thing for the recruiter to call you up and say "I've got a position at in ISP in East Oshkosh doing network installation that I want to put you in for. Okay?" Insist on such courtesies.

It's also a good idea to ask other computer professionals what they know of the firm and whether their opinion of it is good or bad. You can also seek out such information online. Post an inquiry in a forum that computer professionals frequent, asking for opinions on the firm you're considering. The computer consultant's forum on CompuServe, for example, would be a suitable place.

Print Advertisements

One of the first places job hunters turn to is the classified section of a nearby newspaper. Because it's such a popular source of job leads, such advertisements trigger a ton of responses. Although that means you'll face a lot of competition, it's still worthwhile to respond to job announcements that interest you. Just don't be discouraged if you have a lower reply rate from potential employers you contact this way. They may be swamped with candidates and only take time to respond to the top applicants. Your goal, of course, is to be one of those top candidates.

Augment the listings in your local newspaper by picking up copies of (or subscribing to) national newspapers, such as *The Wall Street Journal*, *The New York Times*, and *National Business Employment Weekly*. As an alternative, you can also plan an evening at the library browsing in these and other national publications, photocopying listings that interest you.

If you're planning a move to a new location, consider obtaining a subscription to the largest newspaper that serves the area. You can have it mailed to your current address.

Trade publications should be one of your key print sources of job postings. Because they're focused on the industry in question, you'll have fewer irrelevant ads to wade through. Good leads for computer jobs can be found in publications such as *Linux Journal*, *InformationWeek*, or *Contract Professional*, among others.

When you come across a job advertisement that interests you, clip it and staple or tape it to a standard sized piece of paper to prevent it from getting mislaid. Each advertisement should have its own page, which will serve as a repository of notes regarding the particular ad. This method also enables you to store all of your advertisements in a folder or three-ring binder.

The first thing you should record on the page is the name and date of the publication you found the advertisement in. This will spare you the embarrassment of saying, "I don't know" when an employer asks where you encountered the ad, and it allows you to mention the ad source in your cover letter.

Next, read the advertisement carefully to identify the company that placed the ad and the qualifications sought. Record what you discover on your notes page. If the advertisement still looks appealing after your second read, it's time to find out something about the company. Some advertisements are blind, meaning they don't mention who the employer is, but most often the company offering the job is clearly identified. If you're already familiar with it, great. Otherwise, do a bit of research to find out the basics on products, market, and size. A good resource is *Hoover's Handbook of American Companies*, which you can find at your library or access via the Internet at **www.hoovers.com**. Figure 13.4 shows the *Hoover's* Web site.

To respond to the advertisement, you're going to write a letter. And to do that, you'll need a name at the company. Human Resources Director isn't good enough. Call the company and ask the receptionist for the name and title of the proper person to whom you should send your resumé.

Your cover letter should be succinct, written on quality stationery, and intended to arouse interest in your abilities. As in a good novel, the first sentence is critical. Use it to grab your reader's attention by stating something that's important to him/her. One approach is to open with a mention of your strongest qualification for the job. As you continue, don't just mention your strengths, give examples of how you've applied them. Keep the letter short—two pages maximum. One page is better. Whoever is screening the replies will have many to go through and isn't going to appreciate long, rambling letters. Your closing sentence should be compelling, too. Use it to ask for a personal interview to further discuss the opportunity.

Staple a copy of your response letter to the page bearing the advertisement and your notes. If you're using more than one version of your resumé, attach a copy of the version you sent with your letter as well. Then put everything in your "to follow up" file.

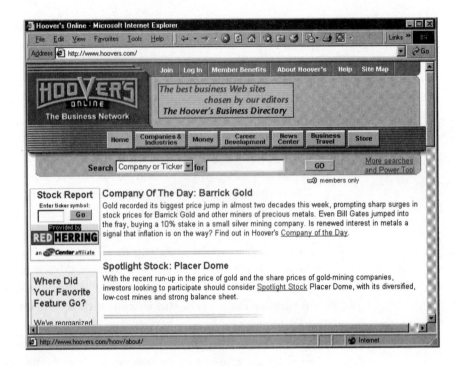

Job Fairs

A job fair offers the opportunity to meet dozens, if not hundreds, of employers in one place over the course of one or two days. It's a chance to do some efficient, condensed job hunting.

But job fairs can be intimidating, too. They can feel like meat markets and you're one piece of meat among hundreds. Nonetheless, attending them can prove well worth the temporary discomfort. Besides the obvious opportunity to connect with a specific job, you'll also be networking, creating and collecting contacts that you can come back to in the future. It's also a great place to learn about new companies, what they're doing, what they plan to do, and the types of jobs they have to fill.

Job fairs are usually advertised in local newspapers, and sometimes you can find them by searching the Internet. Choose one that's geographically compatible with your plans and focuses on technical opportunities. There's no use attending a job fair featuring only local companies if you plan to relocate to the opposite coast.

The advertisement will probably identify the companies that will be in attendance, but if not, call the coordinating organization and ask for a list to be sent to you by mail or fax. This gives you a chance to plan hit lists of primary targets and second choice companies you want to make contact with. Do a little research beforehand on companies that interest you.

Your resumé should be in tip-top shape, and it won't hurt to bring business cards, too. Make sure your certification is listed prominently on both. Consider preparing a second or third version of your resumé that emphasizes different strengths. For example, one version might play up your network management skills while another underscores your expertise with internetworking hardware.

In advance, create a three- to five-minute spiel about yourself and your qualifications. Don't exceed five minutes. The recruiters and hiring managers will speak with hundreds of potential applicants and won't have the patience to listen to rambling, unfocused presentations. You want to say who you are, where your technical strengths lie, and what you've done with them. Include several examples of problems you've solved and how you've solved them. Practice your pitch in front of a mirror until you've got it down cold.

On the big day, dress as you would for an interview. It's unlikely that you'll be hired on the spot, but you need to look your professional best. Bring multiple copies of your resumé and plenty of business cards—more than you think you'll need. It's also a good idea to bring a notepad for jotting down information on companies that interest you. And, of course, bring your list of target companies so you can make sure you visit the booths you've identified as most important.

Start with a company that's on your B list (or not on your list at all). That way you can fine-tune your spiel before connecting with the companies you're most interested in. When you're introducing yourself to a recruiter, watch his body language and wrap it up if he keeps glancing at his watch or gazing over your shoulder, signs that his interest isn't on you.

Collect business cards and company literature and pause between booths to take notes on what you talked about and with whom. Otherwise, it will be difficult to follow up effectively.

Speaking of follow-up, do it within a day or so of the fair. Send a letter recapping your conversation, and include a fresh copy of your resumé. Then, while you wait for the phone to start ringing with interview calls, continue your job search efforts on other fronts.

QUICKTIP

A job fair is an excellent place to get a feel for which technologies are hot and which skills are in demand. If you notice that many recruiters are searching for people with a particular skill, make a note of it so you can consider adding it to your repertoire.

Online Job Hunting

Job hunting via the Internet is efficient and fun, too. You get to browse at all kinds of interesting Web sites, and you can take advantage of the incredibly rich supply of job hunting resources. If a particular company interests you, you can visit its Web site. Most will have a job opportunities section. In many cases, you'll be able to reply online.

The Web is also a huge repository of job postings. Many sites collect thousands of openings in databases, and you can search them by qualifications, salary, geographic location, or other specifications. Some of these sites will even let you register your preferences and then notify you by e-mail if any postings are added that fit your specifications.

You can also utilize the Web to bring employers to you. It really is a worker's market in the computer industry, and recruiters are actively looking for bodies to fill open positions. If you post your resume on one of the many sites that allow you to do so, chances are your e-mail box will soon hold inquiries for you to consider.

A Baker's Dozen: Thirteen Places to Find Computer Jobs Online

The Web as a medium is so conducive to job placement functions that the sheer quantity of job sites can, at times, become overwhelming. Although many of the giant job sites post openings in all industries and areas, others focus on particular job markets.

The following Web sites cater to the high-tech job hunter. Most are specific to computer professionals and a few even specialize in Linux job openings. The others are more broadly based, but contain a high percentage of computer-related opportunities.

* **www.linuxjournal.com** is the *Linux Journal*, which has a career center listing job openings and Linux pros for hire.
* **www.unix-developers.net/** is a good place to search for Linux positions. Just enter the keyword Linux in the search box.
* **jobs.linuxtoday.com/** contains *Linux Today's* job classifieds.
* **comp.jobs.offered** is a Usenet newsgroup of open computer positions.
* **computerwork.com** is a leading online job board and resumé bank, a database of technical jobs and contract opportunities and a potential place to post your resumé.
* **www.computerjobs.com** is the home page of The Computer-Jobs Store, which has job listings for many US major metropolitan areas.
* **www.datamation.com/PlugIn/jobs/itjobs.html** is *Datamation*'s site that links to the recruitment pages of leading IT vendors.
* **www.dice.com** sends you to DICE , a monster collection of consulting and permanent computer-related job postings.
* **www.headhunter.net** is Headhunter.Net, and although it's not strictly limited to high-tech jobs, it includes many positions for computer professionals.
* **supersite.net/computercurrentsjobbank** is the *Computer Currents* professional job bank.
* **www.monster.com** is an online career center with a huge database of jobs from top companies. You can search by industry and geographic area or just browse among the latest postings.
* **www.softwarejobs.com** is The Software Jobs home page. It lists positions available across the country and can be searched by keyword.
* **www.careerbuilder.com** allows you to search and apply for a job online. This site will e-mail you when opportunities that meet your specifications are posted.

❋ **www.selectjobs.com** is the home page of the Select Jobs
Web site. You can search job openings by skills, location, title,
or keywords of your choice. You can also register to be notified
of new openings that meet your qualifications.

When responding to an electronic job offering, be sure to follow
the instructions mentioned in the posting. If a position identification number is mentioned, be sure to include it in your reply. If
you are responding via e-mail, be certain to spell check your message before sending it. E-mail is not an excuse for poor grammar
and spelling.

QUICK TIP

If your electronic mail program doesn't incorporate spell checking, compose your
message using your word processor instead. After you confirm that it's free from
spelling errors, select the text of your message and cut and paste it into the body
of a new e-mail message.

Networking

Don't underestimate the power of your connections to land your
dream job. Tell relatives, coworkers, and friends that you're looking. If you're attempting to be covert, tell only those you can trust
to be discreet. But keeping your job search confidential comes
with a price because it will limit your options to some degree.

Successful networking largely consists of being visible. Attend
professional functions and mingle. If you know someone who
knows someone with connections to a place you want to work,
don't be afraid to ask for an introduction. The worst they can do is
say no, and they'll probably say yes. Seek out professional associ-
ations related to your area of expertise. They may have a referral
service, and if not, are still a good way to meet others who work
in (and hire for) your profession.

Follow Up

Whichever route you use to locate job listings, remember to follow
up on opportunities to which you respond. It's a basic task that's

been stressed in every job hunting guide ever published but it's often overlooked. Send that thank-you letter after an interview, and you could distinguish yourself from all the other candidates who never get around to it. Make that follow-up phone call you promised in your cover letter, and you'll be demonstrating your ability to follow through. Yes, these are somewhat mundane tasks and they take up your time. But they could be just the step that clinches the interview, or the job, that you'd really like to call your own.

Going Independent

If you've been on the brink of a career as an independent consultant, your certification may provide the impetus to make the move. But look carefully before you leap. The benefits of self-employment are potentially limitless, but there are plenty of drawbacks, too.

The independent contractor/consultant needs to be tenacious and organized. You'll have to find your own work, create and adhere to your own schedule, and perform the functions that accompany running your own business. Table 13.1 summarizes many of the pros and cons you'll encounter if you go independent.

TABLE 13.1
Pros and cons of going independent

Pros	Cons
Manage your own career direction	Will have to manage fluctuations in income
Freedom from office politics and red tape	Work and leisure boundaries blur
Potential tax benefits via business tax deductions	You have to wear all the hats: accounting, sales, marketing, production, administration
More control over work/life balance	No externally imposed structure to guide you
Direct responsibility for your income level and success	No corporate employment benefits

Drake Beam Morin, Inc., an outplacement and career management firm, has devoted a section of its Web site to information for people considering self-employment. Visit **www.dbm.com/ career/employment/reality.html** (shown in Figure 13.5) to explore your motivations for self-employment and the realities you're likely to face.

FIGURE 13.5
Self-employment
reality check

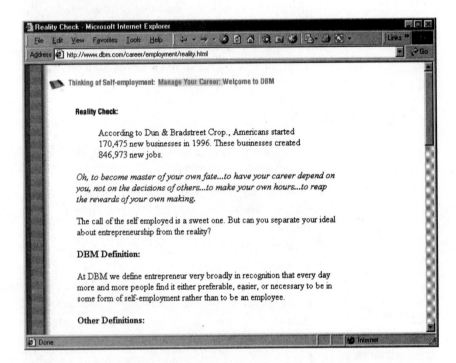

To form a solid picture of the consulting life, there's no substitute for reports from the field. Seek out friends or coworkers who are self-employed or who have been in the past, and take them to lunch so you can get the firsthand scoop. Visit forums and Web sites dedicated to computer contractors and read, read, read. Professionals who frequent these sites are usually willing to share their advice and experiences and can be very helpful to the new consultant, and you'll find lots of articles to advise you. Some of the more helpful sites include:

✳ Janet Ruhl's Computer Consultant's Resource Page (**www.realrates.com**), which is shown in Figure 13.6, is a must-see site for anyone considering going independent. You'll find advice on the ins and outs of the consulting life, current billing rates around the country for various skill sets, suggestions on how to negotiate contracts, and lots more—including contract job opportunities.

FIGURE 13.6
Janet Ruhl's
computer
consultant's page

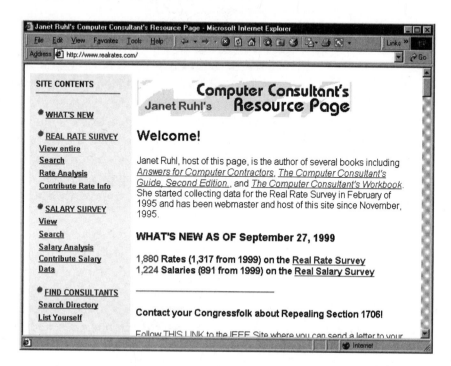

* The discussion forums on the Web site of Contract Professional Forum (**www.cpuniverse.com**) are another good place to seek advice and interact with experienced contractors and consultants.

If you decide to become an independent consultant, don't neglect to capitalize on your certification(s). They are credentials that will add to your credibility with potential clients, which will be especially useful when you're just starting out.

Spare Those Bridges

No matter how aggravating a position you are leaving has been, be careful of how you represent it. Don't knock your previous employer during interviews or to your new employer. Even if every word you say is true, you're conveying an image of yourself as a complainer or worse. Those aren't good traits to have associated with your name. And if you've done it to a past employer, what's to keep you from badmouthing this one a year down the line?

Along the same lines, be wary of exit interviews. While it can be very satisfying to answer a question like: "Is there anything the company could have done to keep you from leaving?" with a retort like "Yes, treat me decently," don't do it. The future is unpredictable, and the day may come when you encounter your boss somewhere down the road. Such comments, however honest, may come back to haunt you. Although confidentiality may be promised during the exit interview process, don't count on it. It's probably not that hard for a manager to tie a particular exit interview with the individual who gave it, even without your name gracing the page.

Finally, throughout your job search, keep records of all your expenditures. You may be able to deduct some of your job-search expenses on your tax return at the end of the year. Items such as resumé printing, postage, unreimbursed travel for job-seeking purposes, and placement agency fees, are generally deductible as miscellaneous itemized deductions on Schedule A (Form 1040). As such, they are subject to the 2 percent limit, which means that they are deductible only to the extent that they exceed 2 percent of your adjusted gross income (AGI). Various and sundry other restrictions also apply. Consult a tax professional if your job-search expenses are significant.

Although few people, if any, would consider a job hunt fun, the results can certainly justify the effort. By moving on to a new position, you may be able to boost your salary, increase your personal satisfaction, and land a job that offers an optimum blend of challenge, reward, and professional growth—the type of job you can look forward to undertaking each day.

Chapter 14

Keeping Current

Once you've obtained your Linux certification, it's important to pay attention to the currency of your skills. However you look at it, continuing professional education is a critical component of any successful career, especially in the computer professions. As this book was going to press, about half of the Linux certification programs required periodic renewal or specified certification update requirements. However, even if your chosen Linux certification vendor doesn't currently insist on continuing requirements, the value of your certification will be enhanced by the fact that you've taken steps to update your skills to keep pace with technological changes.

Professional development efforts prove most valuable when undertaken in a planned, intentional manner. The requirements set forth by individual Linux certification programs outline a minimum path for you to follow. Use them as a starting point, but keep in mind that those requirements are geared to support the individual certification, which may be as narrow as a particular function related to a specific version of a single distribution of Linux. As such, they won't provide an adequate continuing education plan on their own, but they make a good starting point. Choose courses and training events that will serve a specific purpose and add to your skills and/or knowledge in a meaningful way.

Your first step should be to determine what requirements, if any, have been set in place by your sponsor for your certification. You can do this by checking through the literature you have on hand and by visiting the page for your certification on the sponsor's Web site. The Web site is likely to be more current than the printed materials, but don't count on either of these sources to supply complete and timely information. Continuing requirements are subject to change and can suddenly appear in programs where before there were none. This isn't always a bad thing, as it actually adds value to your certification in the eyes of those who might hire you.

Vendor-specific certifications are often version specific. This is especially true of Linux certifications, because Linux is an operating system and evolving constantly. Red Hat Certified Engineers, for example, must renew within a specified time period after new releases. The vendor-neutral Brainbench Linux e-certification, which isn't linked to a specific distribution or version, must be renewed annually.

When version updates are required of certifications that involve multiple initial exams, all it usually takes is passing an upgrade exam. You may or may not receive notice that a new version is imminent, but by keeping your eye on trade magazines and industry publications such as *Linux Journal* you should catch wind of new releases before they hit the market. You can then inquire about certification upgrade requirements and be current and ready to go as the new release hits the streets. This is also a good way to be one of the first to have a complete understanding of the strengths and weaknesses of new versions and distributions of Linux.

Tracking continuing requirements is entirely your responsibility, and there's no guarantee that you will receive any reminders from your certification vendor. It's also up to you to remember that following the guidelines isn't enough—if you don't submit acceptable evidence that you've done so, your efforts won't count. Several certification programs have created online certification tracking systems that you can use once you become a certification candidate, or to which you can refer individuals who want to confirm your certification status. Such systems (see Figure 14.1) store details of every certification test you've taken; you should use them to verify that your efforts have been properly recorded.

Once you've pinned down your particular recertification requirements, calculate the deadlines for meeting them and incorporate them into your schedule. Because these dates can be far into the future, it will help to circle them in red or flag them in some other prominent way. Remember that these dates are deadlines for completing the requirements, not for signing up for the necessary classes. If you're a procrastinator, consider moving your deadlines up several months to give yourself some breathing room if circumstances interfere with your plans.

Staying current involves more than meeting recertification requirements; it's all about keeping your skills up to date and staying at the top of your field. To do this you should invest in periodic training, whether or not it is specifically geared toward recertification requirements.

FIGURE 14.1
Brainbench
(formerly
tekmetrics)
certification
transcript system

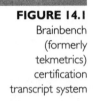

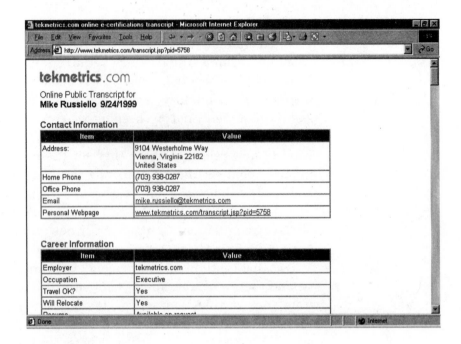

Where to Get Continuing Ed

Continuing education that will help you pass recertification exams can be obtained from many different sources, including:

* Academic institutions, such as community colleges and technical schools
* Independent training companies
* Courses and seminars offered by your certification sponsor
* One-day seminars and conferences
* Employer-sponsored training
* Self-guided study programs

Some certification sponsors don't really care where you obtain your training for recertification, while others require that classes be taken through their authorized training network. It's a good idea to double-check that you don't have to take a specific upgrade course from your sponsor in order to qualify for the recertification exam.

Academic Courses

One of the most common continuing education options is to take classes from a university, college, technical school, or other academic institution. In response to the demand for adult education alternatives, most academic institutions offer evening and weekend classes that will fit into your schedule. You'll also have a wide array of courses from which to choose, which will make it easier to find something that will benefit you professionally, help you meet your recertification requirements, and be interesting, too. Because these are approved college courses, you'll also be able to apply the credits for classes you complete toward a degree program. That means you can get your continuing education to serve double duty: fulfilling both recertification requirements and requirements toward traditional educational goals, such as a master's degree.

The cost of college courses varies widely, depending on the school and level of the course. In general, you can expect to pay up to several hundred dollars per course. If you decide to take classes at one of the ivy league colleges, you can, of course, expect your costs to be much higher. You may also have to pay administrative fees; however, these fees often entitle you to use other facilities on the campus, such as the library and computer lab. If you don't care about receiving a grade, you may be able to attend the course on an audit basis, which will remove test pressures and cut your costs substantially.

It's a good idea to preview the computer lab if you'll be using it in your coursework. In an unfortunate paradox, despite their role as learning centers, many academic computer labs lag behind the commercial sector when it comes to adopting modern technology. If lab work will be an important part of your training, find out before you enroll if the computer equipment is up to par.

Classes will meet two to three times a week for several months, following either the semester or term calendar. In many cases, your classmates will be undergraduate students with less work and life experience than yourself. If you like being a mentor, this may appeal to you, but if you prefer mixing with other experienced professionals, you may find a shortage of them in your class. One way to find out what your fellow students are apt to be like is to meet with the professor for the course and ask.

Chapter 7 goes into detail on the features, benefits, and drawbacks of various learning options.

Independent Training Companies

Independent training companies offer many conveniences for working professionals. Their courses are compact and intense, often spanning just a few days or even a single day. This makes it possible to complete continuing education requirements in a shorter time. Training companies are also more likely to offer up-to-the-minute curriculums, high-end computer equipment, and certified instructors with ongoing interaction in their areas of expertise. All these can translate into an opportunity for you to learn a lot, fast.

Courses and seminars offered by training companies run from one day to a week or more. Prices vary accordingly, and you can expect to pay up to several thousand dollars for a multi-day, hands-on workshop. A one-day seminar will cost much less, possibly even under $100.

Increasingly, training businesses are bringing their courses to the Internet to make them accessible to more potential clients. These courses are often self-paced, include contact with an instructor, and offer interaction with other students via message boards and online conferences. Figure 14.2 shows one of these virtual classrooms.

Whether a course is offered over the Internet or in the classroom, it's important to investigate the quality of the facilities and trainers ahead of time. Although it's possible to complete an inferior course and use it to satisfy recertification requirements, doing so is really a waste of your money and time. The point of recertification is to continue to build your skills, and complying with the spirit of the requirements will serve you much better than just squeezing by.

FIGURE 14.2
Learning online

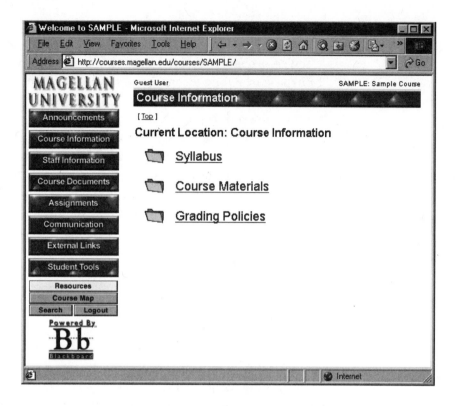

Training Offered by Certification Sponsors

Your certification sponsor will sometimes connect you with the educational opportunities necessary to maintain your certification. The sponsor will either offer the training itself or direct you to authorized training centers that do. If your sponsor operates an annual conference or trade show, attending it may earn some of the credits you need. You'll also get a chance to hobnob with other experts about the ins, outs, and job outlook of your field. In many cases, such conferences are free to individuals certified through the sponsor's program, although you'll still have to pay for travel and lodging. You'll find sponsor-provided training listed on the certification program's Web page and in literature mailed to you.

One-Day Conferences and Seminars

You've probably received invitations to free seminars whose main purpose is selling a company's new product or new version release of an existing product. The seminars are given in major cities across the country, usually in hotel facilities.

Although these events are largely sales events, they do offer an opportunity to learn about new features and usually include demonstrations of many of the product functions. These can prove especially useful to holders of product-specific certifications. Generally, to update such certifications you are encouraged to take an upgrade exam. Attending one of these seminars can give you a feel for how extensive the changes are and may even provide the information you'll need to upgrade. If you're lucky, you might even win the traditional drawing for a free copy of the software.

Company Training

Sometimes organizations provide training to employees by bringing in outside trainers to provide instruction to a whole department. If there is a particular technology that you want to learn about and that you think would also prove valuable to other members of your company, consider mounting a campaign to persuade your employer to provide the training. In a written proposal, explain exactly what the training you're recommending is and how it would benefit the company (for example through increased productivity, less down time, better product support, increased employee retention, or enhanced reseller status). Your document should include a cost benefit analysis showing how the training will benefit the company's bottom line. You should also do some preliminary research exploring who might teach the course and how much it would cost, and include those results in your report. In addition to getting training for yourself, this route has the added benefit of demonstrating that you are concerned with ways the company can maintain or improve its competitive edge, which, on its own, will benefit how the higher-ups view you.

Free Training for Contractors

As certification becomes more widespread, information technology profession-als are increasingly eager to become and stay certified. This is true of contrac-tors, consultants, and traditional employees. Often, continuing education is facili-tated or provided for by a corporate employer, but now contractors can receive that benefit too. Although contractors and consultants don't usually have a single employer, they often deal with recruiting and placement firms. In order to attract and keep top talent, some of these firms have begun to offer free training (mostly through CBT) to attract contractors. In some cases, you don't even have to work for the firm, just register with them for potential future assignments. They get another contractor to call on and you get free training, and maybe even a placement that's just what you've been looking for. One such firm is Aquent Partners (**www.aquentpartners.com**).

Do-It-Yourself Options

One of the most cost-effective routes to continuing education is self-study. In addition to affordability, this option has the advan-tages of being self-paced, widely available, and obtainable in a variety of formats. Unlike instructor-led options, you can also return to the material again for reference or review. Self-study options include:

* Books, manuals, and workbooks
* Video instruction
* Computer-based training (CBT) software
* Internet-based courses
* Hands-on exploration

You can find products in all of these categories by browsing the Internet using one of the popular search engines. Videos, books, and software can also be found in the computer section of major book stores or through advertisements in computer trade publica-tions. The quality of self-study materials varies widely, so make every effort to try before you buy. You'll often be able to accom-plish this by sampling trial versions of software or browsing through printed materials before purchasing. If you cannot do this, verify that a return policy exists so you can get your money back if the materials don't meet your expectations. Ask friends and coworkers who have experience with self-study materials which vendors they recommend and if they've had any bad experiences with particular products or companies.

Many certified professionals find that the best way to keep current with particular technologies is to obtain regular hands-on access to the software and/or hardware. You'll find it worthwhile to uncover a way to get your hands on a variety of Linux implementation and versions on a regular, ongoing basis. This is easiest for those who have equipment at their place of employment and can work with it during breaks, lunch time, or after hours. Individuals who don't have suitable access through an employer sometimes set up the platform and/or software at home—i.e. create a home lab. Doing so makes it possible to experiment with new options and technologies at your leisure without the risk of compromising a critical business computer system. You may already have a home lab setup that you used to earn certification in the first place. Instead of dismantling it, add to it over time and use it to keep your skills sharp.

Training Directories

As the need for continuing technical education has become more pronounced, a number of training resource clearinghouses, which connect students with learning resources, have appeared on the Web. These contain contact information and links to vendors who offer courses and training products. They are a good starting place when you're researching learning options for a particular topic. Yahoo!'s directory pages will also prove valuable in your search. Useful pages include:

* **www.linuxtraining.org/index.html**—Dan York's online compilation of Linux training materials and instruction. Figure 14.3 shows this site.
* **www.trainingnet.com**—This includes computer and non-computer training resources and covers a variety of training formats.
* **www.yahoo.com/Business_and_Economy/Companies/ Computers/Software/Training/**—Yahoo!'s index of comput-

er-training software vendors. It even has a special certification preparation section.

Professional books can be purchased in traditional bookstores or through online outlets such as Amazon.com (**www.amazon.com**) or fatbrain.com (**www.fatbrain.com**).

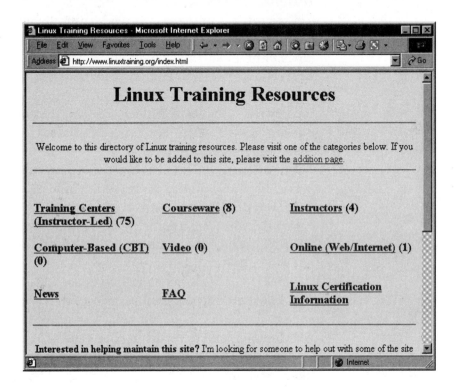

FIGURE 14.3
Linux training
directory

Bonus Benefits

In addition to maintaining your status as a certified professional, keeping up with recertification requirements provides other potential bonuses. Completing continuing education requirements will often serve double duty by providing additional career-boosting benefits not directly related to the certification.

Training venues are a prime networking opportunity. Through them you'll connect with other professionals in your field. By establishing relationships with these people, you'll build connections that can help you in many ways. When you meet another particularly competent professional (whether online or in person), obtain contact information and take note of that person's operating environment and other areas of expertise. Offer your information in return. When either of you encounters a technical dilemma, you'll be able to call on each other as problem-solving resources.

Connections you make through training forums will also build your career network in another important way: by extending your circle of professional acquaintances, you'll build a web of personal connections you may wish to draw on when seeking new employment in the future. Word of mouth is an often underestimated force when it comes to finding excellent job opportunities, and it's one you'll be able to use to great advantage if you know many other individuals in your field.

Continuing education courses can serve double duty in other ways. If you decide to pursue an academic degree at a future time, you may be able to parlay the same courses that earned you recertification into credits applied toward your degree. This has the potential to save you a great deal of time and money.

Going after an advanced degree isn't the only way to get your training to count twice. You may also be able to choose courses that maintain your current certification *and* apply toward obtaining another one. This trick, which requires careful planning and coordination, makes recertification especially painless.

Don't forget to incorporate significant training into your professional resumé. It's an easy way to illustrate your abilities and the initiative you've taken to stay current in the industry, traits that are considered desirable by employers. A good way to include this information is to add a continuing education/continuing professional development heading under the education section of your resume and list the course or seminar titles there, along with the dates you completed them.

Record Keeping

When you investigate the details of the continuing education requirements for your certification, be sure to inquire about the details of submitting evidence that you've met them. If your certification vendor has an online tracking system, that will be the key resource you'll use to verify that your recertification information has been correctly recorded. You should also keep test fee receipts and test score reports just in case their records go awry—as evidence to back up your assertions. Make sure all your course documentation includes dates and descriptions. If you receive a simple, terse receipt, write the details on it yourself before filing it away.

Besides having evidence that you've met recertification requirements, there's another reason to be scrupulous about saving your receipts: tax time. Because this training is undertaken to further your skills in your current career, you may be able to deduct the costs as employee expenses (or, if you're self-employed, as business expenses).

To obtain any deductions you're entitled to, record every expense associated with your educational pursuits, including study materials, tuition charges, and even travel and lodging. If you drive to and from a course, record the mileage and dates, too. If you complete your own tax return, you'll need the information on file to support your claims. If you use a professional tax preparer, you'll need to provide this information so he/she can obtain the deductions for you. Tax preparers don't always remember to ask every question they should, so be sure to bring up your education expenses yourself.

Completing recertification requirements is typically a simple process. These requirements provide a preplanned route for your continued professional development; all you have to do is follow it. Doing so will pay off in numerous ways, including bringing networking opportunities and adding to your sheaf of credentials. On the other hand, if you let your certification lapse because of inattention, you'll pay the price with increased hassle and costs.

Chapter 15

Another Certification?

Now that you've completed your journey to certification, you face
another important career decision: Are you going to do it again?
Just as some people obtain multiple academic degrees in the course
of climbing the career ladder, you can combine various certifications to further boost your career. Earning certifications is typically
faster and less expensive than obtaining academic degrees.

As part of a 1997 Gartner Group study sponsored by Sylvan
Prometric, IBM, Microsoft, Novell, and Sybase, more than 7,000
certification candidates were asked about professional designations they already held. Two-thirds of respondents reported
already holding one or more certifications prior to the one they
were currently pursuing. Less than one third (31%) were earning
their first certification. In contrast, when the same question was
asked back in 1994, more than half of respondents (56%) were in
the process of earning their first certification. These data (illus-
trated in Figure 15.1) indicate a trend toward earning multiple
certifications.

FIGURE 15.1
A trend toward
multiple
certifications

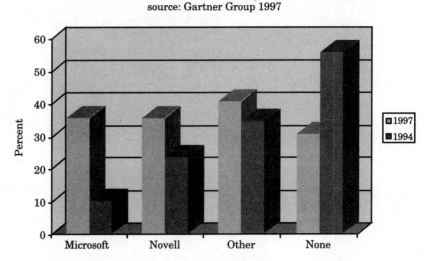

More Can Be Better

There are several reasons you might want to consider going after
additional professional certifications. They include:

* Staying abreast of technological change
* Broadening your market
* Increasing your technical skill level
* Personal pride and a desire to excel

A few technologies endure for long periods, such as the COBOL programming language. But most fade almost as quickly as they become hot when, inevitably, something newer and better comes along. Professional certification programs can be used as tools for technical excellence. Although many in the computer field are skilled at self-instruction, it's difficult to know what you need to learn about a technology that's new to you. A certification program for that technology will outline the path to expertise; all you have to do is follow it.

Adding additional certifications to your professional portfolio can significantly broaden your base of potential clients and employers. You'll be qualified for and able to choose from a wider range of positions and employers. Multiple certifications also tag you as a professional who takes initiative and someone who is a "go-getter." These traits are looked upon favorably by many potential clients and employers.

Some certifications are especially complementary. For example, people who are both Cisco and NT certified will find plenty of employment opportunities. That's because computer environments today are as blended as they are, more often than not incorporating multiple vendors, products, and platforms. Individuals able to integrate the components of these environments have an additional edge in the marketplace.

QUOTE

Benefiting from Multiple Certifications

I have multiple Linux certifications because there is no standard exam. Each Linux exam I've taken has focused on different issues and objectives. Until a standard is agreed upon, I guess I'll just take every certification exam I can in order to demonstrate knowledge of the subject materials.

I see my certifications as a progression throughout my career thus far. I started in a Novell environment and my certifications reflect that. From there I learned TCP/IP and Routing and UNIX System Administration. I think my certifications show a map of where I've been and what I've been able to learn and, in some cases, master. And since I've taken them by choice and not due to job requirements, I believe they also reflect initiative and ambition.

As far as drawbacks, I can see that one person can only hold so much information. In learning each new thing, there is a tendency to lose previous knowledge and expertise. One cannot be good at everything, but I think it is important to have an understanding of all the pieces of the IT puzzle and to be open to possibilities.

—*Jeff Miller, RHCE, dmCLA, MCNE, CCNA, and others*

In addition to the more tangible benefits already mentioned, there's another reason people decide to earn numerous professional certifications: personal fulfillment. Holding professional certifications in more than one area can be a source of pride. It also feeds the appetite for excellence and urge to learn that many computer people possess. Figure 15.2 shows a Web page where certified pros boast of their accomplishments.

Drawbacks

Although adding more certifications to your professional credentials is largely a positive move, there are a few drawbacks of which you should be aware. The most commonly encountered complication concerns logistics. Once you progress beyond your second certification, tracking the continuing education requirements requires more careful attention. You'll have more forms to complete and submit on time, more requirements with which to comply.

QUICK TIP

Individuals who hold multiple certifications may be able to get the education they complete to count double, or more, if it meets the qualifications for several of the programs. There aren't any rules that limit you to applying continuing education activity toward only one certification.

Because of the added complexity of managing several certifications on an ongoing basis, it becomes especially important to use a calendar to track and comply with continuing education deadlines.

VICTOR DUBIN'S CERTIFICATION & NETWORKING PAGE

Certification Wall of Fame

And Current Champs Are:

Anders Gustafsson   6 (SIX) Novell tests a day

Ed Erichson   3 (I&C, D&I, AA) Novell tests a day

Pasha Pergamenchik   Possibly world's youngest CNE & MCPS (14 years old)

Riley K. Fowle	Possibly world's youngest MCSD (19 years old), all four tests in a month.
Herb Martin	All 6 MCSE tests in 11 days. Second place.
Michael Swisher	All 6 MCSE tests in one month, inc one beta
Undell Williams	4 tests in one day - 4.1 Admin, 4.1 I&C, NTS 3.51, NTW 3.51 6 more in three days - S&S, Access 95, D&I, SQL 6 IMP, TCPIP 3.51, Win95
Mark Spain	3 Novell tests in 20 (!!!) minutes - Can you beat it?
Jon Spencer	3 Novell tests(D&I, 3I&C, 3AA in 2 hours 15 minutes,
Pamela Forsyth	(Second) Largest number of certifications from different vendors (5): MCNE, CNX, CLP, CCIE, former CBS
Jens Stark	Fastest single test - Novell NT (200) in 7 (seven) minutes.

Cameron Brendon   **Absolute** record so far: CNE, MCSE, A+ in FIVE!!! months.
                           The guy claims he has personal life too. (G)

Adrian Roni Havas Adrian Roni Havas	**All seven (7)** CNE tests in one hour and 15 minutes, inc 15 minutes brake. Unbeatable since 1993. It seems Rony was really in a hurry. (There were nice old days when sugar was more sweat, water more wet and tests more easy)
Duane D Thilmony of Minneapolis	Six CNE4 tests (525, 605, 801, 804, 532, 200) in 32 days.
Avery Robert	**MS Win95 best score** so far (957 of 1000 in 18 minutes).
David Yarashus	**Largest number of records here** - all that in 2.5 years!!! 1. **Largest** number of different vendor certs - MCNE(Novell), MCSE(MS), CCIE(Cisco), CNX(NGC), Lan Server engineer(IBM), Bay Networks Optivity, 3Com Wizard 2. **MCSE in FOUR (4)** days. 3. **Cheapest** way to CNE (two of seven tests paid, the rest free beta) 4. **Largest** space occupied here (VBG)

My sincere and to them

Your wanna be listed here too? Email me:  71660.117@compuserve.com

HOME   Ms scores | Novell scores | Other scores | Certification News | Preparation Tools | Resources |
              Test Taking Rules | TS Tips & Facts | Links | Wall of Fame | Search Engines | Links to Me | My CV

Broken links? Misprints? Wrong info? Questions? Please feel free to email me at
71660.117@compuserve.com

Earning and maintaining multiple certifications will also add to your professional expenses. It's likely that at least some of the training options you exercise to obtain and maintain the certifications will involve significant expense. Don't forget to apply the money-saving advice in Chapter 5 to earning additional certifications just as you did to earning the first one. That includes going after outside funding and remembering to take any tax deductions you are due.

A final potential drawback you should be aware of only applies when you top three certifications. It's the possibility that some people will look at your list of certifications and think that it's not possible for you to actually be technically competent in all of the areas you hold certifications for, and then to suspect that the certifications represent an ability to pass tests more than professional expertise. You can counteract this potential backlash by finding additional ways to demonstrate that your broad competencies are genuine. If you have plenty of diverse experience included on your resumé, that should take care of it. Otherwise, you may have to do some additional convincing of potential clients.

One way around this potential image problem is to mention only those certifications which are especially relevant when applying for a particular job or contract. You don't have to list every one you hold if you think it will work against you. On the other hand, if you're after a senior position, having multiple certifications on your resume is likely to work in your favor rather than against you.

Selecting Additional Certifications

When choosing additional certifications to pursue, follow the same process that helped you decide which certification to make your first. You'll also need to decide on a strategy—do you want to obtain an array of complementary certifications or go for diversity. Each option has its benefits.

Complementary certifications are those directly related and likely to prove useful within a single work site. For example, holding several networking certifications will make you attractive to the many organizations that operate heterogeneous networking environments. You can think of this as deepening your marketing options within a particular market segment. Multiple complementary certifications often increase your level of expertise in a particular area to the extent where you can command premium rates as a senior person. For Linux, this could mean adding endorsements or certifications for more than one distribution.

Choosing to go with a strategy of diversity, on the other hand, widens your customer base to include additional market segments. For example, if you hold a Sair Linux/GNU Certified Engineer designation and decide to add a security-related certification, you will be increasing your access to additional segments of the computer job market. An added benefit of the diversity strategy is that it makes it possible for you to have more variety in your work, choosing different types of assignments that you find interesting.

Once you've settled on an overall strategy, start browsing through the available programs to determine which ones meet your qualifications and appeal to you in terms of cost and time factors. Places to check include:

* The resource listings included with this book.
* Certification information on your certification vendor's Web site; you may find your next certification goal comes from the same vendor.
* Certification news pages for other sponsors; new certifications are being developed at a fairly fast rate, and if you want to be aware of all your options, you'll need to do your homework and keep up to date with certification news.
* Professional acquaintances who hold certifications; ask them for opinions of the programs in which they have participated.
* One or more of the certification discussion forums mentioned elsewhere in this book; visit these and post a message mentioning your current certification(s) and goals, and seeking advice and suggestions about which program to look into next.

When you've settled on a certification that will enhance your portfolio of professional qualifications, remember to pursue it using the skills you have already learned. Choose learning options that cater to your learning styles and budget. Having already been through the process once, you should know what those are. Go back and do a quick review of the study tips and advice contained in Chapter 9 to refresh your memory on efficient study habits.

The Bottom Line

Cisco certification and other certifications can be a valuable career-boosting tool, or more accurately, set of tools. Like any other tools, certifications can be used properly or improperly. Using an adjustable wrench to pound in a nail may be somewhat effective, but using it to tighten a bolt will be infinitely more so. As with tools, the key to successful use of certifications is to match the tool to the job. This is true whether selecting your first certification, or your fifth.

When you take the time to select and earn appropriate certifications, you're already advancing yourself toward the front of the pack. But if you stop there, you're not getting all that you can out of the credentials. Take those certifications and put them to work for you. Advertise your professional status. Use certifications to land jobs. Employ them to keep your professional edge. Exploit them to launch your career to new heights.

Part 4
References

Certification
Fact Sheets

Brainbench

9104 Westerholme Way, Suite 100
Vienna, VA 22182
URL: http://www.brainbench.com/
Phone: 703-437-4800
E-mail: support@brainbench.com

Brainbench e-Certified Professional–Linux Administrator
Skill Rating: ★★

Date Initiated: 1999

Primary URL: http://www.brainbench.com/cert

Summary: For Linux administrators.

Initial Requirements: Must pass one exam ($25–$50 after free trial period ends). Exam is administered via the Web. The exam contains 40 questions drawn from a larger test bank of questions. Passing score is 2.75 out of a possible 5.0. Scoring 4.0 or higher earns the Master designation.

Continuing Requirements: Must recertify annually.

Online Resources: An outline of exam topic areas is available on the Brainbench Web site.

Offline Resources: Many books on Linux administration are available through book stores, both online and off.

CyberTech Institute, Inc.

6029 Memorial Highway
Tampa, FL USA 33615
URL: http://www.getcertified.com
Phone: (888) 467-1500   **Fax:** (813) 243-8293
E-mail: info@cy-tech.com

CyberTech Linux Certification   Skill Rating: ★★

Date Initiated: 1999

Primary URL: http://www.getcertified.com/coi/describ1.asp?
Subject=LNX131

Summary: For individuals who administer Linux

Initial Requirements: Must pass CyberTech Linux certification
exam ($95). Exam is multiple choice and contains 100 questions.
Exam is administered through CyberTech's own network of test
providers.

Continuing Requirements: None as this book was going to
press.

Perks:

＊ Certificate
＊ Inclusion in directory

Online Resources: Exam fee also brings access to online study
materials for your certification, including an online study guide
and practice tests.

Linux Professional Institute

URL: www.lpi.org
E-mail: info@lpi.org

Linux Professional Institute Certified Level 1 (LPIC 1)
Skill Rating: ★★

Date Initiated: 1999

Primary URL: http://www.lpi.org/

Summary: For individuals who are a step beyond Linux power-user level

Initial Requirements: Must pass three exams. The first two are on general Linux knowledge. The third is specific to a major Linux distribution of your choice. As the exams were still under development as this was being written, pricing information is not available.

Continuing Requirements: None.

Perks: None at this time, but reportedly in the works.

Offline Resources: Many books on Linux are available through book stores, both online and off.

Linux Professional Institute Certified Level 2 (LPIC 2)
Skill Rating: ★★★

Date Initiated: 1999

Primary URL: http://www.lpi.org/

Summary: Still under development, this is LPI's mid level certification for advanced Linux administration and optimization.

Initial Requirements: You must first earn LPIC Level 1. In addition, you must pass two exams: an advanced administration exam and a Linux optimization exam. Details are still under development.

Continuing Requirements: None.

Perks: None at this time, but reportedly in the works.

Online Resources: As they are developed, exam objectives will become available on the LPI Web site.

Offline Resources: Many books on Linux are available through book stores, both online and off.

Linux Professional Institute Certified Level 3 (LPIC 3)
Skill Rating: ★★★★

Date Initiated: 1999

Primary URL: http://www.lpi.org/

Summary: For very advanced level Linux personnel. This is still under development with a long way to go before this certification is available to the public.

Initial Requirements: You must first earn LPIC Level 2. In addition, you must pass two exams, called specializations. Options for the specializations include: Windows Integration, Internet Server, Database Server, Security, Firewalls and Encryption, and Kernel Internals and Device Drivers. Exam details are still under development.

Continuing Requirements: None.

Perks: None at this time, but reportedly in the works.

Online Resources: As they are developed, exam objectives will become available on the LPI Web site.

Offline Resources: Many books on Linux are available through book stores, both online and off.

Prosofttraining.com

2333 North Broadway, 3rd floor
Santa Anna, CA USA 92706
URL: http://www.prosofttraining.com
Phone: 800-776-7638   **Fax:** 714-953-1212
E-mail: learn@prosofttraining.com

Prosoft Linux Certified Administrator   Skill Rating: ★★

Date Initiated: 1999

Primary URL: http://www.prosofttraining.com/certification/lin-uxcertification.htm

Summary: For individuals who administer Linux environments.

Initial Requirements: Must pass Linux Administrator exam ($150). The exam lasts 75 minutes and contains 60 multiple choice questions. Passing score is 75% or better with no less than 70% on either of the two exam modules. Two recommended (but not required) courses are a available to help you prepare: Linux Fundamentals (2 days/$995), and Linux System and Network Administration (3 days/$1295).

Perks:

❋ Certificate

Online Resources: Although exam objectives are not available on the certification Web site, course objectives are.

Offline Resources: The instructor-led courses for this certification are offered through several different vendors, including COMPUSA, ExecuTrain, and IBM. Pricing varies.

Red Hat, Inc.
4201 Research Commons, Suite 100
Research Triangle Park, NC USA 27709
URL: http://www.redhat.com
Phone: 800-454-5503 x294   **Fax:** 919-547-0024
E-mail: training@redhat.com

Red Hat Certified Engineer (RHCE)   Skill Rating: ★★★

Date Initiated: 1998

Primary URL: http://www.redhat.com/products/training_
overview.html

Summary: For individuals who work with Linux, and Red Hat
Linux in particular. This is a system administrator-level certification. Successful candidates will have significant Linux experience
to draw upon. It is especially useful (required) for persons working in Red Hat's Support Partner program.

Initial Requirements: To earn the RHCE certification you must
pass a hands-on lab exam ($749). The closed-book exam consists
of three elements: a written test (1–2 hours); a server install and
network services configuration lab (2 hours); and a diagnostics
and troubleshooting lab (3 hours). It must be taken at Red Hat's
facilities in Durham, North Carolina.

   The lab exam is intended to verify that you can install and configure Red Hat Linux; understand limitations of hardware; can
configure basic networking and file systems; can configure the X
Windowing System; can configure basic security, can set up common network (IP) services, carry out basic diagnostics and troubleshooting, and perform essential Red Hat Linux system administration.

Continuing Requirements: Must recertify with new releases.

Perks:

✳ Certificate

Online Resources: There are many free online sources of Linux
documentation and how-to articles. Red Hat has a free online

preparation guide at **www.redhat.com/products/training_ examprep.html**. Exam schedules are also available on the Red Hat site.

Offline Resources: A corresponding recommended, but not required, course is available through Red Hat and also through Global Knowledge. The class, RHCE 300, runs 5 days and costs $2498, including taking the lab exam on the last day.

Red Hat Certified Engineer II (RHCEII)
Skill Rating: *Unrated*

Date Initiated: Pending

Summary: Although this certification has not been fully defined yet, it is expected to be a more advanced version of the RHCE designation, and to deal with advanced skills and concepts in system administration, networking, and security issues on Red Hat Linux.

Red Hat Certified Examiner (RHCX)
Skill Rating: ★★★

Date Initiated: 1999

Primary URL: http://www.redhat.com/products/training_ rh310.html

Summary: For individuals who wish to become qualified to administer/proctor the RHCE exam. Although it isn't really a trainer certification, it is required in order for you to become an instructor for Red Hat certification courses.

Initial Requirements: Must also attend Red Hat Examiner course ($2498) and pass associated exam. Must hold RHCE or earn this during examiner class. Course and test are administered at Red Hat's Durham, North Carolina location and in Stockely Park, Uxbridge, England.

Perks:

✳ Certificate

Sair, Inc.
503 Heritage Center
Oxford, MS USA 38655
URL: http://www.linuxcertification.com
Phone: 800-777-4210   **Fax:** 601-236-1794
E-mail: kevin@sairinc.com

Linux Certified Professional (LCP)   Skill Rating: ★

Date Initiated: 1999

Primary URL: http://www.linuxcertification.org/

Summary: For individuals who wish to demonstrate distribution-independent Linux knowledge. This certification is typically earned as part of the path toward Sair's Linux Certified Administrator (LCA) certification.

Initial Requirements: Must pass one exam either Installation & Configuration (I&C1) or Systems Administration (SA1). Exams contain 50 questions and last an hour. Passing score is 74% or better.

Continuing Requirements: None at this time. You are expected to move up to a higher-level certification.

Perks:

✳ Certificate

Online Resources: Sample questions and detailed information on the individual exams are available on the certification Web site.

Offline Resources: John Wiley & Sons is scheduled to publish a series of test preparation guides for Sair certifications. Training is also available through Accredited Centers for Education (ACEs).

Linux/GNU Certified Administrator (LCA)   Skill Rating: ★★

Date Initiated: 1999

Primary URL: http://www.linuxcertification.org/

Summary: For Linux systems administrators and power users. This certification is NOT distribution specific.

Initial Requirements: Must pass four exams ($396). Exams are: Installation & Configuration (I&C1), Systems Administration (SA1), Networking (NET1), and Security, Ethics & Privacy (SEP1). As soon as you pass either I&C1 or SA1 you become a Sair Linux Certified Professional (LCP). Exams include true/false and multiple choice questions. Exams contain 50 questions and last an hour. Passing score is 74% or better.

Continuing Requirements: Expected to appear in the future.

Perks:

* Certificate
* Use of logo
* Referral service
* Inclusion in directory
* Beta participation
* Access to restricted forum

Online Resources: Sample questions and detailed information on the individual exams are available on the certification Web site.

Offline Resources: John Wiley & Sons is scheduled to publish a series of test preparation guides for Sair certifications. Training is also available through Accredited Centers for Education (ACEs).

Linux/GNU Certified Engineer (LCE)   Skill Rating: ★★★

Date Initiated: 2000

Primary URL: http://www.linuxcertification.org/

Summary: For individuals who act as Linux system managers. This is the second (middle) level of Sair's Linux certification program. This certification is NOT distribution specific.

Initial Requirements: Must hold LCA. Must pass four LCE exams ($396). Exams are: Installation & Configuration (I&C2), Systems Administration (SA2), Networking (NET2), and Security, Ethics & Privacy (SEP2). Exams include true/false and multiple-choice questions. The exams are still under development and have not been rolled out. Check Sair's site for the latest information.

Continuing Requirements: Expected to appear in the future.

Perks:

* Certificate
* Use of logo
* Referral service
* Inclusion in directory
* Beta participation
* Access to restricted forum

Online Resources: Sample questions and detailed information on the individual exams are available on the certification Web site.

Offline Resources: John Wiley & Sons is scheduled to publish a series of test preparation guides for Sair certifications. Training is also available through Accredited Centers for Education (ACEs).

Master Linux/GNU Certified Engineer (MLCE)
Skill Rating: ★★★★

Date Initiated: 2000

Primary URL: http://www.linuxcertification.org/

Summary: For senior Linux systems managers. This is the third (highest) level of Sair's Linux certification program. This certification is NOT distribution specific.

Initial Requirements: Must hold LCE. Must pass four MLCE exams ($396). Exams are: Installation & Configuration (I&C3), Systems Administration (SA3), Networking (NET3), and Security, Ethics & Privacy (SEP3). Exams include true/false and multiple-choice questions. The exams are still under development and have not been rolled out. Check Sair's site for the latest information.

Continuing Requirements: Undetermined at this time.

Perks:

* Certificate
* Use of logo
* Referral service
* Inclusion in directory
* Beta participation
* Access to restricted forum

Online Resources: Sample questions and detailed information on the individual exams are available on the certification Web site.

Offline Resources: John Wiley & Sons is scheduled to publish a series of test preparation guides for Sair certifications. Training is also available through Accredited Centers for Education (ACEs).

Linux/GNU Certified Trainer   Skill Rating: ★★★★

Date Initiated: 1999

Primary URL: http://www.linuxcertification.org/

Summary: For individuals who want to teach Sair Linux/GNU certification preparation classes at Accredited Center for Education (ACE) sites, colleges and universities, or independently.

Initial Requirements: Must demonstrate proficiency as a trainer. Most people who pursue this certification are already technical trainers with a UNIX background, but that's not required. Often candidates attend the 5-day Train-the-Trainer session ($1,000). Must also pass the exam for the course you are going to teach ($99).

Continuing Requirements: Sair may require additional training from time to time.

Perks:

* Certificate
* Use of logo
* Lapel pin
* Referral service
* Inclusion in directory
* Product discounts
* Access to restricted forum

Online Resources: A schedule of train-the-trainer sessions can be found on the certification Web page.

Appendix **B**

Certification
Quick Reference

Certification Vendor/Name	Distribution(s)	Min Cost	# Exams	Lab Exam	Skill Level	Prereqs
Brainbench						
Brainbench Certified Linux Administrator	Distribution independent	$25–$50	1	No	2	No
CyberTech						
CyberTech Linux Certification	Red Hat, Caldera OpenLinux Lite	$95	1	No	2	No
Linux Professional Institute (LPI)						
Linux Professional Institute Certified (LPIC) Level 1	Distribution neutral combined with choice of distribution specific tracks	Undetermined at press time	3	No	2	No
LPIC Level 2	Distribution neutral combined with choice of distribution specific tracks	Undetermined at press time	2	No	3	LPIC1
LPIC Level 3	Distribution neutral combined with choice of distribution specific tracks	Undetermined at press time	2	No	4	LPIC2
Prosofttraining.com						
Linux Certified Administrator	Distribution neutral	$150–$2,440	1	No	2	No
Red Hat Inc						
Red Hat Certified Engineer (RHCE)	Red Hat, version specific	$749–$2,498	1 multi-part	Yes	3	No
Red Hat Certified Engineer II (RHCE II)—still under development	Red Hat, version specific	Undetermined at press time			4	Unknown
Red Hat Certified Examiner (RHCX)	Red Hat, version specific	$2,498	1 in-class assessment	Yes	3	RHCE

Certification Vendor/ Name	Distribution(s)	Min Cost	# Exams	Lab Exam	Skill Level	Prereqs
Sair						
Linux Certified Professional (LCP)	Distribution independent	$99	1	No	1	No
Linux/GNU Certified Administrator (LCA)	Distribution independent	$396	4	No	2	No
Linux/GNU Certified Engineer (LCE)	Distribution independent	$396	4	No	3	LCA
Master Linux/GNU Certified Engineer (MLCE)	Distribution independent	$396	4	No	4	LCE
Linux/GNU Certified Trainer	Distribution independent	$99	1 in-class assessment	Yes	Unrated	No

Appendix C

Certification Study Aids and Linux Resources

Publications

Linux Certification Books

Linux Exam Prep
By: DeeAnn LeBlanc and Kathleen Scanlon
ISBN: 1576105679 CD-ROM: Yes
The Coriolis Group; 12/1999; $35.99; 650 pages

LPI Linux Certification Fast Track: Level 1 Basic Administration
By: New Riders Development Team
ISBN: 0735709424 CD-ROM: No
New Riders; 11/1999; $39.99; 500 pages

Linux in a Nutshell: A Desktop Quick Reference, Second Edition
By: Ellen Siever
ISBN: 1565925858 CD-ROM: No
O'Reilly & Associates; 02/1999; $24.95; 632 pages

Red Hat Certified Engineer Linux Study Guide
By: Syngress Media
ISBN: 0072121556 CD-ROM: yes
Osborne McGraw-Hill; 11/1999; $41.99; 704 pages

RHCE Exam Cram
By: Kara Pritchard
ISBN: 1576104877 CD-ROM: No
The Coriolis Group; 10/1999; $23.99; 400 pages

Sair Linux & GNU Certification Level 1: Installation & Configuration
By: Tobin Maginnis
ISBN: 0471369780 CD-ROM: No
John Wiley & Sons; 12/1999; $34.00; 304 pages

Sair Linux & GNU Certification Level 1: System Administration
By: Tobin Maginnis
ISBN: 0471369764 CD-ROM: No
John Wiley & Sons; 3/2000; $34.99; 304 pages

Sair Linux & GNU Certification Level 1: Networking
By: Tobin Maginnis
ISBN: 0471369772 CD-ROM: No
John Wiley & Sons; 1/2000; $34.99; 304 pages

Sair Linux & GNU Certification Level 1: Security, Ethics, & Privacy
By: Tobin Maginnis
ISBN: 0471369756 CD-ROM: No
John Wiley & Sons; 2/2000; $34.99; 304 pages

General Linux Books

A Practical Guide to Linux
By: Mark G. Sobell
ISBN: 0201895498 CD-ROM: No
Addison-Wesley; 6/1997; $39.95; 1015 pages

Learning Red Hat Linux
By: Bill McCarty
ISBN: 1565926277 CD-ROM: Yes
O'Reilly & Associates; 9/1999; $34.95; 400 pages

Linux Complete
By: Grant Taylor (compiler), Jeremy Crawford (editor)
ISBN: 0782125670 CD-ROM: No
Sybex; 7/1999; $19.99; 985 pages

Linux, Second Edition: Installation, Configuration, and Use
By: Michael Kofler
ISBN: 0201596288 CD-ROM: Yes
Addison-Wesley; 8/1999; $44.95; 800 pages

Linux: The Complete Reference 3rd Edition
By: Richard Petersen
ISBN: 0072121645 CD-ROM: Yes
Osborne McGraw-Hill; 8/1999; $39.99; 929 pages

Mastering Linux
By: Arman Danesh
ISBN: 0782123414 CD-ROM: Yes
Sybex; 1/1999; $39.99; 928 pages

Red Hat Linux 6 Unleashed
By: David Pitts, Bill Ball
ISBN: 0672316897 CD-ROM: Yes
Sams; 7/1999; $39.99; 1252 pages

Running Linux
By: Matt Welsh et al.
ISBN: 156592469X CD-ROM: No
O'Reilly & Associates; 8/1999; $27.96; 752 pages

Special Edition Using Caldera OpenLinux
By: Allen Smart et al.
ISBN: 0789720582 CD-ROM: Yes
Que; 6/1999; $39.99; 1194 pages

Magazines

Linux Journal
(print and online publication with technical articles, business stories, product reviews, Linux news)
P.O. Box 55549
Seattle, WA 98155-0549
Phone: 888-66-LINUX (for subscriptions)
URL: http://www.linuxjournal.com

Linux Today
(online publication featuring Linux news, product reviews, features, jobs)
2236 Morrison Avenue
Kingsport, TN 37660
URL: http://linuxtoday.com

Web Sites

General Linux Resources

Basic Linux Training
URL: http://basiclinux.hypermart.net/basic/
Sponsor: Henry White
Summary: Free, online introduction to Linux course with lessons and assignments and associated mailing list.

What Is Linux?
Sponsor: IBM
URL: http://learn.ibm.be/linux/
Summary: free online presentation

About.com Focus on Linux
URL: http://linux.miningco.com/compute/os/linux/
Summary: Articles, news, technical information, forum, and tutorials on Linux.

CNET Linux Help
URL: http://searchlinux.com/
Summary: Database of over 250,000 Linux questions and answers.

Justlinux
URL: www.justlinux.com
Summary: Large online Linux resource with applications, documentation, development info, jobs, and more.

Linux Frequently Asked Questions with Answers
URL: http://www.linuxdoc.org/FAQ/Linux-FAQ.html
Summary: Extensive FAQ

Linux Links
URL: http://www.linuxlinks.com/
Summary: Linux portal site. Sections for beginners and advanced users.

Linux.com
URL: http://www.linux.com/
Summary: Huge repository of Linux documentation, news, resources, and community.

Linuxcare
URL: http://www.linuxcare.com/
Summary: Provider of Linux support and training. Product comparisons, online seminars, and other Linux news and information.

LinuxHQ
URL: http://www.linuxhq.com/
Summary: Linux documentation and information, kernel patches, newsgroup archives.

Linux International
URL: http://www.li.org/
Summary: A major source of Linux links to newsgroups, mailing lists, and documentation.

The Linux Documentation Project
URL: http://www.linuxdoc.org/
Summary: Central repository of Linux documentation including man pages, howtos, tutorials, FAQs, and general Linux information.

Linux Mall
URL: http://www.linuxmall.com/
Summary: Marketplace for Linux products from many different vendors, along with links to users groups and other Linux resources.

Open Source IT
URL: http://www.opensourceit.com/
Summary: News, shoptalk, and resources related to Linux.

Linux Ports
URL: http://www.ctv.es/USERS/xose/linux/linux_ports.html
Summary: Major collection of info and links to distributions of Linux that run on various platforms/processors.

Linux Users Groups
URL: http://www.linuxlinks.com/UserGroups/
Summary: Index of hundreds of Linux users groups around the world.

Major Linux Distribution Vendors

Caldera OpenLinux
URL: www.calderasystems.com/openstore/

Debian Linux
URL: www.debian.org/distrib/

MkLinux
URL: http://www.mklinux.apple.com/

Red Hat Linux
URL: www.redhat.com/download/

Slackware Linux
URL: ftp.cdrom.com/pub/linux/slackware

SuSE Linux
URL: www.suse.com

Linux Newsgroups

alt.os.linux—General Linux discussion

alt.os.linux.caldera—Caldera distribution of Linux discussion

alt.os.linux.slackware—Slackware distribution of Linux discussion

comp.os.linux.admin—Discussion on administering Linux systems

comp.os.linux.advocacy—Discussion of merits of Linux vs other operating systems

comp.os.linux.alpha—Linux on the Alpha processor discussion

comp.os.linux.announce—Announcements of general interest to the Linux community

comp.os.linux.answers—Postings of Linux FAQs, How-Tos, other help documents

comp.os.linux.apps—Discussion of Linux software applications

comp.os.linux.development.apps—Discussion of application development and porting of applications to Linux

comp.os.linux.development.system—Linux kernel, device driver, and system development discussion

comp.os.linux.hardware—Linux hardware compatibility and configuration

comp.os.linux.help—Questions and advice regarding Linux (similar to comp.os.linux.questions)

comp.os.linux.m68k—Discussion of Linux on Motorola systems

comp.os.linux.misc—General Linux discussion

comp.os.linux.networking—Networking with Linux discussion

comp.os.linux.powerpc—Linux on the PowerPC

comp.os.linux.questions—Questions and advice regarding Linux (similar to comp.os.linux.answers)

comp.os.linux.setup—Setup, installation, and configuration discussions

comp.os.linux.x—Discussion related to the X Window system

Self-Study Vendors (see also Web Sites)

BeachFront Quizzer
Phone: 888-992-3131
E-mail: info@bfq.com
URL: http://ww.bfq.com/linux.html

Bad Dog Computer and Internet Services
Vendor of numerous self-study titles including videos, CBT, and training bundles.
Phone: 888-567-2496
Email: training@baddogcomputer.com
URL: www.baddogcomputer.com/cisco_training/cisco_training.html

CBT Systems
Phone: 888-395-0014
E-mail: salesinfo@cbtsys.com
URL: http://www.cbtsys.com/catalog/curicula/linux.htm

ComputerPREP
Linux courseware
Phone: 800-228-1027
410 N 44th St, Suite 600
Phoenix, AZ 85008
E-mail: computerprep@computerprep.com
URL: http://www.computerprep.com/

DigitalThink
Online Linux courses
Phone: 415-625-4000
1000 Brannan St, Suite 501
San Francisco, CA 94103
E-mail: info@digitalthink.com
URL: http://www.digitalthink.com/catalog/topics/unix.html

Keystone Learning Systems
Learning Linux Video series
Phone: 888-557-2677
2241 Larsen Pkwy
Provo, UT 84606
URL: http://klscorp.com/

Magellan University
Online Linux courses
Phone: 800-4WWWEDU
4320 Campbell Ave, Ste 230
Tucson, AZ 85718
URL: http://magellan.edu/TechEd/Linux/default.htm

Media@Soft Learning Depot
Red Hat Linux training set on video
Phone: 888-477-0123
E-mail: mpp@mpp.com
URL: http://www.msldepot.com/products/linux/default.htm

Wave Technologies
Self-study pack
Phone: 888-204-6143
10845 Olive Blvd, Suite 250
St Louis, MO 63141
URL: http://www.wavetech.com/whats_new/linex/

Yggdrasil Computing
Linux Installation & Beyond video
Phone: 800-261-6630
URL: http://www.yggdrasil.com/Products/intro_video.html

ZD University
Online Linux training (look under Unix)
URL: http://www.zdu.com

Instructor-led Linux Training Vendors

Batky-Howell
Training at various locations across the U.S.
Phone: 800-868-2202
10333 E. Dry Creek Rd, Suite 150
Englewood, CO 80112
E-mail: training@batky-howell.com
URL: http://www.batky-howell.com/curriculum/linuxcur.html

Caldera Systems Education Center
LPI certification preparation and general Linux courses (online course locator on Web site)
Phone: 888-GO-LINUX
389 South 520 West
Lindon, UT 84042
E-mail: info@calderasystems.com
URL: http://www.calderasystems.com/education/courses/

Eklektix, Inc.
Instructor-led training in Boulder CO.
Phone: 877-419-0786
E-mail: training@eklektix.com
URL: http://training.eklektix.com/

Global Knowledge
Linux, focus on Red Hat
Phone: 919-461-8600
P.O. Box 1039
Cary, NC 27512
E-mail: AM_info@globalknowledge.com
URL: http://am.globalknowledge.com/

Hewlett-Packard Education
Classroom training on Red Hat Linux
Phone: 800-472-5277
URL: http://www.hp.com/education/newlinux.html

IBM Education
Classroom Linux training
Phone: 800-426-8322
E-mail: pnielsen@us.ibm.com
URL: http://www-3.ibm.com/services/learning/linux.html

Institute for Technology Training and Excellence (ITTE)
Linux courses
Phone: 831-662-9164
E-mail: info@itte.org
URL: http://www.itte.org/TRAIN/linux.html

Learning Tree International
Linux installation and support course
Phone: 800-843-8733
1805 Library St
Renton, VA USA 20190
E-mail: uscourses@learningtree.com
URL: http://www.learningtree.com/us/ilt/courses/330.htm

Learn Linux (Aegis Data Systems)
Classroom Linux training
Phone: 214-752-6433
501 Elm St, Suite 350
Dallas, TX 75202
E-mail: training@learnlinux.com
URL: http://www.learnlinux.com

LinuxCare University

Classroom Linux training in San Francisco. Also has training partner network.

Phone: 888-546-4878

650 Townsend St, Suite 3244A

San Francisco, CA 94103

E-mail: info@linuxcare.com

URL: http://www.linuxcare.com/

Prosofttraining.com

Classroom Linux training

Phone: 888-776-7638

3001 Bee Caves Rd

Austin, TX 78746

E-mail: learn@prosofttraining.com

URL: http://www.prosofttraining.com

Red Hat Software

Phone: 800-454-5503

2600 Meridian Parkway

Durham, NC 27713

E-mail: training@redhat.com

URL: http://www.redhat.com/products/training.html

Silicon Graphics, Inc.

Phone: 800-361-2621

E-mail: training@pongo.corp.sgi.com

URL: http://www.sgi.com/support/custeducation/us/linuxpage1.html

Three-Sixteen Training

Classes in Austin, TX

Phone: 512-380-0316

La Costa Corporate Park

6448 U.S. Hwy 290 E., Suite E-105

Austin, TX 78723

URL: http://training.three-sixteen.com/main.html

TrainMe
Training in Orlando, FL
Phone: 407-206-3390
12424 Research Pkwy, Suite 380
Orlando, FL 32826
URL: http://www.trainme.com/

UniForum
Phone: 888-333-8649
E-mail: dmurray@uniforum.org
URL: http://www.uniforum.org/web/education/educ.html

UniTek
Instructor led training in San Jose and Fremont CA
Phone: 510-249-1060
39465 Paseo Padre Pkwy #2900
Fremont, CA 94538
E-mail: info@unitek.com
URL: http://www.unitek.com/

Vortex Data Systems
Training in San Diego CA
Phone: 619-497-6400
7480 Mission Valley Rd, Suite 100
San Diego, CA 92108
E-mail: info@vortexdata.com
URL: http://www.vortexdata.com/

Wave Technologies
boot camp
Phone: 888-204-6143
10845 Olive Blvd, Suite 250
St Louis, MO 63141
URL: http://www.wavetech.com/whats_new/linex/

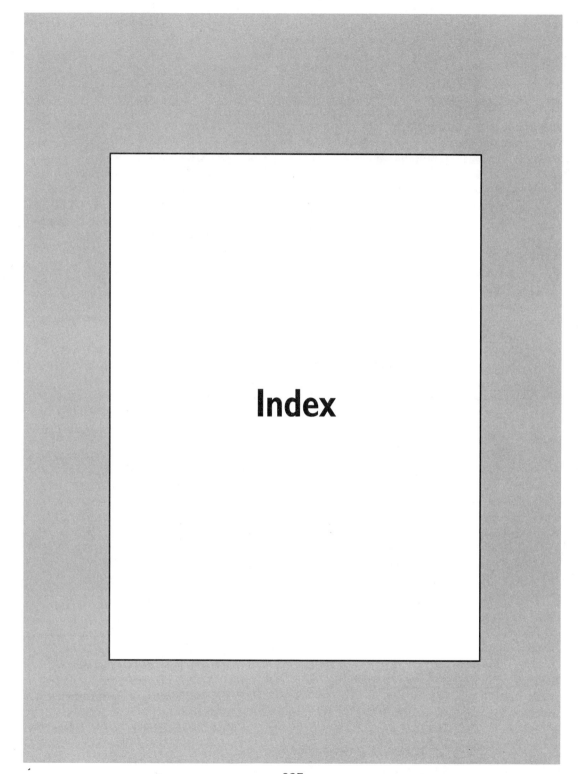

Index

Note: Boldface numbers indicate illustrations.

About the Author

ANNE MARTINEZ is a respected computing writer and regular contributor to *Contract Professional*. She is the author of *Get Certified and Get Ahead*. Her work has also appeared in *Small Business Builder* and many other publications. She holds a degree in computer science and previously worked in the MIS department of a major corporation.